CHRISTOLOGY AND WHITENESS

This book explores Christology through the lens of whiteness, addressing whiteness as a site of privilege and power within the specific context of Christology. It asks whether or not Jesus' life and work offers theological, religious and ethical resources that can address the question of contemporary forms of white privilege. The text seeks to encourage ways of thinking about whiteness theologically through the mission of Jesus. In this sense, white Christians are encouraged to reflect on how their whiteness is a site of tension in relation to their theological and religious framework. A distinguished team of contributors explore key topics including the Christology of domination, different images of Jesus and the question of identification with Jesus, and the Black Jesus in the inner city.

George Yancy is Associate Professor of Philosophy at Duquesne University, USA. His books include *Black Bodies, White Gazes: The Continuing Significance of Race* (2008) and *Look, a White! Philosophical Essays on Whiteness* (2012).

CHRISTOLOGY AND WHITENESS

What Would Jesus Do?

Edited by
George Yancy

Routledge
Taylor & Francis Group

LONDON AND NEW YORK

First published in 2012
by Routledge
2 Park Square, Milton Park, Abingdon, Oxon OX14 4RN

Simultaneously published in the USA and Canada
by Routledge
711 Third Avenue, New York, NY 10017

Routledge is an imprint of the Taylor & Francis Group, an informa business

British Library Cataloguing in Publication Data
A catalogue record for this book is available from the British Library

Library of Congress Cataloging in Publication Data
Christology and Whiteness : what would Jesus do? / edited by George Yancy.
   p. cm.
   Includes index.
1. Jesus Christ–Person and offices. 2. Whites–Race identity. 3. Race awareness.
4. Race–Philosophy. 5. Race relations–Religious aspects–Christianity. 6.
Racism–Religious aspects–Christianity. I. Yancy, George.
   BT205.C53 2012
   232.089'09–dc23
   2012003056

ISBN: 978-0-415-69997-6 (hbk)
ISBN: 978-0-415-69998-3 (pbk)
ISBN: 978-0-203-10612-9 (ebk)

Typeset in Bembo
by Taylor & Francis Books

"The one who showed him mercy."
Jesus said to him, "Go and do likewise."

CONTENTS

CONTRIBUTORS

Victor Anderson is Oberlin Graduate Professor of Ethics and Society at the Divinity School of Vanderbilt University; Professor of African American Studies and Religious Studies in the College of Arts and Sciences. He holds a BA from Trinity Christian College, an MDiv and ThM from Calvin Theological Seminary and an MA and PhD in Religion, Ethics and Politics from Princeton University. Anderson is author of *Beyond Ontological Blackness: An Essay in African American Religious and Cultural Criticism* ([1995] 1999), *Pragmatic Theology: Negotiating the Intersection of an American Philosophy of Religion and Public Theology* (1999), and *Creative Exchange: A Constructive Theology of African American Experience* (2008).

Laurie M. Cassidy is currently Associate Professor of Religious Studies at Marywood University in Scranton, Pennsylvania. Her most recent book is a co-edited volume entitled *Interrupting White Privilege: Catholic Theologians Break the Silence*, which won Catholic Theology Society's book of the year in 2007. Her work as 2009 Luce Faculty Fellow for the Society for the Study of Art in Religion and Theological Studies is forthcoming in a volume from Liturgical Press co-edited with Maureen O'Connell entitled *She Who Imagines: A Catholic Feminist Aesthetic*. Cassidy's research draws on the resources of Christian mysticism for individual and social transformation, particularly in responding to contemporary culture.

M. Shawn Copeland is an Associate Professor of Theology and holds an appointment in the interdisciplinary Program in African and African Diaspora Studies at Boston College. Previously, she has taught at Marquette University and Yale University Divinity School. Copeland is recognized as one of the most important influences in North America in drawing attention to issues concerning the experience of African American Catholics. She has written more than ninety articles, reviews, and book chapters on such topics as Christology, freedom, gender, and race. Copeland is the author of *Enfleshing Freedom: Body, Race and Being* (2010) and principal editor of *Uncommon Faithfulness: The Black Catholic Experience* (2009).

Cheryl Townsend Gilkes is the John D. and Catherine T. MacArthur Professor of African-American Studies and Sociology and director of the African American Studies Program at Colby College (Waterville, Maine). Her research, teaching, and writing have focused on the role of African American women in generating social change and on the diverse roles of black Christian women in the twentieth century. She is currently at work on a book entitled *That Blessed Book: The Bible and the African American Cultural Imagination* and she is also exploring the impact of African Muslims on the formation of African American Christianity during slavery. Some of her essays and articles are gathered in her book *If It Wasn't for the Women: Black Women's Experience and Womanist Culture in Church and Community* (Maryknoll, New York: Orbis Books, 2001). Several of her journal articles have been reprinted in anthologies such as *African American Religious Thought: An Anthology*, edited by Cornel West and Eddie Glaude (Philadelphia: Westminster John Knox Press, 2004).

William David Hart is Professor of Religious Studies at the University of North Carolina Greensboro. Hart describes himself as a critical theorist of religion. He is the author of three books: *Edward Said and the Religious Effects of Culture* (Cambridge 2000) and *Black Religion: Malcolm X, Julius Lester and Jan Willis* (Palgrave 2008), and *Afro-Eccentricity: Beyond the Standard Narrative of Black Religion* (2011). Hart's next project addresses relations among religion, the state, and forms of violence.

Jennifer Harvey is Associate Professor of Religion at Drake University in Des Moines, Iowa. She received her PhD in Christian Social Ethics from Union Theological Seminary in the City of New York. She is the author of *Whiteness and Morality: Pursuing Racial Justice through Reparations and Sovereignty* (Palgrave Macmillan, 2007) and a co-editor of *Disrupting White Supremacy from Within: White People on What We Need to Do* (Pilgrim Press, 2004). Her recent publications include articles pertaining to the movement for reparations among US Protestant denominations.

Moni McIntyre is currently Assistant Professor in the Graduate Center for Social and Public Policy at Duquesne University. Prior to her ordination as an Episcopal priest in 2000, she had been assistant professor in Duquesne's Theology Department. She is the rector of the Church of the Holy Cross in Pittsburgh. She is a retired Navy Captain (0–6) and former Ethics Consultant to the Navy Surgeon General. She teaches bioethics to Navy physicans and dentists in the Advance Medical Department Officer Course in Bethesda, MD. Her publications include three books and numerous articles. Her research interests are in bioethics, nonviolent social change, community organizing, and social movements.

James W. Perkinson is a long-time activist and educator from inner-city Detroit, currently teaching as Professor of Social Ethics at the Ecumenical Theological

Seminary and lecturing in Intercultural Communication Studies at the University of Oakland (Michigan). He holds a PhD in Theology/History of Religions from the University of Chicago, is the author of *White Theology: Outing Supremacy in Modernity* and *Shamanism, Racism, and Hip-Hop Culture: Essays on White Supremacy and Black Subversion*, and has written extensively in both academic and popular journals on questions of race, class, and colonialism in connection with religion and urban culture. He is in demand as a speaker on a wide variety of topics related to his interests and a recognized artist on the spoken-word poetry scene in the inner city.

Anthony B. Pinn (PhD, Harvard University) is the Agnes Cullen Arnold Professor of Humanities and Professor of Religious Studies at Rice University. His research interests include liberation theologies, religion and aesthetics, religion and popular culture, and African American humanism. He is the author/editor of 25 books. Pinn is Director of Research for the Institute for Humanities Studies (Washington, DC).

Rosemary Radford Ruether is Professor of Feminist Theology at Claremont School of Theology and the School of Religion, Claremont Graduate University. She is the author of 45 books and over 100 articles. Ruether's recent book, *Christianity and Social Systems*, was published by Rowman & Littlefield (2009).

Karen Teel is Assistant Professor in the Department of Theology and Religious Studies at the University of San Diego. Her primary research interests are in Christian theological anthropology and Christology. In her book, *Racism and the Image of God* (Palgrave Macmillan, 2010), she engages the works of womanist theologians and ethicists to begin developing a theology of the body that compels Christians, especially white Christians, to resist injustice.

Traci C. West is Professor of Ethics and African American Studies at Drew University Theological School. She is the author of *Disruptive Christian Ethics: When Racism and Women's Lives Matter* (2007), *Wounds of the Spirit: Black Women, Violence, and Resistance Ethics* (1999), and editor of *Our Family Values: Religion and Same-sex Marriage* (2007).

George Yancy is Associate Professor of Philosophy at Duquesne University and Coordinator of the Critical Race Theory Speaker Series. He is the author of *Black Bodies, White Gazes: The Continuing Significance of Race* (Rowman & Littlefield, 2008), which received an Honorable Mention from the Gustavus Myers Center for the Study of Bigotry and Human Rights. He is the author of *Look, a White! Philosophical Essays on Whiteness* (Temple University Press, 2012). He has edited eleven influential books, three of which have received *Choice* Awards. He was recently nominated for the Duquesne University Presidential Award for Excellence in Scholarship.

Josiah U. Young III is Professor of Systematic Theology, Wesley Theological Seminary, Washington, DC. His many books include *A Pan-African Theology: Providence and the Legacies of the Ancestors; No Difference in the Fare: Dietrich Bonhoeffer and the Problem of Racism; Dogged Strength within the Veil: Africana Spirituality and the Mysterious Love of God.*

ACKNOWLEDGMENTS

I would like to thank Lesley Riddle, Senior Publisher, Religion and Anthropology, for her initial show of enthusiasm for this book project. Thanks for your keen insight and your appreciation for challenging and theologically significant books. I would also like to thank Katherine Ong, Senior Editorial Assistant, for her professionalism and patience, and for keeping the project on schedule. You are a pleasure to work with. Kelly Brown Douglas is genuinely thanked for agreeing to write the Foreword to this book, for seeing its theological importance, and for her complex and significant writings across a broad spectrum of important theological issues and themes (race, sexuality, womanism, etc.) within the Black faith tradition. I am honored by your important contribution and assessment of the book. I extend a thank you to the anonymous readers for Routledge who read over the proposal and provided feedback and advanced positive assessments of the book project. I would like to extend my gratitude and deep indebtedness to the scholars whose chapters constitute the very core of the text's theological challenge. Without their incredibly insightful and engaging contributions, the book that you hold would not have seen the light of day. I knew exactly whom I wanted to contribute to the text's theme. I am grateful that each scholar agreed to contribute without hesitation. Working with each of you has been an absolute pleasure. Of course, I owe a special thanks to Victor Anderson for his enduring friendship and enthusiasm for the past projects of mine to which he has contributed. In this regard, I would also like to thank Josiah U. Young, III. He was there for me, along with Victor, when we came together to honor and critique (indeed, to honor and appreciate through critique) the work of Cornel West that resulted in my edited book, *Cornel West: A Critical Reader*. I thank the two of you for walking this journey with me again. I would like to thank James G. Spady for teaching me the spirit of tenacity, the insight to see what needs to be done, and the courage to get it done. I would also like to thank friend and colleague Moni McIntyre. Moni does not really know just how influentially her pedagogy shaped my religious sensibilities. In many ways, this project is itself a product of some embryonic theological insight planted in me while critically thinking through theologies of liberation. You are appreciated. I would also like to thank my extended family, especially those who have always held on to religious faith in the face of obstacles. I would also like to thank James Swindal for his continued support for my work. Manomano M. M. Mukungurutse is thanked for his brilliance and his dedication to nurturing genuine friendship. Mary Louise McCullough is thanked for her dedication to Christian leadership. James Cone is thanked for his theological audacity and fearless speech. I would also like to acknowledge Gavin Walton. Gavin is an impressive and intelligent young man with vision, humility, and honesty. I have had the pleasure of having him as a student in many of my philosophy courses. My hope is that he will continue to strive for excellence and never to compromise what I see as his incredible desire to learn and to make a difference in the world. I would also like to thank my great-uncle William L. Banks for being there. He is an intellectual and spiritual beacon, someone who has worked hard and long hours honing his theological profundity, and is a beautiful servant of those in need. As a scholar, his books inspire and he lives his life with tremendous integrity and faith. Lastly, I would like to thank Ruth, my mother, for allowing a very young kid to pray *for* the devil. While this may sound a bit strange, perhaps even bizarre, unbeknownst to her, she had created a space in my heart to be honest and innocent in my quest. You are loved for this. Susan, Adrian, Gabriel, Elijah, Joshua, and Samuel are all thanked and deeply loved for sharing with me these precious moments in the history of the universe. There are times when I literally ache just thinking about the possibility of losing you to a cosmos that just doesn't give a damn. It is in moments such as these that I remain a *hopeful* theist.

FOREWORD

Kelly Brown Douglas

Whiteness matters. Once again, George Yancy reminds us of the complex ways that it does matter. There are few who have done more to interrogate the significance of race in the United States than George Yancy. He has been tenacious in his investigation of the implications of race for the ways in which we engage our own bodies, other bodies and the world. With each new work, Dr. Yancy reveals another dimension of how race shapes social and individual identities in America. What makes Yancy's work so compelling is the meticulous manner in which he exposes the philosophical, ideological and now theological underpinnings of our racialized narratives and interactions. Most particularly, he has been unrelenting in exposing the multiple ways in which "whiteness" has acted as a "transcendental norm," that is, as a standard for all that which is good and acceptable. In so doing, he has shown the impact that "normative whiteness" has had on bodies that are not white, especially the black body. What Yancy has made clear throughout his extensive work on race, especially through his anthologies and authored books, is that there is no room for complacency when it comes to the significance of whiteness for our human living. Whiteness matters, he reminds us, as long as the human gaze is refracted through race. For Yancy, these things are true: until we fully understand the complex ways in which whiteness matters and functions in our world, dare to name the ways in which whiteness has shaped not simply our social and personal interactions, but also our thinking, it will not be possible to produce a world where all bodies are free to live. For Yancy, the construction of whiteness is no small matter. And so it is that Yancy is unrelenting in exposing the ways in which normative whiteness has infected virtually every dimension of human knowing and being in the world. Thus this edited collection of essays, *Christology and Whiteness: What Would Jesus Do?*

This collection examines the meaning of whiteness, but with a twist. It explores the ways in which being a Christian matters when it comes to the matter of whiteness.

In these essays, the question of "What would Jesus do?" is not a question of "personal piety and private morality" as it often is in public evangelical culture. Rather, it is a question of social justice and Christian integrity.

In this volume, Yancy has managed to bring together an impressive collection of scholars, representing diverse religious disciplines and theological/philosophical perspectives. These scholars wrestle with the meaning of Jesus when it comes to sustaining normative whiteness as well as the relevance of Jesus in the pursuit of racial justice. These scholars leave no stone unturned in their examinations. They forthrightly interrogate, for instance, the significance of the Black Christ in black faith and theology. For some, to claim Christ as black is important for a people whose blackness has been demonized. For others, a black Christ only reinforces the reality of whiteness and ignores the "web of power relationships" which fosters white supremacy. Other essayists have answered the question of "What would Jesus do?" by questioning the relevance of Jesus when it comes to contemporary racial matters. Some have argued that Jesus compels Christians to be actively engaged in the present struggle for justice, because it is clear that Jesus would be likewise involved. Still others are not as confident concerning Jesus' responses to the contemporary situation, and say that we must await the time when Christ will come to make clear where He stands on matters of race. In the meantime then, we must live into the hope of a future where "Jesus would render racism no longer conscious." And then there are those who suggest that the idea of an ethic based on Jesus is detrimental to a fight against injustice because such an ethic invariably gives positive value to suffering. Various others in this collection challenge the way in which the Bible is engaged or not engaged in understanding Jesus and thus in developing a social justice ethic.

As one reads these varied and sometimes divergent perspectives represented in this book, one thing is clear: this collection of essays is not for the faint of heart. It is not for those who have a romanticized notion of Jesus as a gentle and soothing Savior who makes us feel good about ourselves. It is not for those who are afraid to ask hard questions concerning the relationship between Jesus and whiteness. Who these essays are for is those who dare to go to the uncomfortable places and ask themselves the difficult questions of what it means for them to be a racially embodied Christian in a racially divided world. Each of the contributors to this volume takes the risk to interrogate the difference it makes for them to be Christian, given their particular racial identity. So by the time one comes to the end of this volume, the question of "What would Jesus do?" has once again been transformed. The question becomes, "what should *you* do?"

Let me offer now a more personal note. When I wrote *The Black Christ* many years ago, it was not simply an academic exercise. It was for me a part of my journey to reconcile my Christian faith with who I was as a black woman. That journey continues as I continue to learn more about myself and more about the meaning of Jesus. There has been nothing more important to my journey than the opportunity to dialogue with and to learn from others. It is for this reason that I am especially grateful to George Yancy for inviting me to write this foreword, and to be a part of this dialogue. Through reading this book, I learned more about myself and who I am called to be as a black female Christian in a world where race matters. I invite anyone who wants to learn more about themselves and the difference that they can make in a racially defined world to read this book. To be sure, you will not close this book the same as you were when you opened it.

INTRODUCTION

Framing the problem

George Yancy

To love is to make a decision against white racism.

(James Cone)

Where are white Christians in this valley of injustice? What roles do we play—wittingly or unwittingly—in perpetuating the evil of racism?

(Karen Teel)

I am a white person living in a white-supremacist society who still sometimes feels racist feelings in his body, thinks racist thoughts in his head, and acts in subtle (and on occasion, not-so-subtle) racist ways in the world.

(Robert Jensen)

In a church that I have attended for some time now, I think that it is safe to say that less than 10 percent of the church consists of people of color. And while the church is one that is refreshingly open to diversity, one that frequently expresses political and theological views that are against the mainstream, one that openly critiques various forms of hegemony, it remains majority white. I have previously written about the peculiar sensation that, as a black philosopher, I feel while walking through academic conference spaces dominated by white bodies. I have described such a sensation as a complex and multifaceted one that involves a sense of alienation within a sea of whiteness. In every direction, there are white bodies moving and communicating with ease, with no particular sense of being out of place or not at home. The motif of "home" is an important and germane one, as it suggests the sense of familiarity, safety, and being among those with whom one shares something intimate, something familial. Within such a context, one feels relaxed and unperturbed. One might say that the spaces at such academic conferences, for white bodies at least, are inviting and alluring. To be white within such spaces is perceived as commonplace. One is fully engaged, pre-reflectively so, with the mannerisms and etiquette of white social bonding.

Within the context of this particular church, I have often looked around, looked closely at the white bodies that pray, that sing, that worship, that express various theological commitments, and I have felt that sense of alienation, that sense of being surrounded by a sea of whiteness. The church is by no means hostile. On the contrary, it is a welcoming space, one for which I have deep respect. Yet, it is a space where mainly *white* bodies bond, mainly *white* bodies give thanks and engage in other religious speech acts, where mainly *white* bodies break bread together, and where mainly *whites* imagine the divine. Despite the fact that this space is monochromatically white, this does not deny that there may be important and subtle hermeneutic differences regarding various theological issues expressed within this predominantly white space. What stands out for me, what appears so clear to me, are the monochromatic (white) bodies that have come to inhabit this space. There is a sense in which my dark body stands out of place within this space. As this is a space of collective white embodied subjectivities, they recognize this space as their own space through their ease of movement; it is a space that they define, even as it defines them. The fact that they, *as white*, do not feel this peculiar sense of alienation, this sense of being out of place, speaks to the normative structure of the space; it speaks to modes of being white that remain invisible. In short, these white bodies comport themselves within such spaces with no particular need to think of themselves *as white*. Sara Ahmed (2007) writes, "I want to suggest … that whiteness could be understood as 'the behind.' White bodies are habitual insofar as they 'trail behind' actions: they do not get 'stressed' in their encounters with objects or others, as their whiteness 'goes unnoticed.' Whiteness would be what lags behind; white bodies do not have to face their whiteness; they are not oriented 'towards' it, and this 'not' is what allows whiteness to cohere, as that which bodies are orientated around. When bodies 'lag behind,' then they extend their reach" (156). The point here is that such spaces are perceived by whites as open spaces, even if unconsciously. Unlike bodies of color within the context of predominantly white spaces, a white body is able to extend itself into such spaces in a way that "*does not command attention*" (Ahmed, 2007, 156). When my body arrives, I notice it against the backdrop of this whiteness. As the space is predominantly filled with whiteness, and given the operation of the white gaze, I am certain that I am seen precisely against the backdrop of normative whiteness. The "open" space, then, is *lived* as truncated; the monochromatic space does not reflect me. My sense is that, and I agree with Ahmed (2007) here, my being seen as I arrive "tells us more about what is already in place than it does about 'who' arrives" (157). It is what is already in place that allows other white bodies, even white bodies that are new to the church, to congregate with ease. Such bodies might command attention because they are new, but my body commands attention in ways that invoke difference qua race. After all, I am the *black* body, even as I am the "familiar" body.

There is an important and fruitful moment during each Sunday called "Prayers of the People." It is a moment where congregants are given the opportunity to express and share their own burdens, difficulties, pains, and sorrows, and to share how others are in pain and facing difficulties. Some have even used this time to give thanks. After one shares, the minister says, "This is our prayer," and the congregants collectively respond, "God of mercy, hear our prayer." I have also heard congregants raise painful and difficult issues that are political, involving, for example, the horrors of war, death, and dying in other countries. And the congregants collectively respond, "God of mercy, hear our prayer." Within the context of "Prayers of the People," there are even times when the issues of oppression and racial injustice are spoken out against, and again the congregants collectively respond, "God of mercy, hear our prayer." It is during these moments that I wonder if they really believe that they are being heard. Are they really asking God to intervene in human history? What if their discourse travels no further than the community of intelligibility that gives it meaning? What if the discourse of prayer lacks all vertical metaphysical significance and is only an expression of shared community, shared pain and sorrow, a way of engaging in a form of collective, group catharsis? What if theological discourse, prayers, conceptions of the divine, visions of immortality, and "sacred" texts remain socially horizontal, tied exclusively to human persons as *homo narrans* and *homo significans*? What if the religious and theological narratives and symbols that we weave for ourselves are just complex ways that we have learned to cope? Yet, as a *hopeful* Christian theist, I choose to think otherwise; I've decided upon a different *Weltbild*. To say that "I hope" or that I remain "hopeful" means that I stare in the face of a painfully silent and a perhaps infinitely strange and ambiguous universe, and yet I affirm the existence of the divine. This often leads me to feel as if I were standing on a precipice, not knowing what is to happen next, feeling that deep and profound sense of embodied anxiety; it involves looking out on a universe that remains silent in our most dreadful and desperate moments, soaked in our finitude, accepting the fact that physical death is guaranteed, and feeling the utter strangeness that one *is*. Within this context, then, the utterance, *my* utterance, "God of mercy, hear our prayer," signifies openness to divine mystery, or openness to God or divine transcendence, the "more" of which Victor Anderson speaks (2001, 149). It is a hope born of a long and painful history of weeping black bodies that have waited for something *more*. It is a hope that is born of a long line of black relatives who believed in stored-up prayers, who believed in divine historical immanence, who anticipated something *more*. It is a hope not born of calculation, a sort of Pascalian wager. Rather, it is a hope that endures despite doubt and skepticism, despite the reality of massive world suffering, despite the putrefaction and decomposition of human corpses beneath the earth, despite my own inevitable demise, and despite a profoundly complex universe filled with quiet. It is a hope that remains even still.

My understanding of the concept of a hopeful Christian theist aside, however, I have wondered what it would look like for a white person to stand, face her fellow white congregants, and offer the following: "I have been thinking recently about how my whiteness is a site of power and privilege. I have been thinking about how, despite the fact that I define myself as a white anti-racist, I continue to incur white privilege, I continue to carry the weight of white racist training in my body. I notice how when I fight against white racism, it remains in place. I want you to pray for me so that I can become more

aware of the complex and subtle ways that I am unfairly privileged because I am white
in a society that privileges whiteness." I think of the long pause that this sort of honesty
might entail. I think about just how daring and *dangerous* such a prayer would be.
After all, the prayer calls into question the very foundation of North America: white
supremacy. I think about how vulnerable such a person is left feeling, how naked.
I think about how whiteness, within this congregation, would, by implication, be
named and marked as a problem. Within such predominantly white spaces, perhaps
especially white Christian spaces, it is hard to recognize whiteness (*your* whiteness) as
a problem. I think about how whiteness would have been nominated as a problem,
as something that needs to be militated against, as something that is both a deeply
embodied problem and a form of structural sin. As it is a form of structural sin, she
will have implicitly raised the distinction between those who are oppressors and those
who are oppressed; she will have invoked the color line, that powerful Manichean
racial divide that runs throughout every dimension of North American social life.
As Mary Elizabeth Hobgood (2007) writes, "There is no subordination without a
complementary exercise of domination. Whites have the responsibility to interrogate
and resist whiteness as a social location of unjust structured advantage" (40). She
would have raised the importance of metanoia (or conversion) within the larger
context of fighting against white racism, of fighting against *her own* racism. By
nominating whiteness within the midst of other white Christians, she would have
located the problem of whiteness within the walls of the church itself, demonstrating
that whiteness is not some extraneous and vague problem that exists outside the
domain of *ecclesia*, but something rooted right there and all too often invisible. I also
think about the possibility of bad faith subsequent to her confession. I think about
how the proverbial elephant in the room—whiteness—would have been reconfigured
and reduced to *her* problem, as a problem that has to do with her individualist spiritual and moral failings as a white racist, as someone who is different from us "good
white Christians." I wonder if they will see themselves implicated in her entreaty.
After all, they are white. As such, then, through their everyday, taken-for-granted
social existence, they are complicit in the perpetuation of white power and privilege.
At a deeply anti-theological level, where whiteness has functioned and continues to
function as an idol, she will have named the space of whiteness as a site of idolatry,
fanaticism, obsession, and narcissism. Indeed, she will have juxtaposed whiteness as
something antithetical to her conception of the divine. By doing so, she will have
also invited other whites to think of their whiteness as a *problem*, as something
incongruous with their shared theology. It is within this context that philosopher and
theologian George Kelsey theorized white racism as a form of idolatry and poly-
theism, where whiteness becomes a god, one that is worshiped in daily life (Burrow,
2006, 107). She will have created an important slippage between the historical fusion
of white identity with the *Imago Dei*. Within a larger context, Richard Dyer (1997)
theorizes this fusion as the persistence of a Manichean dualism of black and white
"that could be mapped on to skin colour difference; the role of the Crusades in
racializing the idea of Christendom (making national/geographic others into enemies
of Christ); the gentilizing and whitening of the image of Christ and the Virgin in

painting; the ready appeal to the God of Christianity in the prosecution of doctrines of racial superiority and imperialism" (17). It is not by accident that when I was a small boy I imagined God as an old white man with a long white beard. The racial semiotic power of whiteness, and its theological implications, is part of the larger white imaginary vis-à-vis its construction of "Blackness" as that which is evil, dirty, unclean, and sinful.

In the white woman's honesty, she will have indicted whiteness as a historical site of hegemony and as a current practice that continues to express its power and injustice. As Robert Jensen (2005) writes, "Virtually every white person I know, including white people fighting for racial justice and including myself, carries some level of racism in our minds and hearts and bodies. In our heads, we can pretend to eliminate it, but most of us know it is there" (54). Charles E. Curran (2007), a white Catholic theologian, writes, "White privilege is a structural sin that has to be made visible and removed" (81). Curran (2007) also notes, "Acknowledging my failure as a Catholic theologian to recognize and deal with the problem of racism in society and the church is only the first step toward a recognition of white privilege" (80). The point here is that the woman's confession to the congregation would have effectively named the problem of whiteness and named it as something that needs to be confronted within the context of white Christian life, a problem that has serious implications for one attempting to make sense of his/her *white* Christian identity within a white supremacist society. One can hear the response: "God of mercy, hear our prayer." In that collective moment, their prayer would have been on behalf of the white woman and on behalf of their own white Christian identities. Lillian Smith (1949) talks candidly about how she was taught to think about her white skin and God. She says that she and others were taught "to love God, to love our white skin, and to believe in the sanctity of both" (83). Smith (1949) also notes, "I do not remember how or when, but by the time I had learned that God is love, that Jesus is His Son and came to give us more abundant life, that all men are brothers with a common Father, I also knew that I was better than a Negro" (28).

Within predominantly white spaces, as a person of color, it is certainly not unreasonable to wonder about (and worry about) what white people think of you and "your kind." I argue that through a certain hermeneutic lens Christian theology and whiteness—that is, whiteness as a historical process that continues to express its hegemony and privilege through various cultural, political, interpersonal, and institutional practices, and that forces bodies of color to the margins and politically and ontologically positions them as sub-persons—are incompatible. Given this understanding of whiteness, I agree with James Cone (2005) where he says succinctly, "Love is a refusal to accept whiteness" (74). To raise the issue of gender, I would also argue that love is a refusal to accept male supremacy, where women are deemed sexual playthings, sexually fragmented body parts, ontologically subordinate, inferior, and so on. If love is a refusal to accept whiteness, and Christianity is fundamentally predicated upon love, then white Christians have a special duty to reject whiteness even as they, paradoxically, continue to benefit from its power and privilege. As Karen Teel (2010) argues, "Maintaining our own unfairly privileged status, we collude in our own failure to be fully human. To the Christian, this sad state of affairs should be unacceptable" (35). The entire problematic regarding one's white Christian identity in relationship to whiteness is one that ought to be taken seriously. Within this context, Christology becomes a deep existential prism through which to think about what ought to be done about one's whiteness and the problem of whiteness in our contemporary moment. Through a hermeneutic lens that sees Jesus as the embodiment of love and justice for those who suffer, the problem of whiteness, as a site of hegemony, must be approached through the Christological framework of that important Nazarene carpenter who was the very embodiment of caritas. Within this context, it can be argued that whiteness, as a site of imperialist power, functions as a metonymy for the Roman Empire. Jesus did not reap benefits from the Roman Empire, but nurtured a form of *Mitsein* in relationship to those who were the subaltern, outcasts, lepers, Samaritans, those considered "unclean." These bodies were the ones under assault (Hobgood, 2007, 52). Within the context of the trope of "cleanliness"—where to remain "clean" means avoiding those raced bodies in need, avoiding those raced bodies that have been ostracized and pegged as outside of the white polity—whiteness must become "unclean." As a racial and spatial signifier, whiteness maintains its "purity" through processes of insularity, that is, through processes of avoidance and of maintaining distances from those (nonwhites) defined as different/deviant. To traverse this racial distance, to become "unclean," is to challenge the meaning of who constitutes one's neighbor, etymologically, "to dwell near." Hence, through the process of rethinking questions of raced spatial proximity vis-à-vis one's neighbor, whites would need "to dwell near" bodies of color in ways that respect their humanity, autonomy, personhood, and dignity. Whites would need to undergo a form of disorientation, a mode of being "unsafe" and vulnerable in relationship to the black and brown "Other".

And yet, effectively militating against whiteness is no easy matter. As Jensen (2008) notes, "I have struggled to resist that racist training and the racism of my culture. I like to think I have changed, even though I routinely trip over the lingering effects of that internalized racism and the institutional racism around me. But no matter how much I 'fix' myself, one thing never changes—I walk through the world with white privilege. … White privilege is not something I get to decide whether I want to keep. Every time I walk into a store at the same time as a black man and the security guard follows him and leaves me alone to shop, I am benefiting from white privilege" (130–32). Given the complexity of whiteness, the dynamics of *metanoia* would involve a constant process of choosing against whiteness, turning against whiteness, and constantly affirming a Christian anthropology that militates against whiteness as the implied quintessential feature of the *Imago Dei*. Within this context, by *metanoia* I am referring to a dynamic process, a process of constant affirmation, a constant and diligent conversion that is cognizant of human finitude and historical facticity, that is cognizant of the complex trappings of whiteness. Clevis Headley (2004) argues, "Whiteness cannot be dismantled through rational and analytical means. Its suspension must come in the form of a continual affirmed refusal to prolong the ontological and existential project of whiteness" (103). Hobgood (2007) puts it this way, "Exploring the ubiquitous, and for whites often invisible, aspects of white advantage is a lifelong task of gaining religious awareness and engaging moral action" (40). It is important to note that it is not phenotypic white bodies qua white bodies that are intrinsically a theological problem. Rather, the theological problem lies in the ways in which white bodies have become normative bodies that are directly or indirectly involved in the oppression of non-normative bodies of color. The theological problem of whiteness is both a systemic problem and an embodied problem at the level of calcified embodied white racist practices; it is a problem in the form of a politico-social and economic structural phenomenon, and it is a problem at the site of embodied white subject formation.

Over the years, I have been able to identify my understanding of philosophy with greater clarity. This level of clarity has been shaped by my engagement with various existential and sociopolitical concerns on the pedagogical front, for example, within the context of classrooms and larger publics. This clarity has also resulted from wrestling with ideas in the form of writing about them. I have come to think of philosophy as asking of us nothing less than to face both who we are and the world with as much honesty as we can manage, to grieve that world and to grieve our own mistakes within that world, and, yet, to be moved and transformed by the love of wisdom and the wisdom of love. This understanding of philosophy combines both critical, conceptual engagement and praxis. In philosophy courses that I teach where the theme of white racism is a core philosophical issue, I strive to communicate to my white students the importance of naming and marking sites of whiteness, sites that my white students have typically come to accept as racially neutral, as normative spaces. After a critical discussion about the ways in which whiteness functions within the context of their daily lives, in ways that are frequently invisible to them, I encourage my students to learn how to *name* whiteness *when* and *where* they notice it! I also try to get them to see what they previously did not, to develop a critical framework for rethinking the grounds for noticeability. Hence, I encourage them to name whiteness within the context of familiar social spaces. The objective is to instill in them new ways of seeing the world, of noticing everyday white utterances, forms of white body comportment, white gestures, and white social bonding. The objective is to help them to see the ways in which white bodies conceal their status as raced, as sites of power and privilege. I want them to see how *white* bodies pass themselves off as simply *human* bodies, bodies that are "ordinary." And I want them to see how this process works within contexts that are themselves familiar and ordinary. I embolden them to mark whiteness, and thus re-signify it as something peculiar, when gathering with all-white family members during vacations, while socializing with all-white friends, when sitting in classrooms that are all or predominantly white, when watching television, when eating in certain restaurants, and when attending church. The objective is to get my white students to begin to question how certain phenotypic, monochromatic bodies have managed to gather in one space, and to think critically about the normative assumptions that operate within those white spaces. Given that whiteness functions as a transcendental norm, as that which defines nonwhite bodies as different and deviant (as suggested above), I encourage them to create fissures and fractures that help them to see through such a norm and to see how it functions parasitically, resulting in the denigration of nonwhite bodies. Regarding the normative status of whiteness, Laurel C. Schneider (2004) writes, "The invention of race as an absolute signifier of difference—a 'global sign'—was codified in pseudo-scientific theories about biology and evolution that rested on the primacy of whiteness as the standard against which all differences were cited as degeneration and lack" (152). Whiteness, of course, functions, paradoxically, as that which signifies the "superior" *race* while precisely obfuscating its status as *raced*. I remind my white students that coming to see whiteness is something that involves continuous practice because whiteness is a master of disguise, as it were. I explain that whiteness is especially difficult to see because they themselves are white. Moreover, I explain that, as white social actors, they are embedded within structures that privilege them against their will. In short, I help them to see the ways in which they are complicit with forms of white power and privilege, ways in which they undergo processes of interpellation or being hailed, called forth as white, within a white supremacist system. I also explain that, as white, they have internalized forms of white racism that often escape their conscious recognition. Furthermore, I instill in them a level of humility that will encourage them to be willing to bracket their own voices and allow for the insights of people of color to discern what they have difficulty seeing. This, of course, requires vulnerability; it understandably triggers fear. Jensen describes this fear as a form of being haunted, of having one's racist entrails, as it were, exposed. He writes, "What if they can see through us? What if they can look past our antiracist vocabulary and sense that we still don't really know how to treat them as equals? What if they know about us what we don't know about ourselves? What if they can see what we can't even voice?" (Jensen, 2005, 55).

When introducing white undergraduate and graduate students to questions of white privilege, that is, the ways in which they undergo processes of interpellation, I deploy Peggy McIntosh's (1988) seminal article that explores white and male privilege. The article has become staple reading within the area of critical whiteness studies. In that article, McIntosh gives forty-six examples of white privilege. The majority of her examples powerfully identify ways in which white privilege continues to exist. For example, in the first person singular, she writes: "I can go shopping alone most of the time, pretty well assured that I will not be followed or harassed." A significant part of what makes McIntosh's article so powerful is the way in which she conceptualizes the white self as complicit with the systemic operational power of white privilege. I have had white students object to the above example, only later to recant, realizing, for example, that they were probably stopped by security as they entered a store because of their age, choice of attire, or because of their multiple tattoos and piercings. I have never had a white student say that she has been stopped *because she is white.* My objective in using McIntosh's work is to get white students to think about the deeper ways in which their whiteness functions to sustain and contribute to white racism, even as they are, understandably, resistant to the appellation, "racist."

When it comes to internalized forms of white racism, my white students have often overestimated the ways in which they have apparently overcome their own white racism. After discussing the ways in which white racism functions as a form of ambush, that is, of being caught unaware by their racism, and thinking critically through ways in which they themselves have been ambushed by white racism, my students are more open to ways in which white identities are far more complex in terms of how they are shaped by white racism. For example, in 2011, in my course on critical whiteness studies, we read Robert Jensen's book *The Heart of Whiteness*. Jensen describes how, back in the spring of 2002, he shared a panel with prominent *Newsday* editor Les Payne. Aware of Payne's immense experience and impressive record as a journalist, Jensen nevertheless discloses that as he sat down next to Payne he felt this incredibly powerful sense of superiority to Payne. Jensen (2005) crucially adds: "If it seems odd that I would feel superior to someone older and more experienced, whom I knew to be more talented and accomplished than I am, here is another relevant fact: Les Payne is black" (67–68). Jensen (2005) adds, "I am white and Payne is black, and that feeling of superiority was rooted in that fact" (68). I would only add that that specific sense of superiority is rooted not in the "fact" of phenotype, but in the historical ways in which black and white bodies have been shaped through the prism of racial and racist discourse, the way in which those bodies have been constituted through various myths and racial and racist narratives. It is not about the so-called ontological differences that install the sense of "superiority" (or "inferiority"). Rather, it is about the powerful and enduring *social* ontology of race, its larger institutional forms and its interpersonal manifestations at the level of micro-social processes that sustain and reinforce myths regarding the so-called ontological differences.

Jensen's example is particularly powerful, as my white students are often reminding me how they *know* that they are not racist. Given that I teach at a Catholic institution, I can only imagine that they see themselves as "good Catholics," those who are living transformed lives that are above the fray of white racism. Part of the problem is that the majority of my white students have never really thought critically about racism before, and certainly not about their own whiteness. Yet, at the core of their "self-certainty" resides a fundamental ignorance about the ways in which they *become* white, that is, the ways in which they come to embody, intentionally or unintentionally, various racist perceptual practices, judgments, sensibilities, and assumptions, and how these perpetuate white power and privilege. Jensen was profoundly shaken by the realization that he harbored such racism. He writes, "Why all of this drama? Because I'm supposed to be one of the 'good' white people, one of the antiracist white people. I am politically active, and have worked hard to incorporate an honest account of race and racism into my teaching, writing, political work, and life. But in that moment, I had to confront the fact that a basic psychological feature of racism was still very much part of me" (Jensen, 2005, 69). If Jensen was asked before the panel event with Payne to share his thoughts about him, Jensen would no doubt have praised Payne's talents and spoken about him with high praise. Asked how he compared to Payne, Jensen would have probably said that there is no comparison and that Payne is clearly the more experienced journalist and public speaker. My interpretation is that it was not about what Jensen "knew" to be true about himself through the process of self-reflection, that is, prior to sitting next to Payne. Rather, it was about the formative racist dynamics that exceeded the site of an epistemic white subject possessed of so-called full self-knowledge. Jensen's experience demonstrates how white racism is embedded within one's embodied perceptual engagement with the social world and how white racism is woven into, etched into, the white psyche, forming an opaque white racist self, which impacts on (and often overshadows) everyday mundane transactions—like being part of a panel discussion where the other discussant is black. Jensen is always already linked to the domain of otherness in the form of prior social relationships involving formative, in this case, racist influences. Jensen is challenged by "the otherness that marks the boundaries of the self 'within'" (Cornell, 1993, 41), that is, the opaque self, a dense aspect of the white self that is embedded within the white psyche. So, just as the white subject undergoes white racist interpellation within the context of white racist systemic structures and practices, the white self also undergoes processes of interpellation vis-à-vis the psychic opacity of the white racist self. One responds, as it were, to the hail of one's "immanent other"—the opaque white racist self—just as one responds to the hail of the interpellative structural forces that confer white racial power and privilege.

From the above, it should be clear that being a white *Christian* does not *ipso facto* mean that one will be able to deal successfully and effectively with confronting whiteness and avoiding the perpetuation of whiteness with absolute ease. Sally N. MacNichol (2004) captures the complexity and tensions involved in attempting to dismantle whiteness when she notes, "In permanent rebellion against the white supremacy that distorts all human persons who live within its defiling and destructive grasp, I write in anger and in sorrow, and *against* the fear that I will reproduce the same old white racial narcissism I wish to escape" (189). Jensen (2005) also writes with a sense of honesty and angst when it comes to confronting whiteness: "If any white person wants to take seriously an honest struggle with whiteness, it doesn't lead directly to some land of love and harmony. In my experience, it is a long, difficult road" (94). And yet, as a white Christian, one must choose. Within this context, God-talk is inextricably linked to praxeological engagement; it involves taking sides, being on the side of those bodies of color who continue to suffer under the hegemony of whiteness. This praxeological engagement is about rethinking the very concept of neighbor, the very meaning of "dwelling near." I have often said to my white students that part of the problem with white racism in North America is that whites come to know people of color through myths and stereotypes. There is no real desire to know us, to touch us in ways that are not mediated by distortion. Whiteness is an orientation to the world. As such, then, people of color are out of reach. Ahmed (2007) writes, "What is reachable is determined precisely by orientations we have already taken. Or we could say that orientations are about the directions we take that put some things and not others in our reach" (152). Whiteness is a site of distancing from the *Imago Dei*. To engage in acts of de-distancing vis-à-vis bodies of color, one affirms the unity of the *Imago Dei*. From a Christological perspective, one sides with Jesus against whiteness. To affirm liberation from white oppression is to affirm "the existential significance of the Resurrected One" (Cone, 2005, 119–20). To invoke the existential within this context is again to place emphasis on choice and the complexity of choice; the complexity of embodiment; the complexity of historical facticity; the complexity of heteronomous forces; the complexity of the white psyche vis-à-vis whiteness; and the complexity of beginning again as one fails. On my view, the choice is fueled by hope, a hope that is often linked to a felt absence. And yet, one that reaches out for and aspires to a felt presence (Green, 1999, 95).

So, why this book? Many white Christians would no doubt reject a priori any association with white supremacy in the form of the KKK, neo-Nazi groups, skinheads, or systems of racial and racist governance that intentionally valorize certain phenotypic bodies, in this case, white bodies, as superior over others, in this case, bodies of color. Such groups or forms of racial and racist governance would be anathema to a theological perspective based on love through the affirmation that all are made in the image of God. The life of Jesus, one that is read through a certain hermeneutic, exemplified in acts of profound love and community, is morally and spiritually incompatible with the sheer, unadulterated hatred upon which such groups are founded. Indeed, such a system of racial and racist governance would belie Jesus' sense of a community adorned in the spirit of Agape. However, many white Christians, while rejecting white supremacy, and white forms of hegemonic governance, continue to benefit from a system that provides them with unearned privilege and power in virtue of being white. Hence, while many white Christians reject blatant forms of white supremacy, American cultural and political reality permeates with racial balkanization, racial hierarchies, racial privileges, and unequal racial power. Given this, it is morally and theologically incumbent upon white Christians to make sense of the ways in which whiteness functions to confer upon them unearned privileges, privileges that impact, in profoundly negative and egregious ways, on the lives of black people and other people of color. In short, then, how does one reconcile the aim to exemplify the life of Jesus while simultaneously reaping unjust benefits from being white, which have negative implications for those who are not white? What are white Christians to do? Thinking about this question is part of the motivation behind this book. *Christology and Whiteness: What Would Jesus Do?* is not designed to make white people feel good about themselves; this is too easy and too close to replicating various forms of white narcissism. Rather, the text is designed in part to *trouble* the comfortable world of white Christians. It is also designed to encourage honesty and critical thinking when it comes to white Christian identity formation.

What Would Jesus Do? is not treated as a facile and popular mantra, even as the question (WWJD) has acquired something of a commercial value, appearing on bracelets. Rather, the question is treated as a powerful impetus for white Christians to rethink their white Christian identities with greater political cognizance in relationship to theological/religious insights that evolve out of attempting to make sense of whiteness within the context of what so many believe to have been Jesus' liberation praxis. As a caveat, one that I have alluded to above, it is important to note that this text *does not* argue that the religious or moral standing of white people is somehow problematic because of "light skin." This would simply reverse the ideology of white supremacy and the ways in which black people (those with "dark skin") were demonized. It is whiteness—that normative and political site of privilege and power—that is deemed problematic, especially in relationship to a conception of Jesus whose life and message were implicative of overcoming domination and oppression. As another important caveat, this text is in stream with scholars in critical race theory and critical whiteness studies who argue for a form of "race realism," that is, the view that although race is ontologically empty and epistemologically bankrupt and does not refer to anything "real" in the physical world, race is, nevertheless, a socially constructed category that has real and profound *socio*-ontological, existential, political, and psychological implications for those who are categorized as white and nonwhite. Hence, while whiteness is a social construction, it has deep political and axiological implications on the lives of those who are not privileged by it and of those who are privileged by it. Indeed, whiteness is a very complex historical, political, cultural, aesthetic, and epistemological site of power.

Christology and Whiteness: What Would Jesus Do? is specifically designed to address the problem of whiteness from the perspective of Christology. Personally, my objective was neither to argue for the historical reality of Jesus nor for his metaphysical status as divine. For me, this is a point of narrative embarkation, a place woven out of *hope*, *love*, and *desire*. The text specifically asks theologians, religionists, and social ethicists whether Jesus' life and work can or cannot address the question of contemporary forms of white privilege. There is an emphasis placed on exploring the fruitfulness or lack thereof of theological, religious, and ethical resources within the narrative (for some posited) life of Jesus to address such issues as contemporary forms of whiteness. The text, then, constitutes a specific religious, theological, ethical challenge to white Christians. As readers of the text, whites (Christian or not) are invited to think about ways in which they are complicit in perpetuating whiteness as privilege and power and ways in which they are complicit in perpetuating a particular form of structural evil. Lastly, the text constitutes a critical corpus of theological, religious, and ethical scholarship *par excellence* in the form of critical reflections on the question of Jesus' praxis in relationship to contemporary manifestations of whiteness. Hence, the text significantly contributes to contemporary critical approaches to whiteness and Christology.

Summary of chapters

In Chapter 1, Karen Teel insightfully suggests that whites in the United States turn upon themselves the question regarding how it feels to be a *problem*. She explicitly names the *problem* of the color-line as a site of white supremacy. She describes whiteness and then suggests that white Christians should be compelled, given their belief in Jesus, to confront it. She also examines Charles M. Sheldon's 1896 book, *In His Steps: What Would Jesus Do?* In examining the "What Would Jesus Do?" movement, she is cautious about the tendency to overemphasize individual moral or spiritual improvement at the expense of a more thoroughgoing systemic critique of whiteness. She also critiques the assumption (implicit in a white person's asking "What would Jesus do?") that if Jesus were here today, he might be a white Christian. Lastly, she argues that, in order to fight effectively against whiteness, it is essential that white Christians cultivate a particular existential and Christological discomfort, as she powerfully says, *in their own skins.*

In Chapter 2, Laurie M. Cassidy engages the question "What would Jesus do?" as a heuristic that is explored communally, critically, and in a daily struggle in order to see that what whites have been taught is invisible—their privilege and others' suffering. She does this through the site of North American media spectacle and how this mediates knowledge of self, others, and the world. She argues that media spectacle, regarding photographs of human suffering, presents a nexus of moral and ethical issues for the viewer and the viewed. She maintains that the spectacle of human suffering is a re-inscription of social roles of race, gender, and class dominance and subordination. Contextualizing photographs of suffering within the phenomenon of media spectacle, she explicates the power and privilege that is invisible in the act of gazing upon photographs of suffering. Lastly, she explores the question "What would Jesus do?" in regard to photographs of human suffering. Drawing on political theology and Catholic social teaching, she concludes that, like Jesus, Christians must be active agents, not spectators, in order to realize the call of Christian discipleship.

In Chapter 3, Cheryl Townsend Gilkes locates Samaria and Samaritans as important and memorable aspects of Jesus's ministry. She pulls from Jeremiah Wright's contention that "in the Bible, the Samaritans were the spooks!" She also emphasizes Wright's point that the narrative of Jesus and the woman at the well involved "a race problem in John 4." Gilkes examines the stories of Jesus's encounters with Samaritans and in Samaria, and of Jesus's use of a Samaritan in a parable. She argues that Jesus's insistence on traveling through Samaria highlights the importance of the agency of the privileged in struggles for social justice. She also argues that the use of the Samaritan in a parable about love and neighborliness not only provides an important lesson on human responsibility but also is an example of the humanizing power of the privileged. Her point is that Samaria and the Samaritans were used by Jesus to signal the disestablishment of the primacy of Jerusalem and Mount Zion as the proper places of worship. Jesus made an actual effort to engage and stand with Samaritans, even tolerating being labeled a Samaritan himself. She goes on to argue that the outsider status of Samaritans and their conflicts with the Judeans place them in a parallel situation to people of color in the United States and their efforts to acquire humane and just treatment in a white supremacist society. Like whiteness, Judean-ness carried the privilege of control of the holiest shrines and the material and social profitability associated with providing access to sacred spaces. Jesus, by insisting upon visiting Samaria and through his engagements with Samaritans, provides a model, according to Gilkes, for disestablishing the dominance and hegemony of whiteness and, ultimately, the mountains (high places) of race and the idolatry/falsity of whiteness.

In Chapter 4, Moni McIntyre situates "The Black Church" as a well-known phenomenon in the United States. She shows that the Episcopal Church, riddled with racism, was one denomination that fostered black churches when it refused to welcome African Americans to otherwise white congregations. She shows how the Church of the Holy Cross in the Homewood section of Pittsburgh, Pennsylvania tells a story of what Jesus, the human face of the God of Truth, would *not* have done. First, relying on selected biblical passages, she posits Jesus as a liberator of the oppressed. She then describes the general state of affairs in the segregated Episcopal Church of the nineteenth century and focuses in particular on the origin of the Church of the Holy Cross as issuing from that segregated body. Lastly, she presents a positive analysis of the Holy Cross as a congregation that Jesus might indeed bless today, despite its inescapable and undeniable elements of whiteness.

In Chapter 5, Jennifer Harvey explores the possibility that, for Christians racialized as "white" in the context of white supremacy, a move into liberative, anti-racist praxis requires an initial careful (and counterintuitive) "disidentification" with Jesus. She argues that the results of whiteness on and the relationship of whiteness to white bodyselves mean that for the white Christian to ask what Jesus would do as a means of identifying with Jesus is a problematic enterprise that might actually re-inscribe whiteness. She interprets the constitution of the white racial subject as a social process that has deeply and inextricably formative implications for the subject him or herself. She demonstrates how two theological responses to Jesus' nature, life and ministry (the "What Would Jesus Do?" movement and the argument for Jesus as the Black Christ) intersect with white racial identity development in ways that forestall liberative praxis. Given the pitfalls created by the move to identify with Jesus, she argues that a better question for the white Christian seeking an anti-racist, anti-white supremacist practice would be: "What would Zacchaeus do?"

In Chapter 6, Rosemary Radford Ruether examines the shaping of the term "white" in American law and culture to define the legal and cultural superiority of the North-West European settlers of the English colonies against Africans and indigenous peoples. Ruether shows that the term "white" not only defined an ethnic identity of these people, but assumed a moral and cosmological dualism of good and evil, and thus implied the necessity of seeing Christ as "white" theologically. She then examines the critique of the "white" or European Christ of Western domination by African American, African, Latin American and Asian theology, as a critique of whiteness in the form of domination. She concludes her chapter with the argument that we need a Christology where Christ is identified with those who continue to suffer because of various political, social, and economic injustices. This means, according to Ruether, taking Christ's liberation message seriously: to free people of color from the multiple ways in which whiteness/white supremacy destroys their lives and to unmask and free whites from the idolatry of contemporary expressions of whiteness that imprison the spirit and militate against Christ's message of love and justice.

In Chapter 7, Traci West identifies Christological teachings that are serviceable to anti-black white racism, and what kinds of theological strategies are needed to intervene. She explores a comparative approach to the history of white supremacist Christological teaching that samples critical African scholarship on the role of Christianity in the European colonization of Africa, as well as African American scholarship on the Christian conversion of those enslaved. The primary focus of her chapter, however, is a discussion of the contemporary moral consequences of making truth-claims about Christ interchangeable with lies about social hierarchy and how such Christology can provide support for violence linked to race and sex/gender. Finally, she provides suggestions about Christology that can create a healthier moral climate related to sex/gender and race for black Christian self-understanding.

In Chapter 8, Josiah Young opens his chapter with the observation that the gospels and Paul's epistles do not speak of racism directly. Indeed, he notes that first-century writers probably never imagined evil events such as the Middle Passage and the Holocaust, thinking that they were living at the very end of the age. Nonetheless, Young argues that one can infer from the gospels and from Paul that the *risen* Christ has opposed and opposes racist ideology and practices. Yet, as history shows, racism has not stopped. To this reality, Young poses very complex questions: Does this mean that anti-racist christologies are on tenuous ground until Christ's arrival ("parousia")? And without the *irrefutable* presence of the Christ in the midst of history, like a force field invulnerable to transience and corruption, isn't every anti-racist Christology a candle in the dark? Young's chapter probes these questions in focusing on pericopes and historical christologies that indicate the limitations of anti-racist hermeneutics and the precariousness of pre-millenarian hope. Young concludes, though, that while the New Testament is a first-century anthology, neither that limitation nor hope's precariousness rule out a Christ who is coming in opposition to racist injustices.

In Chapter 9, James W. Perkinson draws from the work of black theologian James Cone, who argues that the God of the oppressed is already active in the circumstance of exploitation. Perkinson points out an important hermeneutic truth, that is, that our inchoate sense of what Jesus is doing now informs how we "read" what he was doing back in the day. Perkinson first lays out his position on whiteness that forms his response to the question, "What would Jesus do?" He argues that his response will unfold in relation to a juxtaposition of ancient text and contemporary conundrum. Deploying a call and response approach, he argues that his first reflection on whiteness will establish the call and that the response will coalesce in terms of a particular reading of the Good Samaritan mode of "parable-telling," in which Jesus throws up an explicit category of ethnicity to expose an inchoate text of purity/impurity that organizes first-century Palestinian space and governs social behavior. He then re-evaluates the centrality of Jesus' Temple-exorcism as critical to Jesus' struggle to break open the hegemonic structure of perception and discourse that used the Torah to control and sanction political economy and debt. Lastly, Perkinson characterizes the way whiteness/color have functioned as modern analogues to purity/impurity to give ideological ramification to our own globalizing structures of development/ under-development and wealth/poverty. He argues that confronting the power of whiteness today is as tricky and fraught as the struggle Jesus engaged in first-century Palestine to "call out" the branding potency of impurity-perceptions and galvanize a social movement of resistance capable of restoring dignity to an impoverished peasantry while inverting the meaning and direction of stigmatization.

In Chapter 10, William David Hart explores Howard Thurman's classic text, *Jesus and the Disinherited*, as a possible resource for thinking about whiteness. Hart is interested in several powerful and overlapping, but discrepant questions: Is Jesus a useful point of departure for addressing whiteness, or, as Hart phrases this differently, what are the limits of a Jesus-based social ethic? Can Thurman's *Jesus and the Disinherited* be updated to tackle the white problem, or be read as already addressing the issue before it was named? Whose Jesus and which interpretation—can "we" rescue Jesus from Christology and should we? Thurman already recognized the extent to which Jesus—especially the Jesus of Christology—had become an empty if not a negative signifier. Can "we" rescue Jesus from this emptiness and negativity? More important, should we? Hart's chapter constitutes a sympathetic but skeptical engagement with the question: "What would Jesus do?"

In Chapter 11, Anthony B. Pinn begins his chapter by pointing out that the history of white supremacy and the struggle against the ramifications of that history have in part been worked out through the nature and meaning of Jesus' physical presence on earth. He argues that this Christological emphasis has involved not only an aesthetic of physical and spiritual beauty, but also a system of ethics that is inherent in the question: "What would Jesus do?" Pinn maintains that efforts to challenge whiteness as normative through the aesthetics presented in the story of Jesus' "look" and through efforts to mimic Jesus' system of ethics fall short. Pinn argues that this is because they are based on biblical mythology that can be manipulated and made to support any position on whiteness. In other words, for Pinn, a positive blackness predicated on Jesus Christ's person and ethics does little to contest a positive whiteness. For Pinn, the symbolic importance of Jesus' life and ministry can be used to support either a critique of whiteness discourse or an embrace of such a discourse. In addition, for Pinn, both discourses of whiteness and discourses of blackness are too limiting, for both present limited ways to identify one's humanity. In other words, one's humanity is recognized only to the extent that it can be defined relative to this one marker. More specifically, both fail to wrestle with the fundamental nature of moral evil, which Pinn construes as a denial of the right to physically and discursively occupy time and space in complex and transformative ways. Instead of attempting to counter the damage done by whiteness discourse through the process of claiming Jesus' blackness, either as a "symbolic more" or ethical mandate, it is more significant to recognize the limits of Christology as a model for human self-understanding.

In Chapter 12, M. Shawn Copeland begins by attending to the Spirituals made and sung by enslaved Africans and their ebonization and reconfiguration of the (white) Jesus of slaveholding Christianity. Copeland then revisits historian and activist Vincent Harding's "Black Power and the American Christ," which appeared at the crest of the black power movement and well before the advent of critical whiteness studies. Harding provided a sketch of the major features of American colonialism, that is, the structure of racial privilege, the introduction of a system of preferential patronage rooted in assimilation and existential self-denial, and the institution of mechanisms of control and suppression. For Copeland, what is at stake in this reflection is black identification with the historical Jesus and the impact of a black messiah on the sacramental and social economy. Copeland, following Harding's question, would rather we reject the *American* Christ and choose the Suffering Servant of God. In the spirit of praxis, she argues that those of us who would rather live with the Suffering Servant of God must be willing to uncover and dismantle white hegemony and to enter into concrete solidarity with a suffering world, to embrace the little ones as comrades and equals, and to cast our lot with the black Jesus who challenges and changes the sacramental imagination and economy.

In Chapter 13, Victor Anderson engages in a critical discussion of the relationship of Christian supersessionism, which is the idea that Christ's saving works supersede all prior covenants, promises, and dealings with biblical Israel because Christ is the fulfillment or recapitulation of God's soteriological aim to reconcile creation and all people to God. According to Anderson, this aim is mediated not only in the person and work of Christ (Christology) but especially in the gospel that Jesus preached. Anderson argues that the gospel of Jesus is a scandalous gospel that carries its own history of supersessions, which mimetically join Christology and whiteness. Indeed, Anderson says that behind this mimesis of representations of "white Jesus" lay histories of mimetic desire, rivalry, violence, and scandal in the gospel of Jesus. This is the critical relationship between Christology and whiteness. According to Anderson, supersessionism organizes the history of peoples by progressive ages and stages until arriving at civilization, which means Western European civilization and culture (whiteness). In the last section of his chapter, Anderson shows how this mimesis of salvation and dissimilitude is satirically carried over into the scandalous gospel of Reverend Ruckus in Aaron McGruder's *Boondocks'* episode, "The Passion of Reverend Ruckus."

References

Ahmed, Sara. "A Phenomenology of Whiteness," *Feminist Theory*, 2007, 8 (2) 149–68 http://fty.sagepub.com/content/8/2/149.

Anderson, Victor. "Is Cornel West also among the Theologians? The Shadow of the Divine in the Religious Thought of Cornel West," in George Yancy (ed), *Cornel West: A Critical Reader*, Malden, Massachusetts: Blackwell Publishers, 2001.

Burrow, Rufus Jr. *God and Human Dignity: Personalism, Theology, and Ethics of Martin Luther King, Jr.*, Foreword by Lewis V. Baldwin and Walter G. Muelder, Notre Dame, Indiana: University of Notre Dame Press, 2006.

Cone, James H. *A Black Theology of Liberation: Twentieth Anniversary with Critical Responses*, Maryknoll, New York: Orbis Books, 2005.

Cornell, Drucilla. *Transformations: Recollective Imagination and Sexual Difference*, New York: Routledge, 1993.

Curran, Charles E. "White Privilege: My Theological Journey," in *Interrupting White Privilege: Catholic Theologians Break the Silence*, eds. Laurie M. Cassidy and Alex Mikulich, Maryknoll, New York: Orbis Books, 2007.

Dyer, Richard. *White*, New York: Routledge, 1997.

Green, Garrett. "The Hermeneutics of Difference: Barth and Derrida on Words and the Word," in Merold Westphal (ed), *Postmodern Philosophy and Christian Thought*, Indianapolis, Indiana: Indiana University Press, 1999.

Headley, Clevis. "Deligitimizing the Normativity of 'Whiteness': A Critical Africana Philosophical Study of the Metaphoricity of 'Whiteness,'" in George Yancy (ed), *What White Looks Like: African-American Philosophers on the Whiteness Question*, New York: Routledge, 2004.

Hobgood, Mary Elizabeth. "White Economic and Erotic Disempowerment: A Theological Exploration in the Struggle against Racism," in Laurie M. Cassidy and Alex Mikulich (eds), *Interrupting White Privilege: Catholic Theologians Break the Silence*, Maryknoll, New York: Orbis Books, 2007.

Jensen, Robert. "White Privilege Shapes the U.S.," in Paula S. Rothenberg (ed), *White Privilege: Essential Readings on the Other Side of Racism*, New York: Worth Publishers, 2008.

——*The Heart of Whiteness: Confronting Race, Racism, and White Privilege*, San Francisco, California: City Lights Publishers, 2005.

MacNichol, Sally N. "We Make the Road by Walking: Reflections on the Legacy of White Anti-Racist Activism," in Jennifer Harvey, Karin A. Case and Robin Hawley Gorsline (eds), *Disrupting White Supremacy from Within: White People on What We Need To Do*, Cleveland, Ohio: Pilgram Press, 2004.

McIntosh, Peggy. "White Privilege and Male Privilege: A Personal Account of Coming to See Correspondences through Work in Women's Studies," in Richard Delgado and Jean Stefancic (eds), *Critical Whiteness Studies: Looking Behind the Mirror*, Philadelphia: Temple University Press, 1988.

Schneider, Laurel C. "What Race is Your Sex?" in Jennifer Harvey, Karin A. Case and Robin Hawley Gorsline, (eds), *Disrupting White Supremacy from Within: White People on What We Need To Do*, Cleveland, Ohio: Pilgram Press, 2004.

Smith, Lillian. *Killers of the Dream*, New York: W.W. Norton & Company, 1949.

Teel, Karen. *Racism and the Image of God*, New York: Palgrave Macmillan, 2010.

1

WHAT JESUS WOULDN'T DO

A white theologian engages whiteness

Karen Teel

Over one hundred years ago, W. E. B. Du Bois (1996) declared that "the problem of the Twentieth Century is the problem of the color-line" (pp.1, 13, 35). He summed up the attempts of many white people to make conversation with him, an African American, by pointing out that what most of them really wanted to know was this: "How does it feel to be a problem?" (Du Bois, 1996, pp.3–4). He reports that he never responded to this question beneath the questions, and one suspects that most white people he describes never admitted, even to themselves, that this was in fact the question they were really asking.

In the U.S. today, "the problem of the color-line" remains. To be perfectly precise, the "problem" has never been people of color, but rather white notions of white superiority. In this chapter, I contend that it is past time for contemporary white people to turn our question "How does it feel to be a problem?" back on ourselves.[1] Nearly one hundred fifty years after the demise of legalized slavery, over forty years after the Civil Rights Movement officially ended segregation, and having elected a biracial man as our nation's president in what some please to call a "colorblind" or "post-racial" era, white people still maintain a death grip on a disproportionate share of resources, opportunity, and power in the U.S.[2] What is wrong with us?

By way of answering this question, this chapter renames "the problem of the color-line" for the twenty-first century as "whiteness": a system of structural injustice and inequality with roots at least as far back as the beginning of race-based slavery in the "New World" colonies. As a white Roman Catholic theologian, I am particularly concerned with white U.S. Christians, whose predecessors created this system and who today should be actively engaged in dismantling it, but by and large are not. I consider this problem in four parts. First, I describe whiteness and suggest that white Christians might be compelled, by way of our belief in Jesus, to address it. Second, I ask whether striving to imitate Jesus can generate an adequate response. Briefly exploring the book that gave rise to the "what would Jesus do?" movement, I caution that this approach tends to emphasize individual moral or spiritual improvement at the expense of systemic critique and change. Third, following the theology of James H. Cone and others, I interrogate the assumption implicit in a white person's asking "What would Jesus do?": that if Jesus were here today, he might be (like) a white Christian. Fourth, having considered what Jesus would do in our situation—or to be more precise, what Jesus would *not* do—I argue that in order to fight effectively against whiteness, white Christians must cultivate a particular existential and Christological *discomfort in our own skins*. Unless we feel viscerally that we are part of the problem, we may not be compelled to address it. I conclude with the hope that we will begin alerting our white Christian brothers and sisters to the need to resist and subvert our whiteness.

Whiteness: a white Christian problem

Whiteness, which Du Bois was the first to theorize,[3] can today be defined as a system of hegemonic power that operates to benefit people perceived to be white and to disadvantage people perceived to be of color.[4] Whiteness has developed through a long and tortuous history (see, for example, Roediger, 2005, 2007), a history that some scholars contend has its root in an ancient and fundamental perversion of Christianity's Jewish origins.[5] There can be no doubt that it began at least as long ago as the European Christians who, even before thinking of themselves as "white," created the U.S. system of race-based slavery. "Whiteness" is a properly and peculiarly white Christian theological problem that demands a white theological response.[6]

In the decades since legal slavery met its demise, whiteness has metamorphosed through Reconstruction and the tragedies of segregation and lynching into the varied forms of white supremacy and racism that persist today. Whiteness can be manifested in attitudes and acts of personal racism, but it is primarily a system of social or structural injustice: the inequalities that persist even though the laws have changed, even when no one consciously intends a racist outcome. Social scientists document this phenomenon.[7] When a white person gets a job interview before an equally well-qualified black person (Bertrand and Mullainathan, 2004), whiteness may be working. When a white felon finds employment before a person of color without a criminal record (Pager, 2003), whiteness may be working. When people in communities of color are more likely than people in white communities to fall victim to high-cost mortgage lending practices (Been et al., 2009; Boehm et al., 2006), whiteness may be working. When a non-African American child finds an adoptive home before an African American child (Maldonado, 2005–6), whiteness may be working. Whiteness operates to benefit white people, regardless of our individual wishes. This makes us a problem. So, guided by Du Bois, let us ask ourselves: how does it feel?

In many white circles, this question would be a non-starter. White people have a notoriously difficult time seeing whiteness, for we are barely aware of ourselves as "raced."[8] While biologists agree that race is not a biological reality, it remains a very real social phenomenon (see, for example, Townes, 2006, pp.63–65; Bonilla-Silva, 2006). In terms of the self-understanding of many whites, to be white in the United

States is *not* to be "colored": black, brown, yellow, red, mixed. To be white, we think, is to have no race. To be white, we think, is to be a unique, individual expression of universal humanity, while to be raced is to be conditioned, contingent, a less-than-adequate representation of universal humanity. By and large, white people believe that to be white is to be "normal" and therefore requires no reflection; when we do notice whiteness, we may insist that we are really observing something else. As noted, social science research indicates that to be white in U.S. society is to receive all sorts of advantages that accrue from the social valuation of white skin over non-white skin, not from personal merit.[9] Yet we often take these advantages for granted. We may notice them only if they are eliminated, and then we may complain bitterly about injustice; witness the ongoing debates over affirmative action. To be white is to have unbelievable power, power that is unearned and undeserved and unjust, and, typically, to be virtually unaware of it.

Since whiteness is systemic, and operates regardless of individual intention, a white person who happens to notice that *all is not well* might logically conclude that if she does not approve of whiteness and does not intentionally collude with it—that is, if she is not part of the problem—then she is not responsible for its effects. She could even argue that if she were a racist, she would not through that personal failing become responsible for systemic whiteness; to renounce her own racism and try to do better would be enough. In Christian terms, she might believe that such an effort could absolve her of the sin of racism.[10] It is certainly true that being (relatively) pale does not necessarily mean actively or willfully promoting injustice. Indeed, to name the unjust structures in society as stemming from whiteness is not to claim that we whites who are alive today created them. It is rather to recognize that this system confers benefits upon us, regardless of whether we want them. Whiteness has taken on a life of its own, and no one person or group can hope to solve it.[11] Thus, if asked, "What is the responsibility of individual white people to the problem of whiteness?" or, "What should white people feel about whiteness as a problem?" some would say, "Nothing at all."

I contend, however, that even though we contemporary whites did not create the system, and may in principle oppose it, our responsibility to it is very great. One cannot be white in the U.S. without receiving the privileges of being white in the U.S.—that is, without being part of the problem. Can any white person honestly say that he has never thought, in relation to a person of color, something along the lines of "Oh, you poor nonwhite thing!" (Du Bois, 2003, p.56)? Activist Tim Wise (2008) testifies to the fact that even a white person who has built a career fighting racism can still experience the rising in his mind, unbidden, of a purely racist thought (pp.165–67). To be white in the U.S. is to be shaped by whiteness.

Moreover, regardless of what goes on inside our heads, whiteness is something that white bodies *perform*. Because of my skin color, my default position is on the side of whiteness. As I go about my everyday activities, I am logically associated with the hegemony of whiteness and receive its benefits, unasked for, unearned, and largely unnoticed. Whenever my actions fail to visibly contradict whiteness, I melt into the masses of white people who have not done enough, are not sufficiently aware of the problem, and even deny that it exists. Colluding with whiteness can be something my body does freely, because I choose it; there have been times when I have "leaned on my whiteness" to get something done the easy way.[12] But more often this is not the case. It is precisely in the context of the larger society in which whiteness is over-privileged that my body takes on this meaning. My consistent complicity in whiteness, intentional or unintentional, reliably distorts my own and others' freedom into unfreedom. How does this feel? Horrible!

White Christians such as myself, then, must engage whiteness as a systemic injustice that we both encounter and enact. Christianity—a religion of radical justice and love, yet also inescapably bound up with the origins of whiteness—ought to have a lot to say about how to do this. A few white thinkers, including theologians, are beginning to address whiteness, including practical suggestions for how white people should proceed once we have decided to resist its insidious power (see, for example, Harvey et al., 2004; Cassidy and Mikulich, 2007; Nilson, 2007; Wise, 2008).[13] While indispensable for those who have ears to hear, I want to draw attention to the fact that such suggestions do not grab the attention of the majority of white Christians, who in all likelihood consciously intend to do no racist or white supremacist harm, and who have no inkling that we should or could be doing anything to prevent or to remedy such harm. Unfortunately, as Robin Hawley Gorsline has observed, "*No one—no white person—has to do anything for white supremacy to continue*" (2004, 53, italics in the original). White supremacy, or whiteness, flourishes in an environment of white disengagement. As I see it, then, before we ask what white people collectively ought to do about the problem of whiteness, the logically prior question is how to get white Christians to notice that there is such a problem, and that we must decide whether to undertake the struggle against it.

In my limited experience of trying to draw white people's attention to what I am here calling whiteness, I find that neither rational argument nor moral suasion (not that these are opposed!) reliably obtain. Many whites are aware of the wealth, income, and opportunity gaps in this country but think that these gaps generally result from some people's having worked harder than others.[14] If one disagrees, even bringing relevant social-scientific evidence to bear, one must be prepared to face charges of insanity. Pointing out that whiteness costs white people something, as some thinkers do quite persuasively (see, e.g., Wise, 2008, pp.147–71), is also insufficient; again, one may simply be called crazy, or worse, boring and irrelevant. When compared to the apparently painless present that we white people enjoy and the discomfort that inevitably accompanies an awakening to reality, we do not perceive the potential benefits as valuable enough to pull us out of apathy and into action. We need to be shocked into it.

While I hope there will be many ways to accomplish this, here I am writing as a white theologian concerned with white U.S. Christians' responses to whiteness. As such, one possible method that occurs to me is to try to confront ourselves and one another with images of Jesus that challenge our assumptions about him, and about ourselves in relation to him. In order for ordinary white Christians to start taking whiteness seriously, we need to meet a *discomfiting* Jesus who accosts us where we are, reaches into our ignorant complacency, seizes hold of us, and thrusts us into the maelstrom of whiteness. In the remainder of this chapter, I experimentally propose one way that we might begin to discover and deploy such a Christology.

What would Jesus do?

The heart of Christian faith is the hope of a personal, life-giving relationship with God through Jesus of Nazareth, who was executed as a criminal by the Roman Empire and proclaimed by his followers to be the risen Christ. At our best, Christians are followers or disciples of this Jesus. We strive to listen to him, do what he wants us to do, even emulate him. Finding that racism has a hold on our minds, even our souls, and that the benefits of whiteness accrue even against our will, white Christians might think it sensible to ask: What would Jesus do in my situation, as a white person who wants to shoulder her responsibility vis-à-vis the problem of whiteness?

Since Charles M. Sheldon's 1896 book *In His Steps*, efforts to follow Jesus have been popularized through this question, which formed the book's subtitle: "What would Jesus do?" *In His Steps* enjoyed wide circulation and has been retold twice (Clark, 1950; Sheldon and Morris, 1993); the most recent version generated the familiar WWJD bracelets and bumper stickers and, in 2010, *WWJD: The Movie*. Surely a Christian could never go wrong in striving to imitate Christ, especially in racially charged situations where it seems obvious that kindness and compassion should replace hatred and misunderstanding. Yet an analysis of *In His Steps* reveals that, for white people mired in whiteness, asking "What would Jesus do?" can be dangerously misleading.[15]

The central character of *In His Steps* is a pastor in a small, average town. As the book begins, Reverend Henry Maxwell witnesses the death of an unemployed man who had come to him asking for help, but whom Maxwell had turned away. Conscience-stricken, Maxwell challenges himself and his affluent congregation to pledge, for one year, to make no decision and take no action without first considering the question, "What would Jesus do?" (Sheldon, 1896, p.15).

The group that joins Maxwell on this quest includes such prominent townspeople as the newspaper editor, a railroad manager, a young singer, and an heiress. They make sacrifices: the newspaper loses circulation upon dropping questionable advertisements and "sensational" news (e.g. of boxing matches), and the singer gives up a lucrative job offer for a gig at the local mission. They support one another: the heiress endows the newspaper with a sizeable sum for operating expenses. All derive considerable satisfaction from following the desire to "do something that will cost me something in the way of sacrifice ... to suffer for something" (Sheldon, 1896, p.56). Their efforts to improve their town meet with modest, though not overwhelming, success.

To this privileged reader at least, the sincerity of Sheldon's characters renders them surprisingly compelling. Yet a troubling thread weaves throughout the story. Without exception, all the characters assume their ability to do what Jesus would do, and plunge ahead with no reflection on what this might mean. Although they observe what we now call the gap between the haves and the have-nots, the characters never think of questioning their own privilege.[16] For example, at one point, the heiress wonders what Jesus would do with a million dollars. She exclaims,

> It maddens me to think that the society in which I have been brought up ... is satisfied year after year to go on dressing and eating and having a good time ... and, occasionally, to ease its conscience, donating, without any personal sacrifice, a little money to charity. ... When I honestly try to imagine Jesus living the life I have lived ... and doing for the rest of my life what thousands of other rich people do, I am under condemnation for being one of the most wicked, selfish, useless creatures in all the world.
>
> *(Sheldon, 1896, pp.44–45)*

Despite this revelation, the only response she can imagine is donating a *lot* of money to charity, along with a good deal of her time.

Thus, the heiress's understanding of what Jesus would do, reflected by all Sheldon's characters, is limited to the idea that Jesus would be virtuous and kind, helping people however he could. This is not an inaccurate reading of the gospels, but it is incomplete. Jesus not only engaged in ministry among people who were poor and marginalized, but also condemned the system that dehumanized him and the people he served (see, for example, Wink, 2003). The characters of *In His Steps* hearken to Jesus' call to compassion, but they fail to take up his trenchant critique of the powerful. As a result, they are patently unable to address or even understand structural issues.

Here the ending of the story is perhaps most telling. Far beyond his comfort zone, Reverend Maxwell preaches at a meeting of working-class men. One of the men, unemployed, widowed, and struggling to feed his children, asks what he should do when the entire system seems designed to work against him and, no matter how he tries to imitate Jesus, things don't go his way (Sheldon, 1896, pp.226–27). If Jesus had to choose either to steal or to let his children starve, what would he do?

Reverend Maxwell is deeply disturbed. He himself has never faced such a choice. Previously he has provided for needy people from his own resources, but he can't invite hundreds of men to stay with him, or employ them all. He can find no answer, and the meeting is commandeered by socialists who name the structural issues quite eloquently. Not taken with socialism, Maxwell goes home and uneasily concludes that what is needed is more Christians doing what Jesus would do. If there were enough of them, then perhaps unemployment, hunger, and so on could eventually be overcome. Unable to imagine a movement that would change structures, he rather uncertainly seizes hold of this "perhaps." As promoted by *In His Steps*, then, the strategy of asking "What would Jesus do?" is limited in its ability to inspire social change.[17]

This is not inevitable. Latin American liberation theologian and Catholic nun Ivone Gebara, for example, describes her spirituality as an effort to live according to the question "What would Jesus have done in this situation?" (Gebara, 1999, ch. 5, especially pp.175–76). She observes that Jesus did focus in his ministry on solving individuals' immediate problems, but she also identifies as touchstones Jesus' "stance in favor of the poor and outcast, his firm resistance to oppressive powers, and his lack of dogmatism … the value of the body, especially the bodies of the poor and their basic needs" (Gebara, 1999, p.176). Faithfully asking "What would Jesus do?" has led Gebara to a perceptive and effective critique of oppressive social structures. Unfortunately, many white Christians do not reach this level of spiritual sophistication and commitment. Certainly the characters of *In His Steps* never imagine engaging in what we might properly describe as "firm resistance to oppressive powers." A century ago, Walter Rauschenbusch, architect of the Social Gospel movement, was already voicing this critique:

> In our own time the books of Mr. Charles M. Sheldon have set [the ideal of imitating Jesus] forth with winning spirit, and we have seen thousands of young people trying for a week to live as Jesus would. But it is so high a law that only consecrated individuals can follow it permanently and intelligently, and even they may submit to it only in the high tide of their spiritual life. To most men the demand to live as Jesus would, is mainly useful to bring home the fact that it is hard to live a Christlike life in a mammonistic society. *It convicts our social order of sin, but it does not reconstruct it.*
>
> (Rauschenbusch, 1916, p.46, emphasis added)

In His Steps suggests that asking "What would Jesus do?" can inspire Christians to read the gospels carefully and cultivate intimate relationships with God. Yet this seemingly innocuous question displays an insidious ability to distract white Christians from broader issues. Insofar as it fails to prompt us to critique our own social positions, it can allow us to skim right over the problem of whiteness, to think and act as if it is not there, to remain oblivious to—or at least helpless in the face of—unjust social structures. In other words, it can enable the continuation of the white unreflectiveness about whiteness that I lamented earlier. As a method for white Christians to discover how to address whiteness, asking "What would Jesus do?" lends itself to answers that address symptoms, not the disease itself.

The cure, I believe, may lie in Reverend Maxwell's anxiety over whether asking "What would Jesus do?" can change society. Unable to clarify this uneasiness, he sets it aside, and the last we see of him, he is preaching his "What Would Jesus Do?" message in Chicago. If we sit with his discomfort awhile, however, I think it can tell us something about Jesus, and about what it means for white people to follow Jesus in the U.S. today.

Who would Jesus be?

The minister and the heiress are never quite satisfied trying to do what Jesus would do. Their dis-ease, as they bump up against the limits of this strategy for change, demands further investigation. As noted, the problem seems to be their assumption that Jesus is simply a virtuous, kind, compassionate helper. We need to know more about him if we want an answer to our question: If Jesus were here in the U.S.

today, acting in a manner consistent with his previous conduct, what would his stance be with regard to whiteness?

One route to an answer might be evident if Jesus had addressed whiteness explicitly in his teaching and healing ministry. But two thousand years ago, whiteness as I have defined it did not exist. Even the scholars who locate its genesis in the beginnings of Christianity trace it to the emergence of Christian supersessionism, not to the time of Jesus. Thus, to inquire how Jesus would engage whiteness is anachronistic; some work is required to transform this into a sensible contemporary question. To this end, in this section I consider, first, whether Jesus would be white if he were here today; and, second, how this modern-day Jesus might go about opposing whiteness.

Would Jesus be white?

Like the heiress and the minister of *In His Steps*, contemporary Christians who ask "what would Jesus do?" presume that we can determine what Jesus would do if he were here, because there is a good chance he would be (like) us. We aren't asking how Jesus would act if he returned to earth today as a Galilean Jewish man. We are asking what Jesus would do *if he were us*. This practice evokes the ancient Christian beliefs that salvation is equally available to every person, and that the resurrected Jesus has promised to be with his followers always as we carry out his commands (Mt. 28:19–20). Given these convictions, to ask what Jesus would do if he were me, or standing right next to me, is not unreasonable; white Christians rarely question it. But if we want to oppose whiteness, I think we need to trouble the presumption that we can be like Jesus because he might be like us.

Perhaps the best-known theologian to consider the question of who Jesus would be if he were here today is James H. Cone. Upon completing his training in the classical European theological tradition, Cone began teaching in the African American community. He found immediately that that tradition had no answers for the existential questions his students were asking about oppression, in the context of their Christian faith (Cone, 1975, pp.5–7). This was in the late 1960s. Most objectionable laws were being changed, but changing laws does not instantly transform entrenched attitudes and systems of privilege, and progress was slow. For Cone, the riots of Detroit and Newark signified that black people's existential situation afforded them little hope. Was Jesus truly on their side? Recognizing these questions as properly theological, Cone began to utilize the method of correlation, seeking to match (or correlate) the questions to theological answers.[18] African Americans' high regard for the Scriptures, for Jesus as savior, and for God as liberator led Cone to search the Bible.

He found a God who champions the victim, most saliently in the Exodus story, and a Jesus who was not only on the side of oppressed people but who was himself oppressed. Because most Jews in first-century Palestine, including Jesus, were not Roman citizens, being Jewish rendered one marginalized.[19] The historical person of Jesus was not from a privileged Roman class; he engaged in a ministry to the poor and outcast of society; and he died the death of a common criminal, condemned by the local government, without the possibility that a citizen would have had of appealing his sentence to Rome. Moreover, first-century Palestinian Jews were probably darker skinned. The historical person of Jesus was not white, historically or analogically: he was neither European nor privileged. Noting that this and none other is the context in which God chose to become incarnate, and mindful of the Christian belief that God does not do things by accident, Cone surmises that this taking on of oppressed human flesh must have been intentional.

Continuing further, Cone declares that if God's choice to become incarnate as a marginalized person was intentional, then insofar as marginalization is still a feature of human society, Jesus' non-whiteness has current significance. Jesus' historical situation is mirrored in the present situation of blacks in the U.S. Cone concludes that if Jesus were alive today in the U.S., he would be black: "He *is* black because he *was* a Jew" (Cone, 1975, p.123). Indeed, Cone argues that, for black people, salvation means to be liberated from oppression; for white people, it means to reject whiteness and "become black with God"—working for the liberation of people who are oppressed (Cone, 1990, pp.63–66). It is important to note that Cone does not say that Jesus could *only* be black today, in a reductive or exclusive sense. Rather, he says that if God were to become incarnate in the contemporary U.S. situation of white supremacy, God would assume the flesh of a member of an oppressed group, not a privileged one (Cone, 1990, p.7). If we want to find Jesus, we should look for him in African American or other marginalized communities.

A chorus of voices has picked up this dramatic insight. Going beyond Cone, womanist theologian Jacquelyn Grant, referencing the tridimensional oppression— race, gender, and class—experienced by many black women, maintains that "Christ among the least must also mean Christ in the community of black women" (Grant, 1989, p.217). Kelly Brown Douglas, also a womanist, argues that Christ would be a black woman who would struggle against any injustice, not only the three articulated by Grant (Douglas, 1994, pp.106–10, at p.109). From a Latin American context, Jon Sobrino (2008) declares that the crucified and resurrected Christ demonstrates God's partiality toward the victims of oppressive human structures, and warns that privileged people can hope to be saved only if we cast our lot definitively with these victims. James W. Perkinson (2004), one of the few white scholars to take up Cone's challenge, urges white Christians to become "post-white." On these and other analyses, while we cannot say for sure who Jesus would be if he appeared in the U.S. today, we can be certain that he would not be white.[20]

What does this mean for white people? If we fail to recognize the seriousness of the problem of whiteness, we might conclude that a God who becomes a person of color is inclusive, generous, a patron of multiculturalism. It could be a way for God to nudge us to get over our prejudices, to realize that "other" people are just as valuable as we are. But this interpretation would be sorely inadequate, for the thinkers described above indict whiteness and all it stands for. The Jesus they describe would not be on our side. He would be for the people we have marginalized. Indeed, Cone believes that God's blackness liberates by bringing hope to black people, and a warning to white people: God opposes whiteness and will not let it stand (see Cone, 1990, pp.66–74).

This vision is persuasive, particularly in the face of white bodies' complicity with whiteness. God could not take on a white body because white people would mistake God for one of us, part and parcel of whiteness. A white body would not manifest a critique of unjust power structures in the way that Jesus' dark body did in the first century and would still need to do today. For white Christians wondering what to do about whiteness, therefore, the question "What would Jesus do?", with its attending presumption that he might well be like us, is not only distracting, it is nonsensical.

How would Jesus oppose whiteness?

For white Christians, the idea that whiteness is so destructive that Jesus could not risk a white skin today is a sobering one. It should give us pause, and a good dose of humility. Nevertheless, we still need to know what to do about whiteness, and to this end, it may yet prove fruitful to ask: How would a contemporary, non-white Jesus oppose whiteness?

If Jesus were a person of color in the U.S. today, whiteness would indeed be a phenomenon with which he would have to contend. Yet, while whiteness is powerful, it must not be confused with ultimate reality or with the meaning of black (or any "minority") existence. Consider novelist Zora Neale Hurston's insistence on depicting black people at home, in church, on the front porch of the general store: on their own merits, in situations where they were not defined by the white gaze but could simply live and "work out their salvation" (Phil. 2:12) among themselves. Jesus, then, would see whiteness for what it is; when the opportunity arose he would vigorously oppose it, but he would not allow it to define himself or those around him.

Further, curing white people of our whiteness would not be Jesus' *primary* concern. Although it is not their responsibility to enlighten us, people of color have consistently and generously done so: they "have told white people over and over, and with increasing precision and moral urgency ... what it is like to live under this system of domination. They have repeatedly showed us ways in which we remain complicit" (Harvey et al., 2004, p.9). And they sometimes give helpful advice on how to move forward. For example, in the course of doing her theological ethics, womanist thinker Emilie M. Townes provides pointers for white people trying to dismantle whiteness (Townes, 2006, pp.77–78). Townes remains clear, however, that her ultimate concern is for people who are victims. Whenever she must choose between restoring victims to full personhood and rehabilitating the violent, she will choose the victims. She has no interest in "rescuing the killers" (Townes, 2006, pp.150–58). It is reasonable to suppose that Jesus wouldn't either. I am not suggesting that a black Jesus couldn't or wouldn't save white people from our whiteness, but that salvation may look very different from what many of us expect. Our task may be to accept graciously all the help that is offered, and use it to figure out how to "rescue" ourselves.

If this sounds harsh, remember that in his ministry as portrayed in the gospels, Jesus has only fleeting and tangential contact with powerful groups such as the Pharisees and Romans. He carries out his healing and teaching ministry among the poor, outcast, and marginalized of society. Indeed, most of the "authorities" who happen to take notice of Jesus never understand who he is, and they wind up condemning him to death. The Roman centurion at the cross, exclaiming "Truly, this was the son of God!" (Mt. 27:54 NAB), is the exception, not the rule. These powerful people are the closest analogue in Jesus' time to white people in positions of privilege today. A contemporary non-white Jesus, then, might have only fleeting and tangential contact with privileged whites; if we were to encounter the Messiah, most of us might never realize it. Just as in the gospels, Jesus' engagement with the powerful might well be no more than a footnote to his main work of redemption among the marginalized.

What Jesus wouldn't do

At this juncture, it should be clear why the question "What would Jesus do?" is problematic for white U.S. Christians today. As *In His Steps* shows, the question may encourage personal morality, but it does not reliably lead to a critique of structural injustice. Moreover, if Jesus would not be white in the contemporary U.S., asking what he would do as a white person becomes nonsensical. In fact, when such naïveté perpetuates the structural power of whiteness, and by extension the victimization of the marginalized, it is deadly. White Christians should not assume that we can stand, just as well as anyone else, in the place Jesus would occupy if he were here. On the contrary, our intentional and unintentional complicity with whiteness renders us far less able to do so than people who daily suffer whiteness's effects and know all too well what resistance requires. Instead of imagining ourselves at the center of the drama, as Jesus himself, white Christians should be asking, more cautiously and humbly, "What would Jesus *have us* do?"

The first step, which I have been advocating, may be simply to grapple honestly with this idea that Jesus would not or could not be white today. White Christians who do so will begin to feel profoundly uneasy. To struggle effectively against whiteness, this is exactly what we need: a Christology that renders us *uncomfortable in our own skins*. Insofar as they collude with injustice, we must cultivate insight into our white skins as problematic places to be, sites of intense discomfort. This should not be confused with hatred of the body, which I do not promote and to which I strongly object. I have argued elsewhere that human bodies, like souls, deserve respect, for every body is made in the image of God (Teel, 2010). But beyond simply *having* the image of God, there is a difficulty with *manifesting* that image that is peculiar to those of us with white skin (Teel, 2010, pp.163–64). Our bodies effortlessly undermine any desire we have to be antiracist that fails to issue in concrete action, for "neutral" white bodies reinforce the status quo. Indeed, uncritical white bodies are seldom truly neutral, for our everyday acts constantly accrue the advantages of whiteness, like interest compounding in a forgotten bank account; we are no less beneficiaries for being oblivious.[21] Thus, my goal is not white masochism, but a keen awareness of how our skins function within the "system of advantage based on race" (Tatum, 1997, p.7) that our ancestors created and we perpetuate.[22]

Once we realize that our white bodies collude with injustice, we will begin to develop new instincts. Recognizing when whiteness is working, like Reverend Maxwell we will become uneasy. We will learn "how it feels to be a problem." This knowledge may produce physical discomfort: we may wish we were somewhere else; we may feel itchy all over; we may feel anxious or nauseous; we may want to jump out of our skins. Whatever the particular feeling, we must encourage it until we become unable to sit still in the face of whiteness. Then we will learn to stand up and speak up, disrupting its power. Whenever we convince ourselves to do nothing, we must reflect critically on our failures and strategize to do better next time. Learning to feel and act upon this discomfort in our own skins is a conversion to which we are called and a skill we must practice. As we learn to combat our bodies' tendency to collude with whiteness, we may hope to become dynamic signs of the image of God, if not quite the presence of Jesus in the world today.

In proposing that we cultivate discomfort in our own skins, I am trying to make a Christological argument that white Christians should strive for a particular way of feeling. In doing so, I echo and hope to amplify the call to conversion articulated by thinkers such as James H. Cone (2001), M. Shawn Copeland (2002), James W. Perkinson (2004), and Jon Nilson (2007). Theologian and philosopher Bernard Lonergan describes conversion as overcoming bias and expanding one's horizon of knowledge to encompass more of reality.[23] He notes that conversion "can mean that one begins to belong to a different social group or, if one's group remains the same, that one begins to belong to it in a new way" (Lonergan, 1971, p.269). While I do not believe that white Christians are ready, collectively, to *begin belonging to a different social group*, I do hope that those of us wishing to confront whiteness efficaciously can *begin to belong to our social group in a new way*. As this new belonging takes shape, friendships and family relationships may shift and we may experience real loss. Yet, to remain silent in the face of death—no exaggeration, when it comes to whiteness—is unthinkable.

Imagine, if you will, that Jesus is here, in the twenty-first-century U.S., working among his people.[24] Several whites approach Jesus eagerly to ask what we must do to enjoy a place in the reign of God. We have kept the commandments since our childhood, we say. Jesus looks at us with love and tells us that one thing we lack: we must relinquish the power of whiteness and give it to the poor (Lk. 18:18–30). Like the rich young man, white Christians cling to powers and possessions that rightly belong to others. In our own time and place, we must allow Jesus' call to conversion to wrench us out of our white comfort zones. If we wish to share in his life, we must embrace the discomfort that following him brings, lest, like the rich young man, we go away sad.

"Mama, I'm walking to Canada ... "

I have prescribed a conversion in white U.S. Christians' theological imaginations, in our understanding of who we are—or, more precisely, who we are not—and what we are called to do. Collectively, we may not be prepared to hear, much less heed,

Jesus' call to hasten the end of whiteness. But some of us are ready to confront our "problem" status, to cultivate discomfort with our bodies' collusion with injustice. This means facing up to our unearned privileges and taking responsibility for resisting them. As we do so, white Christians also need to guard against thinking of ourselves as isolated followers of Jesus, and work to urge one another toward conversion.

This may be the hardest challenge of all. As our understanding of our role in U.S. society is transformed, we will be tempted to succumb quietly to alienation from our white Christian brothers and sisters who don't yet "get it." But it would be far better to invite them to come along with us. Confronting whiteness with those close to us means much more than challenging racist or otherwise ignorant statements. For example, in conversation with other whites, we can carefully raise questions and refuse easy answers: Why are so few people of color coming to this church, or working in this department, or attending this university? What are the experiences of those who are here? Are they different from ours, and if so, how and why? Again, if, as a white Catholic, I regularly attend a gospel mass, I ought to be willing to explain to my white Catholic friends and family who think I merely have "exotic" taste in music that being part of this vibrant worshiping community is vital to my spiritual health, that in truth, black Catholics are saving my own Catholic faith. By not giving up on each other, generously offering our experiences, and braving the discomfort such conversations bring, we can follow in the footsteps of the courageous people of color who have been doing these things for centuries in the hope of turning more white Christians against whiteness. In our own way, we may emulate Alice Walker's "traditionally capable" womanist, who says, "Mama, I'm walking to Canada and I'm taking you and a bunch of other slaves with me" (Walker, 1983, p.xi).

In theology, I see at least two possible avenues for bringing people along. First, white scholars should be intimately familiar with the work of scholars from under-represented groups, who have long been calling us to confront the problem of whiteness. Our shameful practice of addressing their thought in token fashion—in asides, footnotes, or toward the ends of our writings—is by now well documented. In her lyrical refusal to "rescue the killers / of dreams and visions of a world better than this," Townes includes "the killers / who create optional reading lists / that signal to me / that some actual or alleged scholars really believe / that there are optional peoples, cultures, lives, ideas, hopes, realities / and secondary lists are little better / when they traffic peoples' yearnings and expectations as ideologies and abstractions" (Townes, 2006, p.151). We must alter this pattern; at least for a time, these colleagues' work should be our starting-point. Second, we need role models for the white fight against whiteness. White theologians should work to develop a "litany of the saints" of white Christians who have resisted whiteness, beginning with St. Peter Claver, if not further back. Sally Noland MacNichol has begun to compile such a list (MacNichol, 2004, p.197). In these ways, perhaps, we can live into the truth of the mama's reply: "It wouldn't be the first time" (Walker, 1983, p.xi).

Whether we are trained theologians, ordinary laypersons, or ordained ministers, white Christians must learn to see ourselves not simply as individuals trying to imitate Jesus but as a community in "permanent rebellion" (MacNichol, 2004, p.189) against the power of whiteness. Adding our strivings to the ongoing efforts of people of color will increase our collective chances of bringing about greater justice. Cultivating discomfort in our own skins, learning "how it feels to be a problem," we can take personal responsibility for changing the system and call one another to account. If he were here today, Jesus would not be white, so he would not have to do these things. But I believe that he would be delighted to see us doing them.

Notes

1 When speaking of white people and whiteness, I use the first person in order to include myself explicitly as white, and to encourage readers who are white to reflect consciously on their own racialized identities; I cannot speak for everyone. I owe an immense intellectual and spiritual debt to people of color and hope that they will find this work useful. Yet white people created the United States' "race problem," and we need to take a proactive stance toward ameliorating it. For these reasons, which will become clearer as the reader proceeds, I have whites in mind here as my primary audience.

2 In the interest of specificity, I focus here on black–white relations as my primary framework. I think, however, that the analysis I am developing in this chapter could be adapted to white relations with Hispanics, Asians, Native Americans, etc.

3 Joe R. Feagin states that Du Bois "developed the first important Whiteness study" in his essay "The Souls of White Folk" (Du Bois, 2003, p.23). "Souls" appears in *Darkwater* (Du Bois, 2003, pp.55–74).

4 Although whiteness is usually discussed as a system of unearned privilege, involving factors that confer advantages on white people, some commentators also investigate the cost that whiteness exacts from white people. See, for example, the writings of white activists Lillian Smith (1949), Mab Segrest (1994, 2002), and Tim Wise (2008, especially pp.147–71).

5 In various ways and using varied terminology, theologians Kelly Brown Douglas (2005), J. Kameron Carter (2008), and Willie James Jennings (2011) all argue that what I am here calling whiteness first began to develop when Christianity became distinct from Judaism, specifically in the emergence of Christian supersessionism.

6 In a Catholic context, Jon Nilson (2007, pp.10–12) reminds us that theologians of color have been pointing out this need since at least the 1970s.

7 For the sake of brevity, I provide one or two pertinent studies per example; interested readers may easily locate others.

8 The argument in this paragraph depends largely upon Emilie M. Townes's extended analysis in "Invisible Things Spoken: Uninterrogated Coloredness," chapter 4 (pp.57–78) in Townes, 2006.

9 Peggy McIntosh's well-known article on the "invisible knapsack" (widely available on the Internet, or see McIntosh, 2002) catalogs some of these advantages.

10 Since their 1979 pastoral letter *Brothers and Sisters to Us*, the U.S. Catholic bishops have repeatedly named racism as a sin. For a discussion of this history, see Massingale, 2010, pp.43–82.

11 The need for a coalitional approach may not be immediately obvious to white people. In a telling anecdote, white antiracist activist Tim Wise recalls a young woman who expressed her desire to spend a few years solving "this racism thing" so that she could also "save the rainforests" before getting a "real job" (Wise, 2008, p.90).

12 I am certain that this happens far more often than I am aware, although obviously I cannot report on most instances. Here is one example. I was once able to negotiate a significantly lower-than-advertised rent for an apartment in a majority-Hispanic neighborhood because the landlord was so delighted at the prospect of renting to a "good" (code for "white, well-off") family. In this situation, my whiteness worked out to be worth about a 15 percent discount. Conversely, the cost to the landlord is clear: had I taken the apartment, his prejudice in favor of white tenants would have cost him two

hundred dollars a month in rental income. It is worth noting that this transaction, which depended on the idea that Hispanic tenants were less desirable, would have occurred entirely between two white people, with benefits transferring from one white party to another. The landlord eventually found Hispanic tenants. I wonder what rent they are paying?

13 George Yancy (2008, pp.227–50) describes whiteness, particularly of white people who aim to be antiracist, as "insidious," sneaking up and "ambushing" us, despite ourselves. Thus someone who thinks of herself as antiracist may make a racist remark and then wonder how it could have come out of her mouth, or entered her head in the first place.

14 Some might cite the "Occupy" movement, which began as "Occupy Wall Street" in September 2011 and continues at the time of this writing, as evidence that some white Americans are waking up to the pervasive structural inequalities that plague our society. This movement, however, seems to be founded on a white objection to the rapid widening of income and wealth disparities in recent years, rather than arising from an understanding of historic inequalities between whites and people of color, the roots of which go back at least as far as slavery and colonialism. Genuine social transformation would require the latter, and it is not at all clear that it is forthcoming. Nevertheless, insofar as some middle-class white people are becoming aware of their own disenfranchisement, the movement could represent a small step in the right direction. I am grateful to Tracy Tiemeier, M. Shawn Copeland, and George Yancy for helping me to think through this question.

15 While all three books follow similar plotlines, the issues that I wish to address come into sharpest relief in the original.

16 Sheldon's main characters all seem to be white. Race is not mentioned in reference to any of them until the 1993 book, when one couple taking the pledge is identified as black. A Latina eventually joins that group as well.

17 Problematizing *In His Steps* in the context of the social gospel movement, James H. Smylie (1975) points out that in Sheldon's later works, "he affirms aspects of the socialist movement" (p.44).

18 Cone adapts this method from the theology of Paul Tillich; on this point, see Stewart, 1983–84.

19 For Cone's argument about Jesus summarized in this and the following paragraph, see Cone, 1990, pp.110–28; 1975, pp.99–126.

20 Extending Cone's analysis, one may well ask whether God would today choose to become incarnate in the U.S. at all. Probably not, but I consider the U.S. anyway, because it is my context, Cone's context, the context of whiteness, and the context of many of the people who find it pertinent to wonder, "What would Jesus do?"

21 My thanks to George Yancy for pressing this point.

22 My narrow focus on race in this chapter is for the sake of brevity and has not been intended to exclude GLBT or any other issues. For example, for straight Christians who want to combat homophobia, cultivating discomfort in the heterosexual body could be extremely fruitful.

23 These notions are discussed throughout Lonergan's writings. For example, on bias see Lonergan, 1958, pp.191–206, 218–44; on conversion as the decision to widen one's horizon see Lonergan, 1971, pp.267–69.

24 The premise of Sheldon's sequel to *In His Steps*, titled *Jesus is Here!* (1914), is that Jesus appears in the flesh in the U.S. This is not the second coming, but a visitation in which Jesus stays with friends (affluent and poor), encourages the faithful in the churches, and speaks publicly against social evils such as poverty and exploitation. Here Sheldon's Jesus calls attention to structural inequities, though the other characters remain largely unable to critique their privilege.

References

Been, Vicki, Ingrid Ellen, and Josiah Madar (2009). "The High Cost of Segregation: Exploring Racial Disparities in High-Cost Lending." *Fordham Urban Law Journal* 36 (April): 361–93.

Bertrand, Marianne, and Sendhil Mullainathan (2004). "Are Emily and Greg more Employable than Lakisha and Jamal? A Field Experiment on Labor Market Discrimination." *American Economic Review* 94.4 (Sep): 991–1013.

Boehm, Thomas P., Paul D. Thistle, and Alan Schlottmann (2006). "Rates and Race: An Analysis of Racial Disparities in Mortgage Rates." *Housing Policy Debate* 17.1: 109–49.

Bonilla-Silva, Eduardo (2006). *Racism without Racists: Color-Blind Racism and the Persistence of Racial Inequality in the United States.* Second edition. Lanham, Maryland: Rowman & Littlefield.

Carter, J. Kameron (2004). "Christology, or Redeeming Whiteness: A Response to James Perkinson's Appropriation of Black Theology." *Theology Today* 60: 525–39.

——(2008). *Race: A Theological Account.* New York: Oxford University Press.

Cassidy, Laurie M. and Alex Mikulich, eds. (2007). *Interrupting White Privilege: Catholic Theologians Break the Silence.* Maryknoll, New York: Orbis.

Clark, Glenn (1950). *What Would Jesus Do? Wherein a New Generation Undertakes to Walk in His Steps.* St. Paul, Minnesota: Macalester Park.

Cone, James H. (1990). *A Black Theology of Liberation, Twentieth Anniversary Edition.* Maryknoll, New York: Orbis; originally published J. B. Lippincott, 1970.

——(1975/1997). *God of the Oppressed.* Seabury; revised edition, Maryknoll, New York: Orbis.

——(2001). "Theology's Great Sin: Silence in the Face of White Supremacy." *Union Seminary Quarterly Review* 55.3–4: 1–14.

Copeland, M. Shawn (2002). "Racism and the Vocation of the Christian Theologian." *Spiritus* 2.1: 15–29.

Douglas, Kelly Brown (1994). *The Black Christ.* Maryknoll, New York: Orbis.

——(2005). *What's Faith Got to Do with It? Black Bodies/Christian Souls.* Maryknoll, New York: Orbis.

Du Bois, W. E. B. (2003). *Darkwater: Voices from Within the Veil.* With an introduction by Joe R. Feagin. Amherst, NY: Humanity Books; originally published New York: Harcourt, Brace, and Howe, 1920.

——(1996). *The Souls of Black Folk.* New York: Penguin; originally published A. C. McClurg & Company, 1903.

Gebara, Ivone (1999). *Longing for Running Water: Ecofeminism and Liberation.* Minneapolis: Fortress.

Gorsline, Robin Hawley (2004). "Shaking the Foundations: White Supremacy in the Theological Academy." In Harvey et al., *Disrupting White Supremacy from Within*, 33–62.

Grant, Jacquelyn (1989). *White Women's Christ and Black Women's Jesus.* American Academy of Religion Series 64. Atlanta: Scholars.

Harvey, Jennifer, Karin A. Case, and Robin Hawley Gorsline, eds. (2004). *Disrupting White Supremacy from Within: White People on What We Need to Do.* Cleveland: Pilgrim.

Jennings, Willie James (2011). *The Christian Imagination: Theology and the Origins of Race.* New Haven: Yale University Press.

Lonergan, Bernard J. F. (1958). *Insight: A Study of Human Understanding.* San Francisco: Harper & Row.

——(1971). *Method in Theology.* Toronto: University of Toronto Press.

MacNichol, Sally Noland (2004). "We Make the Road by Walking: Reflections on the Legacy of White Anti-Racist Activism." In Harvey et al., *Disrupting White Supremacy from Within*, 188–215.

Maldonado, Solangel (2005–6). "Discouraging Racial Preferences in Adoptions." *UC Davis Law Review* 39.4: 1415–80.

Massingale, Bryan M. (2010). *Racial Justice and the Catholic Church.* Maryknoll, New York: Orbis.

McIntosh, Peggy (2002). "White Privilege: Unpacking the Invisible Knapsack." In *White Privilege: Essential Readings on the Other Side of Racism*, ed. Paula S. Rothenberg, 97–101. New York: Worth.

Nilson, Jon (2007). *Hearing Past the Pain: Why White Catholic Theologians Need Black Theology.* Mahwah, New Jersey: Paulist.

Pager, Devah (2003). "The Mark of a Criminal Record." *American Journal of Sociology* 108:5 (March): 937–75.

Perkinson, James W. (2004). *White Theology: Outing Supremacy in Modernity*. New York: Palgrave Macmillan.

Rauschenbusch, Walter (1916 [originally published 1912]). *Christianizing the Social Order*. New York: Macmillan.

Roediger, David R. (2007). *The Wages of Whiteness: Race and the Making of the American Working Class*. 3rd ed. London and New York: Verso.

——(2005). *Working Toward Whiteness: How America's Immigrants Became White—The Strange Journey from Ellis Island to the Suburbs*. New York: Basic Books.

Segrest, Mab (2002). *Born to Belonging: Writings on Spirit and Justice*. New Brunswick, New Jersey: Rutgers University Press.

——(1994). *Memoir of a Race Traitor*. Boston: South End.

Sheldon, Charles M. (n.d. [written 1896]). *In His Steps*. New York: Grosset & Dunlap.

——(1914). *"Jesus Is Here!" Continuing the Narrative of* In His Steps *(What Would Jesus Do?)*. New York: Hodder & Stoughton/George H. Doran Co.

Sheldon, Garrett W., with Deborah Morris (1993). *What Would Jesus Do? A Contemporary Retelling of Charles M. Sheldon's Classic,* In His Steps. Nashville, Tennessee: Broadman & Holman.

Smith, Lillian (1949). *Killers of the Dream*. New York: W. W. Norton.

Smylie, James H. (1975). "Sheldon's *In His Steps:* Conscience and Discipleship." *Theology Today* 32.1: 32–45.

Sobrino, Jon (2008). "The Resurrection of One Crucified: Hope and a Way of Living," trans. Paul Burns. In *No Salvation Outside the Poor: Prophetic-Utopian Essays*, 99–108. Maryknoll, New York: Orbis.

Stewart, Carlyle Fielding III (1983–84). "The Method of Correlation in the Theology of James H. Cone." *Journal of Religious Thought* 40.2 (Fall–Winter): 27–38.

Tatum, Beverly Daniel (1997). *"Why Are All the Black Kids Sitting Together in the Cafeteria?" And Other Conversations About Race*. New York: Basic Books.

Teel, Karen (2010). *Racism and the Image of God*. New York: Palgrave Macmillan.

Townes, Emilie M. (2006). *Womanist Ethics and the Cultural Production of Evil*. New York: Palgrave Macmillan.

United States Conference of Catholic Bishops (1979). *Brothers and Sisters to Us: U.S. Catholic Bishops' Pastoral Letter on Racism*. United States Conference of Catholic Bishops. www.usccb.org.

Walker, Alice (1983). *In Search of Our Mothers' Gardens: Womanist Prose*. Orlando: Harcourt.

Wink, Walter (2003). *Jesus and Nonviolence: A Third Way*. Minneapolis: Fortress.

Wise, Tim (2008). *White Like Me: Reflections on Race from a Privileged Son*. Revised and updated. Brooklyn, New York: Soft Skull.

WWJD: The Movie (2010). Motion picture. Produced by Kevan Otto. Nasser Entertainment.

Yancy, George (2008). *Black Bodies, White Gazes: The Continuing Significance of Race*. Lanham, Maryland: Rowman & Littlefield.

2

GROTESQUE UN/KNOWING OF SUFFERING

A white Christian response

Laurie M. Cassidy

Imagine you have just gotten your morning coffee and while standing at the kitchen counter you look at the front page of the newspaper. While you sip your coffee, your gaze focuses on a photograph of a small, naked, emaciated Black[1] girl-child. The child appears to be crawling, while being watched by a vulture. What do you do next? The privilege is yours.

Mary Hobgood (2007) has called on white theologians to engage a variety of "theoretical approaches in the intellectual and political struggle against racism" (p.40). My chapter uses visual cultural tools to make visible the invisible white privilege(s) at work in photographs of human suffering. To gaze at a photograph of suffering is not unique to being white, but functions to make white privilege a cultural "common sense." Drawing upon Bernard Lonergan's concept of culture, Bryan Massingale clearly demonstrates racism as a set of meanings and values that inform the way of life in America. Racism defined as a culture unveils how it is a matrix of meaning within which human beings in a society are socialized (Massingale, 2010, p.42). The power of this starting-point to analyze photographs of suffering is to underscore how culture makes meaning of the social, political, economic and religious systems that condition everyday life. Culture (de)forms the unconscious and taken-for-granted way that racism and white privilege operate in daily existence.

The morning ritual that I described above is not uncommon, and the event is very meaningful for understanding how white privilege works in contemporary American culture. Living in America, we all encounter photographs of suffering human beings.[2] We take for granted the *intimate* access we have to *distant* tortured and starved bodies with tear-streaked faces, crying out in anguish. In photographs we gain "up close" knowledge of the world of suffering, while simultaneously remaining outside the frame and invisible. This dynamic of "up close and far away" gives us a sense of knowing about the world while remaining ignorant of our relationship and responsibility to the suffering people we see (Sontag, 2003, p.99).[3]

If you find the example of reading a newspaper too "old school," then take a moment to consider that photographs of suffering "others" are presented to us through phone "apps", on television, in magazines, as well as in various virtual formats.[4] This intense and immediate knowledge could destabilize our privileged white existence, but does it? Let's return to the example of the morning ritual. After seeing the photograph of this starving Black child what do you do? Do you sit and weep? Do you turn the page? Do you shower and prepare for work? Our daily routines repeatedly expose us to the anguish of "others," which normalizes their suffering and reinforces our position of white privilege.[5]

For those of us who profess to follow Jesus, this morning routine challenges fundamental elements of the practice of Christianity. For example, to begin the day with knowledge of another's suffering without compassionate response is reminiscent of the people who pass the wounded man on the road in the parable of the Good Samaritan (Luke 10:29–37). Moreover, in Matthew's gospel we hear Jesus explain that compassion toward a suffering human being is equivalent to treatment of the Christ. "I tell you solemnly, in so far as you did this to one of the least … you did it to me" (Matthew 25:40). In Matthew's account of the Last Judgment what differentiates the blessed from the cursed is their response to suffering human beings.

Photographs of human suffering raise a staggering number of questions in regard to how human beings respond to each other at this moment in history. I have written about these questions before.[6] I have argued that photographs of suffering are morally ambiguous, and that ambiguity demands that the viewer question the image to discover its moral character. However, I have changed my mind.[7] My argument here is a shift in my thinking. I no longer believe these images to be morally ambiguous. These images are one part of the larger cultural process of representation that normalizes suffering "others." These photographs, even when intended not to, reinforce the idea that we are not "them." A number of things have caused this shift. For example, over the past seven years I have found undergraduate students to be growing more unable (at least publically) to engage the implicit and multiple levels of meaning in photographs. Also, reading scholars of visual cultural studies has convinced me of the virulent way that systems of oppression are being globally reinscribed even when the photographic message appears to expose or interrupt these systems. And critical race theory continues to challenge the theological categories I have learned regarding goodness, innocence, and responsibility. My argument here is about examining the experience of gazing upon another's suffering—ironically, something that would appear to bring to light our privilege. The larger issue of my inquiry is how Christian practice(s) allow for the radical transformation of the gaze of white privilege.

To develop my argument here I will explore a moment that we take for granted, seeing a photo of suffering in the newspaper over a morning cup of coffee. This reflection is to make visible the invisible, to notice how we participate in cultural processes of representation that reinscribe white privilege in ordinary, everyday events. Being a middle-aged woman, and being white, my daily life is filled at every turn with everyday interactions of penalty and privilege. As a Christian, my struggle is to be aware of the complex ways in which I both internalize and am complicit in multiple systems of oppression. I will demonstrate that in exploring our everyday experiences of contemporary culture we discover how we are connected to each other and how such knowledge may move us toward more adequate understanding(s) of the complicity of white privilege. The cultural reflection I propose is at the service of "the necessary deeper critical work required to unearth the various ways in which one is actually complicit in terms of racist behavior" (Yancy, 2008, p.232).

I will reflect on this vignette of morning coffee in a number of ways. First, I will briefly map out why analyzing visual culture is critical to understanding and dismantling our daily enactment of white privilege. Second, I will return to the photograph that I describe at the opening of this chapter. I will analyze Kevin Carter's 1993 photo of a Sudanese child.[8] Carter's photograph was deemed the "icon of starvation," but the image misrepresented the actual material conditions of Sudanese famine. To study this photograph as cultural text of white privilege reveals how global power relations are reified in everyday life.[9] The photograph's creation, perspective and use are like a text which, when analyzed, reveal the workings of white privilege. Finally, I will explore what Christianity may offer us to resist the voyeuristic formation of contemporary American culture.[10]

To gaze on a photograph of suffering is always to be outside the frame, a stance that reinforces that I/we are not the suffering person we see. However, these photographs are often the only way that we "know" about human suffering. This situation is a moral dilemma, a bind, and a place of radical contradiction for Christians who are white. How do we respond to our neighbor if the very way that we see and know our neighbor is a cause of their objectification, their dehumanization, their suffering? I will suggest a practice of Christianity that may allow us to become vulnerable to the moral contradiction of our white gaze. For Christians, this vulnerable stance toward our own radical complicity as white may hold the possibility of being saved.

Grotesque un/knowing

Let's return to the moment of having coffee in the morning and reading the newspaper. How many times have you only looked at the photographs and captions because you don't have time to read the articles? In contemporary North American culture the knowledge of suffering human beings is often dependent solely upon visual images. In a course on social suffering, my students were shocked to find how often the photographs did not cohere with the text of the news article. In this section, I will draw upon Charles Mill's idea of the Racial Contract to demonstrate that photographs of suffering are often a cultural reinscription of the epistemology of ignorance. In the United States, photographs of suffering are part of the cultural process, making common sense of the systems that make suffering people not us. This "knowledge" of human suffering for those of us who are white protects "*a type of moral certainty, arrogance and innocence*" (Applebaum, 2010, p.34).[11] The "knowledge" that we get from photographs of human suffering is often a masquerade; a knowing that is unknowing, a remembering to forget.

Charles Mills (1997) brilliantly diagnoses the perverse nature of how we whites are socialized into "knowing" the world. To be white, we agree to an

> officially sanctioned reality (that) is divergent from actual reality ... one has an agreement to *mis*interpret the world. One has to learn to see the world wrongly, but with the assurance that this set of mistaken perceptions will be validated by white epistemic authority, whether religious or secular.
>
> *(cited in Applebaum, 2010, p.37. Italics in text.)*

For Mills (1997), this covert contract maintains the privileges of whites over non-whites (p.14). As a straight, able-bodied, middle-class, white woman, I contend that the inverted epistemology of white privilege that Mills so aptly describes also involves interlocking systems of dominance and subordination. Critical reading of photographs of human suffering offers us insight into the real-time actions of what Patricia Hill Collins (1998) describes as the matrix of domination (p.225). Interrogating Mills' idea of an epistemology of ignorance through the lens of the matrix of domination opens up deeper understandings of the multiple systems of oppression being culturally reinscribed in photographs of suffering.

Let me return to the vignette of reading the paper in order to understand how photographs are a cultural formation in the un/knowing of our place and participation in the matrix of domination. The photograph I alluded to at the opening of this chapter is of a Sudanese girl-child, naked, alone and in the bush. As I will document in my analysis in the next section, the grotesque nature of this knowledge is that it reinscribes not only racist ideologies, but also imperialist, colonialist, and sexist ideologies as well—simultaneously in one image. One way in which it reinscribes these ideologies is by making it appear as if they do not exist. The photograph demonstrates these ideologies and makes them invisible at the same time. At its best, the image of this little girl draws me in and I feel heart broken, or I may feel outrage. However, such reactions allow me to remain ignorant of my complicity in her situation. My altruistic reactions reinforce my sense of innocence. Eve Sedgwick (1980) contends that white epistemology is not a passive ignorance, as if I just don't know about the "big picture" at work in this little child's suffering (p.225). This is actually an activity and way of knowing the world (Mayo, 2002, p.85). In other words, in looking at this photograph I don't have to ask any questions about how my white existence conditions the suffering of this little girl-child. Looking at the photograph is an activity that functions to make me feel innocent, while blinding me to complicity—through the very "knowledge" of her suffering.

When I analyze photographs of suffering with students, some will say, "Damn, professor you are thinking way too much about this!" And they object to the analysis, protesting, "You can't prove the photographer had all these bad intentions!" These comments highlight white privilege at work. Part of the privilege of my ignorance is "having the privilege not to need to ask ... certain questions" (Applebaum, 2010, p.37). I don't have to ask how my existence is radically interconnected with this girl-child in Sudan. I believe that Mills is describing this phenomenon when he writes about the Racial Contract as "simply a failure to ask certain questions, taking for granted as a status quo and a baseline the existing color-coded configurations of wealth, poverty, property and opportunities ... " (Mills, 1997, p.73). Moreover, as Barbara Applebaum (2010) makes clear, this ignorance "is a type of knowledge that protects systemic racial injustice from being challenged" (p.37).

My students' protests are very helpful in proceeding deeper in critically reflecting on how these photographs function culturally to reinscribe the very unjust social relations that they appear to challenge. To hold out the humanitarian motives of the photojournalist, or the photograph's use by a relief agency, or, moreover, in the empathetic affect of the viewer misses the core problem at work. All of these points are individualistic and blind us to the radical sense of interconnection, complicity, and responsibility at work in photographs of suffering. As white people we need to ask ourselves if looking at such photographs makes us authentically understand our privilege and complicity in the world. When I hear white people say, "Wow that photograph makes me count my blessings!" then I know that we do not understand. It is relevant to ask if the photograph challenges our Racial Contract, or is the photograph at the service of protecting us from any challenge to our privileges. Let's return to the photograph of the young Sudanese girl-child, considered an icon of starvation. If these photographs challenged the Racial Contract, then the existence of this Sudanese girl would be able to speak to us, to question us. If photographs of suffering were interruptive of white privilege they would offer knowledge with the possibility of radically changing systems of social relationships.[12]

At this point it is fair to ask, "Don't these photographs document actual humanitarian crises, and give necessary witness to the abuse of human rights?" In order to answer that question we need to inquire into how this specific photograph by Kevin Carter helped us to understand and respond to this Sudanese girl-child's actual situation.

"The icon of starvation"

Kevin Carter's Pulitzer Prize-winning photograph of a Sudanese girl crawling to a feeding station was ironically deemed "the icon of starvation" in Africa.[13] Within Orthodox Christianity the icon functions as a meeting-point between the believer and all the blessed, the angels, the saints, as well as Mary the Mother of God and Christ. Some scholars describe the icon as a window on the Divine.[14] It is important to note that this window is a two-way looking-glass. The icon not only functions for our gazing upon the Divine, but also for us to experience God's gaze upon us. To gaze and be gazed upon, like the lover and beloved, can be transformative. The icon is understood to be a meeting-place for an encounter of two subjects, in relationship. As I analyze this photograph as a cultural representation I invite the reader to consider what it would be like if this image were truly an icon. What if the people we gaze upon in photographs of suffering were gazing back at us?

Carter's photo depicts a small Black female child, barely larger than an infant. The little girl is naked except for a bracelet on her wrist and a necklace around her neck. "She appears bowed over in weakness and sickness, incapable, it would seem, of moving; she is unprotected" (Kleinman and Kleinman, 1996, p.4). Ominously present in the frame is a vulture. No family appears in the photo to protect the little girl and "to prevent her from being attacked by the vulture, or succumbing to starvation and then being eaten" (Kleinman and Kleinman, 1996, p.4).

The historical context of the photo and the photojournalism of Kevin Carter demonstrate the photograph as an interpretation of reality—as a representation. Kevin Carter, a white South African, was a photojournalist who worked for the *Johannesburg Star*.[15] In March of 1993, Carter and a colleague went north from South Africa to photograph the rebel movement in famine-stricken Sudan.

> Immediately after their plane touched down in the village of Ayod, Carter began snapping photos of famine victims. Seeking relief from the sight of masses of people starving to death, he wandered into the open bush. He heard a soft, high-pitched whimpering and saw a tiny girl trying to make her way to the feeding center. As he crouched to photograph her, a vulture landed in view. Careful not to disturb the bird, he positioned himself for the best possible image. He would later say he waited about 20 minutes, hoping the vulture would spread its wings. It did not, and after he took his photographs, he chased the bird away and watched as the little girl resumed her struggle. Afterward he sat under a tree, lit a cigarette, talked to God and cried. "He was depressed afterward," Silva recalls. "He kept saying he wanted to hug his daughter."
>
> *(McCleod, 1994, pp.70–73).*

After the photo was bought and printed by *The New York Times* hundreds of people wrote and called to inquire about this Sudanese child (McCleod, 1994, pp.70–73). The paper reported that it was not known whether she had reached the feeding center (Keller, 1994, B8). Papers around the world reproduced the photograph and the image generated political will to aid Sudan and helped NGOs to raise money to stop hunger in Africa (Kleinman and Kleinman, 1996, p.4). In 1994 the photograph won the Pulitzer Prize, and was deemed the "icon of starvation" (Kleinman and Kleinman, 1996, p.5).[16]

Within a few months of winning the prize Carter committed suicide, leaving a note saying, "I am haunted by the vivid memories of killings and corpses and anger and pain ... of starving or wounded children, of trigger-happy madmen, often police or killer executioners ... " (MacLeod, p.73).

The notoriety of the photograph and the public nature of Carter's death generated a firestorm of controversy about this photo, about photojournalism, and about how photos of human suffering function in contemporary culture (Harwood, 1994, A25).[17] What did Carter do after he took the photo? Was the photo posed because he waited so long for the vulture to spread its wings? How could Carter allow the vulture to get so close to the little girl without doing something to protect her? "Inasmuch as Kevin Carter chose to take the time, minutes that may have been critical at this point when she is near death, to compose an effective picture rather than to save the child, is he complicit?" It was suggested that Carter was a predator, another vulture on the scene of this little child's anguish (MacLeod, p.73). Even Carter's friends wondered aloud why he had not helped the little child (MacLeod, p.73).

Few photographs of suffering so explicitly reveal the multiple layers of interdependence between the suffering subject, the photographer, the news outlet, and the viewer, as does Kevin Carter's photo of this Sudanese child.

> But what of the horrors experienced by the little Sudanese girl, who is neither a name nor a local moral world? The tension of uncertainty is unrelieved. Only now, with the story of Carter's suicide, the suffering of the representer and the represented interfuses. Professional representation as well as popular interpretations would have us separate the two: one a powerless local victim, the other a powerful foreign professional. Yet, the account of Carter's suicide creates a more complex reality. The disintegration of the subject/object dichotomy implicates us all.
>
> *(Kleinman and Kleinman, 1996, p.7)*

The history of the photograph challenges the subject/object dichotomy and points the viewer to the larger processes that the image represents and reinscribes. The claim that we are all implicated by the photo rests on the idea that the photograph of this little Sudanese girl is implicitly revealing to the viewer the power relationships that conditioned her suffering and death. The photo is a text about the white privilege that makes her suffering possible.

The photograph of this Sudanese child is problematic because its power is in its compelling capacity to make it appear as though the viewer is close enough to touch her, to hold her, to feed her, and to rescue her. This photograph is a representation which appears not to be. The representation of this child masquerades as "natural immediacy and presence" (Mitchell, cited in Dikovitskaya, 2006, p.16). In *The Politics of Representation*, Michael Shapiro (1988) explains this dilemma:

> In simple terms, then, representation is the absence of presence, but because the real is never wholly present to us—how it is real for us is always mediated through some representational practice—we lose something when we think of representation as mimetic. What we lose, in general, is insight into the institutions, actions and episodes through which the real has been fashioned, a fashioning that has not been so much a matter of immediate acts of consciousness by persons in everyday life as it has been a historically developing kind of imposition, now largely institutionalized in the prevailing kinds of meanings deeply inscribed on things, persons, and structures.
>
> *(p.xii)*

My intent is to understand the workings of privilege that deeply inscribe themselves upon the representation of this child's suffering. In documenting the anguish of this

Sudanese child, what does the photo say about the causes of her suffering? How does this photograph enable the viewer to reflect "on how our privileges are located on the same map as [her] suffering ... [?]" (Sontag, 2003, pp.102–3). And what moral claim does it make upon the agency of the viewer?

First, Carter's photograph first appeared in the *New York Times* in March of 1993. Carter's photo accompanied an article by Donatella Lorch (1993) entitled, "Sudan Is Described as Trying to Placate the West." Lorch's article documented food aid allowed by the Sudanese government for the starving people in the South. At the time of this aid more than a million people were suffering from famine and were at risk of starvation in southern Sudan. In her article, Lorch (1993) gives an accounting of this nightmare of social suffering.

> Forced to leave their lands and with their cattle herds virtually decimated, hundreds of thousands of mostly nomadic southern Sudanese are either on the brink of starvation or face severe malnutrition, relief workers say. In the area around the town of Kongor, 625 miles from Khartoum 145,000 displaced people face starvation, and more than 15 are dying each day. About 100,000 more cattle herding Dinka, have been pushed to camps along the Kenyan border. In some areas there are no children under 5 years of age.

The famine suffered by the southern Sudanese was (and has been) the result of political violence and chaos resulting from the civil war in Sudan. The article explained that famine was used as a tool of "ethnic cleansing" by the Sudanese government in Khartoum to subjugate the people in the South (Lorch, 1993). Moreover, in 1993 the United Nations Human Rights Commission had "accused the Sudan of widespread executions, torture, detention and expulsions and had voted to appoint a special investigator" (Lorch, 1993).

Lorch's article documented the first convoy of aid, which she judged to be placating the Western governments. This gesture was deemed a response to the United States' government's threat to place Sudan on the list of countries that sponsor terrorism (Lorch, 1993).

The caption of Carter's photo read, "A little girl, weakened from hunger, collapsed recently along the trail to a feeding center in Ayod. Nearby, a vulture waited" (Lorch, 1993). For this photograph to accompany Lorch's article of famine as systemic violence is problematic in a number of ways. The article is documenting the systemic causes of the suffering of the people in southern Sudan. The famine is not a "natural" occurrence, but is the result of human intent (Dreze and Sen, 1991).[18] The famine is a systemic form of violence, and it is interpreted today as a weapon of genocide in Sudan. However, the photo situates the suffering of this little girl against the horizon of "nature." The child's nakedness, the presence of the vulture, the dried grass and trees in the background give the impression of her starvation as the result of the crop failure and cycles of nature, absent of any collective human intent.

The vulture embodies danger and evil, but the greater dangers and real forces of evil are not in the "natural world": they are in the political world, including those nearby in army uniforms or in government offices in Kartoum.

(Kleinman and Kleinman, 1996, p.4).

The photo represents the causes of suffering in a manner that contradicts the documentation of the article it accompanies.

In addition, the child is alone, her community and local world are absent (Kleinman and Kleinman, 1996, p.7). To represent this child absent of any local world functions in two ways; first, to represent famine as the suffering of the lone individual is uniquely Western (Kleinman and Kleinman, 1996, p.7).[19] Modern conceptions of pain and suffering in the West have been deemed as existing only in the individual's nervous system or in personal consciousness (Morris, 1997, p.38).[20] This representation of suffering and human anguish is unable to account for the social suffering of collective groups of human beings on a massive scale. For instance, "[t]he Holocaust cannot be accurately described as the suffering of a single Jew repeated six million times" (Morris, 1997, p.38).

To represent the famine in Sudan as an individual's experience is to reduce the radically social experience and impact of this suffering. This child's suffering is not the result of any unique characteristic, but because of her belonging to a social, political, and cultural group in southern Sudan who are also part of a global community (Desjarlais et al., 1995).[21]

In addition, the next inference of the viewer to seeing this child alone is to assume that there are no families, no communities, no local institutions or programs to assist her. "The local world is deemed incompetent, or worse" (Kleinman and Kleinman, 1996, p.8).[22] This child is helpless without outside immediate assistance.

There is, for example, the unstated idea that this group of unnamed Africans (are they Nuer or Dinka?) cannot protect their own. They must be protected, as well as represented, by others. The image of the subaltern conjures up an almost neocolonial ideology of failure, inadequacy, passivity, fatalism, and inevitability. Something must be done, but *from outside* the local setting.

(Kleinman and Kleinman, 1996, p.7. Emphasis in text.)

The authorization for foreign aid and intervention to help this Sudanese child comes from indignation at the absence of her local world; foreign aid is evoked by erasing local voices and acts (Kleinman and Kleinman, 1996, p.7).

What is most troubling is the "racial knowledge" that this picture reinscribes about suffering in Africa (Goldberg, 1993, pp.148–84). This child's representation is not without precedence but is rather part of the archive of images of Black suffering children in Africa who appear desperate and victimized in the Western media.[23] The image of this little child's suffering body becomes an overcrowded intersection of views of the racialized suffering "Other." Her suffering—her Blackness—and her predatory surroundings make her "not us." The photo in one image links together the ideology of the primitive with suffering and Blackness in such a way that all these together in one body appear naturalized.[24]

To view this photograph within the cultural history of the United States is even more problematic. This small, crouched and starving female child in Sudan is caught up in a photographic genealogy of representing Black children as animals. The image of the Black child as pickaninny bears an uncanny resemblance to Carter's image of this small Sudanese child in the African countryside being pursued by a vulture.

> Black children depicted as pickaninnies were small and almost subhuman if not animal like. They were often mistaken for animals and were often pursued by hunters and other animals—dogs, chickens and pigs.
>
> *(Townes, 2006, p.142)*[25]

Emilie Townes (2006) explains the (im)moral implication of such representations of Black children in white people's imagination. The image of the pickaninny generated a (mis)belief that "Black parents were inherently indifferent to their children's welfare" (Townes, 2006, p.143). Such a view of Black parents and children made it easier for white people to not feel any sense of responsibility for the welfare of Black children. Moreover, as Townes (2006) so keenly reveals,

> The existence and maintenance of these caricatures prevented or made difficult any acknowledgement or examination of how elite White-controlled economic factors might have contributed to the slovenly appearance and substandard education of Black children.
>
> *(p.143)*

The process of representing a Black child that denies dignity is also an obfuscation of how the white viewer is essentially related to this child's suffering.

My analysis of this photograph raises many questions. Are we to dismiss all photographs of suffering? Are we to judge all photojournalism as corrupt? Should we stop looking at any documentary photography? What are we to do? What I hope the reader can see is that photographs of suffering can be very informative, but not in the way that they are explicitly intended. For white people, exploring our experience of looking at the photograph and also critically engaging the photograph as a text may offer insights into our relationship to the people pictured. Such reflection and engagement brings together theory and practice, because it is taking theoretical insight and behaving differently in our everyday life. Returning to our experience of the ritual of reading the paper and sipping morning coffee can be very instructive to concretely understanding our everyday enactments of white privilege.

Our task becomes how to engage and be engaged with photographs so as to shift our position of unmarked/invisible privilege to a position of shared vulnerability with those human beings in the photograph. Our struggle as white people to shift our position to shared humanity and vulnerability is a journey that I explore in the next section of this chapter.[26] This shift begins by questioning. Susan Sontag explains that questioning photographs is necessary because "We understand very little just looking at the photographic witness of some heart breaking arena of indignity, pain and death. Seeing reality in the form of an image cannot be more than an invitation to pay attention, to reflect, to learn, to examine rationalizations for mass suffering offered by established powers ... " (Sontag, 2001, p.16). A photograph can not "do the moral work for us, but it can start us on the way" (Sontag, 2001, p.16). Sontag (2001) states emphatically, "There are questions to be asked" (p.16). The moral work begins as we question how our own power and privilege is connected to the suffering of the people in the photograph.

Contradiction and complicity: a starting-point for white Christians' discipleship

> Jesus looked around and said to his disciples, "How hard it is for those who [are white] to enter the kingdom of God!" ... "It is easier for a camel to pass through the eye of a needle than for a [white person] to enter the kingdom of God." They were more astonished than ever. "In that case" they said to one another "who can be saved?" Jesus gazed at them. For [white people] he said, "it is impossible, but not for God: because everything is possible for God."

> *(Mark 10:23–27)*

When asked to write this chapter, I was to address the question "What would Jesus do?" This question is tricky for Christian white people. One reason is we have been taught, ironically, when reading Gospel stories, to identify with Jesus. But for most of us, we don't identify with a first-century Palestinian Jewish person living under Roman occupation. Rather, as white people we identify with a Christ-figure who is powerful, and usually is imagined as white—and not Jewish.[27] As Jim Perkinson (2004) declares, "But the very modern form of god-in-the-flesh. The very epitome (scandalously!) of Christianity—incarnation caricatured—the Jesus of the blue eye and fair hair" (p.192). What would it be like as a white citizen of the United States to pray to Jesus as a Jewish person suffering Roman occupation?[28] Traci West illustrates this problem when she describes intercessory prayers in Christian worship. She points out that when praying for "others" white people are always the ones who are not suffering, do not need help and are the ones doing the saving. To pray in this way reinforces our innocence, and makes us blind to the very suffering to which we are complicit.[29] Part of the Racial Contract is never having to explore or question the way in which my practice of Christianity legitimizes my white dominance. In other words, the seditious inner reach of white privilege is that as a white Christian I never have to question my privileged place in the gospel story.[30]

I begin my Christian response with this gospel passage about salvation not for rhetorical flourish but because this text expresses the existential experience of white Christianity. If neighbor love is the fundamental Christian response, how do white people respond to the photographs we see of suffering? The very act of looking at the photograph is an enactment of the gaze of whiteness privilege. Our gaze reconstitutes the power relations that create this suffering! If salvation is more than an abstract concept, and moreover a transformed relational reality, then God saves us in ways that create the possibility of new kinds of relationships. Jesus did not simply preach better ideas, but invited people into a radically different relationship with God, with each other and with themselves.

Some theologians have responded to my research about photographs of suffering by saying, "This is untenable, you have left us with no option—this is just a bind that allows people to do nothing!" or "We have to do something more than ask questions!" These reactions bespeak the bind, express the experience of having no way out that is a very valuable starting-point for exploring white Christian discipleship and what it might mean to be saved. Reactions like these are a way in which we distance ourselves from the pain of this bind, of the contradictions that are fundamental to our everyday life as white Christians. The desire to alleviate suffering is not the problem, the problem is that, as white people, we have an urgency to act so as to overcome our discomfort, we need to be in control, we need to have an action plan. History is littered with the plans (and human bodies) of the powerful who have created plans to bring about a better world. Edward Schillebeeckx drew upon the Frankfurt School of Critical Theory to highlight how utopian ideals can become oppressive for suffering people. The theological stakes of theses utopian plans of those in power is that we equate the plans with God's salvation.[31] In our case, as white people in the United States, our "action plans" to end suffering have been constructed without collectively questioning ourselves in ways that concretely contend with complicity in our everyday existence.

What I describe in this section is a response to our situation in seeing other people suffering in photographs, but it involves us first. I propose a way of being with our everyday experiences of white complicity so as to create the possibility of being open to God's saving grace. I argue that it is our willingness to be with the radical contradiction of our white everyday existence—in its pain, confusion, powerlessness, and vulnerability that is "doing something." It is tempting to look at a photograph of suffering and think that systems of oppression are "out there" and not be aware of the fact that these systems are inside me/us. As Nancy Pineda-Madrid explains, "We cannot view the world merely as an experience of the present nor merely as an experience external to ourselves; rather, we must realize that it lives within us and within our communities" (Pineda-Madrid, 2011, p.126).[32] To begin questioning within my everyday white context is at the service of a way of knowing how I/we participate in the world with others who suffer, and taking responsibility for my/our part in the relationship.

In contrast to doing "nothing," this stance is an acknowledgement of our need for God's grace at the very place of this bind. Part of the illusion of innocence is that we are good, and as Christians we are "saved." Therefore, as people who are saved, we desire to go out and help suffering people, as a way of following Jesus. My description of how innocence, goodness, and salvation are equated may sound quite theologically simplistic. However, I believe that it is an accurate account of assumptions that are operative in how we try to fix and solve problems. What I am suggesting is that to acknowledge our complicity and that we are not innocent is a way to realize salvation in the bind and contradictions of our white existence. We may indeed have faith in Jesus Christ's saving us, and believe in this as an "objective" reality. However, God's gift needs to be realized subjectively in relationship to the complicity of our white privilege.[33] Salvation is God's gift of freedom from all forms of human enslavement. Also God's gift is freedom for being "new creations" in relationships with God, with others, and our selves (Schillebeeckx, 1980, p.513).

Looking at a photograph of human suffering, salvation for the people we see is salvation from all forms of oppression. Salvation for us, who gaze upon them, involves being saved from the blindness of our own privileged white existence. We cry out, like the blind man on the road to Jericho, to see (Mark 10:46–52). And like some of the blind people cured by Jesus, our coming to sight may be a process (Mark 8:22–26). For us as Christians, these stories are our stories, and these stories offer us a way to know God's saving power in the bind of our white existence.

This willingness to engage in this stance in everyday life is a radical interruption of white privilege because it is not pretending to know how not to be white, or how not to be complicit. The stance, I suggest, is to be changed in our capacity to be in different kinds of relationships that cause the suffering upon which we gaze. This stance opens us to a way of relating beyond dominance and subordination, which is at the heart of white privilege.

This radical starting-point, this way of being conscious of our everyday complicity, is a way of being open to God's saving power. To claim that this stance makes us open to God's saving power is to say that we are opening ourselves to God's making us able to be in relationship to ourselves, other people, and God in a new way—a way out of the bind of white privilege. This stance is reminiscent of Jesus' description of being reborn. Jim Perkinson (2004) describes this rebirth from within the context of our white identity.

> [T]o crawl back through the history and up into the womb of the beginning and come out again, a second time, wet sticky, needing everything, an unformed newborn—accompanied by one's whiteness as a late after-birth, "good" only for a burial or the med lab ... Maybe this is the litmus test for a reformulated, a reinitiated, a re-evolved white identity: is it good for testing and then offering to the worms? That *is* our destiny. We should not be shocked, that is the destiny of all flesh. It is time whiteness became *mere* flesh, just like any other.
>
> (p.192)

What I am suggesting is that the experience of sipping coffee and reading the paper can be a way that we acknowledge we are mere flesh, we are human and, as white people, in radical need of God's grace. For example, how do we, as white people in America, imagine young children in Africa, particularly Sudan? Do we think of them as well-fed, healthy, laughing, playing soccer, living in middle-class homes in urban areas while dreaming of going to university? We all have pictures in our heads of each other. I am not suggesting that we should not have these pictures in our mind—it is part of the human existence. As white people, our work is in understanding how these images function, and how these images connect us to history, to other people and to the suffering in the world.

Let me take a phenomenological turn in order to offer a concrete awareness of the gospel idea that "It is easier for a camel to pass through the eye of a needle than for a [white person] to enter the kingdom of God" in regard to dealing with the complicity of viewing a photograph of suffering. I would invite the reader to reflect upon a time of looking at a photograph of human suffering. Looking at the photograph may give me a feeling of gratitude to know what is going on in the world. I may feel that in seeing the image I am more of a global citizen, which is not necessarily a bad thing. Then a whole host of other thoughts and feelings may arise. I acknowledge the horror of the person's plight and move on to another activity. I may feel tired, overwhelmed, and may feel a frustrated sense of powerlessness and guilt. I may feel compassion and want to do something for this person, and feel good about myself that I feel compassion, but also feel disturbed about the fact that I don't know what to do with my compassion. There is a range of thoughts and feelings that unfold in viewing a photograph of suffering. As this process unfolds there are "forks in the road" where the viewer has a number of options.[34] For example, to turn the page, go and pray, seek more information, or go for a walk. To choose among various options at each step of the viewing process is a privilege. For example, I may seek more information about the plight of the person in the photograph, and then be distracted by another task or activity. And all of these thoughts and feelings toward the suffering person are "intra-personal." All of these reactions and rumination are happening inside me. Even if I feel compassion but do not alter the way I live, if my life is the same after seeing the photograph, is this not grotesque?

As Barbara Applebaum (2010) argues, for white people, our ethical starting-point must be our complicity. Building upon Applebaum's insight, I am arguing that for white Christians this starting-point, existentially, can be a stance to a practice of Christianity. To examine my complicity is to be drawn out of my "intra-personal" rumination. I need to confront the way I live, and begin to examine how the concrete material conditions of my own existence are a participation in the suffering I see in the photograph. Even for white Christians who acknowledge participation in systems of oppression, the acknowledgement may be abstract. The struggle is to account for how our daily lives are concretely conditioned by this participation. For example, why is it that in the United States the water in our toilets ordinarily comes from the same source as water drink from the tap? In the United States we use clean drinking water for all our water use. Each day we sit and defecate into this fresh clean drinking water, unaware that so many people do not have clean drinking water. Returning to the existence of the small Sudanese girl-child, her plight was in no small part determined by the political abuse of food and water. Water is one way that fundamentally connects me to all other human beings, and the drinking water in my toilet reveals the complicity of my daily activities.

I will illustrate this stance in regard to the experience of looking at photographs of suffering. For white Christians, questioning our own gaze is not a theoretical question, but a deeply theological one. From the perspective of the Racial Contract, knowledge of human suffering depicted in photographs is not only a critical question for visual cultural studies, but is also a critical question for the practice of Christianity. The problem is that this mediated knowledge is rooted in what Shawn Copeland calls the "ocular epistemological illusion" (Pfeil, 2007, p.113).[35] This illusion "equates knowing with simply looking at that which is visible" (Pfeil, 2007, p.113). The problem with the visual as a basis for knowledge is that "[s]uch a foundation for knowing is easily seduced to support the Eurocentric aesthetic 'normative gaze' with its attendant racist, sexist, imperialist, and pornographic connotations" (Copeland 1997, p.112).[36] In other words, the illusion of this gaze is that the knowledge generated from this viewpoint *is reality*, not a mediated picture of reality. This gaze is inherently privileged because this gaze assumes a universalizing capacity in knowing the world, without accounting for any of the layers of mediation that have created the representation before one's eyes.

For white Christians, the danger of such a universalizing view of reality is that it is idolatrous. As Jim Perkinson (2004) has passionately detailed, "[w]hiteness is first of all 'theological'" (p.192). This absolutizing gaze is the fundamental stance of the practice of theology.

> Whiteness is the demon *in* the eye of theology, what looks out *from* that eye, as it devours the world in its rapacious organizing gaze ... Modern "looking" is always part of the White gaze ...
>
> *(Perkinson, 2004, pp.192–93)*

This privileged gaze holds a dangerously ironic twist in regard to "knowledge" of suffering human beings. David Theo Goldberg (1997) writes that this gaze gives the viewer the illusion of knowing, while the person—and the reality of their suffering—may actually remain invisible. "Invisibility also happens when one does not see people because one 'knows' them through some fabricated preconception of group formation" (Goldberg, 1997, p.80).[37] The photograph becomes a known commodity, while the suffering person and the viewer's relatedness to this anguish are obfuscated. What Copeland and Goldberg describe is the spiritual sickness of ignorance and arrogance of white privilege.

Our arrogance and ignorance suggests a practice of Christianity that Meg Guider (2002) describes as involving

> a willingness to approach, rather than avoid and evade, the discomfort, frustration, awkwardness, unmasking, exposure, misunderstanding, and vulnerability ...
>
> *(p.132)*

Drawing upon Nicholas of Cusa, Alex Mikulich (2007) insightfully describes this "knowing" as a form of "un-learned ignorance" (pp.160–75). Mikulich (2007) is reinterpreting Nicholas of Cusa through the work of M. Shawn Copeland in order to offer white Christians ways in which to theologically understand self-knowledge in the journey of becoming anti-racist. For Nicholas of Cusa, unlearned ignorance is dangerous for Christians because through "pride and presumptuousness [they] close themselves off from the path of divine wisdom" (Mikulich, 2007, p.162). This kind of knowing/ignorance "involves a fundamental absence to oneself, others, God, and the whole of God's creation" (Mikulich, 2007, p.162). As Mikulich describes, for Christians, turning from such "un-learned ignorance" is a spiritual journey, and, most fundamentally, a conversion. Mikulich's work lends a theological logic to inter-rogating how white Christians know the world. To explore our white knowing as a form of un-learned ignorance involves a stance toward the world that is characterized by humility, recognition of the radical limits of our knowing, and utter dependence upon God's grace. Such a faith stance demands that we listen, be open to critique, and question our own certainty about the world.[38] This approach to Christianity engages "What would Jesus do?" as a heuristic that is explored communally, critically, and in a daily struggle to see that what we have been taught is invisible—our privilege and others' suffering.

For white people to explore the potential of this starting-point, the experience of discomfort, vulnerability, and unmasking in following Jesus, let us return to the vignette of sipping morning coffee and reading the newspaper.[39] Think for a moment of the levels of interconnectedness and complicity with other people and other creatures that we realize simply by using an ordinary American kitchen. Experiencing this embedded complicity is to understand what salvation means, and Jesus' good news in relationship to the bind of our everyday lives. This is to say, we open ourselves to Jesus' revelation of God's passionate love, to the extent that we come to a lived awareness of our concrete interconnected existence. Just as racism and oppression are not "out there," neither is God's saving power. We meet God's saving power in history to the extent that we can be open to the reality of our white, everyday existence in all its complicity.

As we sip our coffee and see a photograph of a suffering Sudanese girl-child what is our experience? Do I ask, "Well what can I do?" Asking this question too quickly regarding what we can or I should do, we may be distancing ourselves from our own whiteness because in this question we move away from ourselves and from the radical nature of our white complicity.[40] In other words, by asking what should I/can I do, we shift the focus from our imbeddedness in systems that make this suffering possible. These questions evade the question of who I am as a white person and how my existence here, sipping coffee, reading the paper, is constructed by the very privileges relating me to this suffering person that I see in the photograph. Asking questions of responsibility, such as "what can I do?" allows me to hide behind an illusion of innocence. The suffering person becomes less important than my urgent need to feel innocent by "doing something" (Applebaum, 2010, p.183).

Before we explore our responsibility, it is crucial to explore our experience of complicity. One reaction to this photograph may be to be overwhelmed, or to be numb, and the need to turn the page. This reaction may reveal a great deal about our everyday embodied experience of white complicity. I have discussed the impact of being overwhelmed with students as they view photographs of suffering. They admit that the feeling of being overwhelmed generates a feelings of hopelessness and powerless, accompanied by a belief that this is "just the way it is." To explore the experience of being overwhelmed when looking at photographs of suffering enables us to discover how "the system of racism is perpetuated and maintained by and through individuals" (Applebaum, 2010, p.183). Our experience of being overwhelmed serves to reify the systems that make "others'" suffering "normal."

This experience of being overwhelmed and numb is the very way that white people suffer from and perpetuate our privilege. Being overwhelmed and numb makes us out of touch with our bodies. Alienation from the body is described by Mary Hobgood as one of the key ways that elites are hurt and oppression is perpetuated in the U.S. system of white privilege. For Hobgood (2007), "[t]he deepest possible religious awareness is for us to 'feel our own flesh as vital and vulnerable' and to be aware of our dependence on others" (p.41).[41] Drawing upon the work of Beverly Harrison, Hobgood (2000) writes that this connection to our bodies is the source of erotic power: "The erotic is the source of our energy and all our doing. It is the opposite of numbness and passivity" (p.117). Could the image of this suffering Sudanese girl child be calling into question a way of life that keeps us numb to the very life energy needed to be fully human?

Let's return to the idea of these photographs as icons, and how we might engage them in a way that the human beings we see are subjects, not objects. Human beings are ends, not means, and deserve to be respected "with a reverence that is religious."[42] The Catholic bishops of the United States suggest that this reverence should inspire awe that arises "in the presence of something holy and sacred."[43] While this teaching arose in relationship to national economic concerns, it also has profound implications in relation to the cultural production of images of human beings. Such reverence is particularly fitting in regard to photographs of human suffering. The bishops' teaching may suggest a reverence and awe as we look at photographs of human beings who suffer. Such a reverential gaze upon this young Sudanese child creates a relationship in which the viewer and the viewed are persons. From within the gaze of reverence this image can become an icon of God's suffering and objectified Black body in the world.

This gaze is an expression of the stance of openness and humility that allows for the uncertainty of my white view of reality. This stance acknowledges that the representation is just that, a representation, and my reverence is for the subject, the person that is captured within this frame. The activity of questioning is a practice that enables us to interrogate how our privileges may be located on the same map as the subject's suffering (Sontag, 2003, pp.102–3). For example, one critical question is: "Does this image interrupt or reinscribe the stereotypes of people who look like this or share this social position?" This question has a dual function. First, the question makes us stop and examine the images within our minds that determine perceptions of this person/s and their situation.[44] This inquiry is the first step in acknowledging shared human vulnerability. To inquire into these stereotypical images in our minds is to acknowledge the human vulnerability to be conditioned and impacted upon by the communities in which we live.

The second function of this first question is that it shifts us from passive receptors of the representation, to engaged participants in a message of the photograph. To inquire into the nature of how the suffering person is being represented is to begin to understand the photograph as a text and to "read" its message about the causes of and possible responses to this anguish.

Another question we might ask is: "Is this suffering avoidable and how so?"[45] To question the image in this way resists any way that the photograph may imply that this suffering is "normal" or destined for this person or group of people. To interrogate the historical causes of the suffering that we view holds the possibility of reconstructing the ties that bind us to the suffering person as a human being and realizing the claim that they make upon us.

Another question that holds this dynamic relational quality is: "If I or a loved one were in this photograph, how might I want this image to be different?" This question is a deeper step in the journey of shared human vulnerability because we now begin to imagine ourselves, and our relations, as inhabiting this same social space of suffering. Would it be acceptable for us to be photographed naked and violated? Would it be acceptable for us to be captured at the moment of shattering pain or grief? Would it be acceptable for our loved one to be pictured as tortured, or dismembered? Even to mentally consider these images as possible may be painful. This consideration of how we might want the knowledge of our suffering to be communicated has a heuristic quality. The question creates a space in the white viewer's moral imagination that acts as a bridge between our humanity and the humanity of the person who is viewed.

For us as white people, salvation understood from within the context of gazing upon a photograph of human suffering has profound implications for how we understand Christian discipleship. As we gaze upon photographs of human suffering the experience is one in which we share in a common need for salvation with those upon whom we gaze. Our task is not to save the people we see. I'm not sure that they need our saving them. But they do need us to understand ourselves and our connection to them as subjects, and to be responsible for our existence. Salvation understood within the bind of our white existence means becoming open to a radically different relationship to God, to ourselves and to the people upon whom we gaze. We can't fix this or solve this bind. To pretend that we can make our way out of this bind on our own is to claim that we can save ourselves. For us as white people, our task begins in understanding our very real and concrete connection and relationship to the people upon whom we gaze. Understanding our human, interconnected existence begins with making conscious the complicity of our everyday existence. The understanding of our complicity that is required is of our lived material and embodied experience, not just as a concept. This starting-point opens up space for God to transform us so as to relate in a radically different way. This journey of salvation may indeed be in our learning how to be truly responsible. This all may sound impossible, "but nothing is impossible for God."

Notes

1 Throughout this chapter, in referring to racial identity I will use lower case "w" for white and upper case "B" for Black. Drawing upon the legal scholarship of Cheryl Harris, Alice McIntyre explains that "Although 'white' and 'Black' have been defined oppositionally, they are not functional opposites. 'White' has incorporated Black subordination; 'Black' is not based on domination … 'Black' is naming that is part of counterhegemonic practice." Cheryl Harris, "Whiteness as Property," *Harvard Law Review* 106 (1993): 1709–1791 at 1710. I want to thank Alice McIntyre for this insight, this explanation and for her commitment to this practice in her writing (McIntyre, 1997, p.171, n. 1).

2 In this chapter I will use the words "we" and "our" for two reasons. First, what I am describing is a systemic issue that we enact as persons, but is not an individual phenomenon. Looking at a photograph of a suffering human being is to take part in a large and complex collective cultural process of representation that reinscribes privilege. Second, I use collective pronouns "to situate the reader as active and responsible in the context of the argument I am advancing." For this second point I am indebted to Nancy Pineda-Madrid (2011), p.154, fn. 1.

3 Susan Sontag comments that the dynamic of up close and far away in viewing photographs of suffering produces a strange combination of pity and sympathy, which mystify the viewer's connection to the suffering person.

4 These different venues deserve sustained analysis and constructive engagement by Christian theologians and ethicists. Scholars in media studies, linguistics and visual culture point out the different ways that photographs of suffering function in sites such as a museum exhibit, a calendar, Live Aid concert, and CNN broadcast. See further Lilie Chouliaraki (2006). What I am arguing here is that all of these venues mediate our knowledge of suffering "others" and are part of the culture reinscription of privilege.

5 For more on this point see the excellent article by Anna Szorenyi (2009).

6 For an extended discussion of some of these questions see Cassidy (2010).

7 I want to thank Alex Mikulich, Ph.D. for his generous and careful reading of this essay as well as for his insightful feedback.

8 To view this image, please see the following URL- www.corbisimages.com/Enlargement/ Enlargement.aspx?id=0000295711001&tab=details&caller=search. It is problematic that I, as a white North American social ethicist, will focus on a photograph from Africa to argue that representation inscribes racist power relations. Barbara Andolsen and Shawn Copeland have pointed out that North American Christian social ethicists and theologians often use examples in Africa rather than the United States to obfuscate their own involvement in white privilege. I join with this critique and intend my analysis to show how this representation is an expression of this obfuscation. This photo serves as a "spectacle of the other" which reveals the global implications of North American white privilege. See George Frederickson (1987) and bell hooks (1992).

9 Kevin Carter's photograph accompanied the article by Donatella Lorch (1993).

10 For the purpose of this chapter I will be focusing upon how this culture formation impacts on whites. This voyeuristic cultural formation impacts on all of us in American society—however, in different ways.

11 Italics the author's. I am indebted to Barbara Applebaum's insight on the virulent dynamic of white complicity.

12 If you have seen photographs in a recent campaign by Care you may challenge my argument. Care's recent photographs have people of color, looking straight into the camera, with the caption "I am powerful." Reading the intent of the campaign, one discovers that Care is trying to educate donors into seeing the people that Care serves as agents. This is a helpful shift. Inquiry into the significance of these photographs and this campaign deserves its own chapter. My concern is that such a campaign is still at the service of a liberal paradigm of socio-economic and political relations. Which is to say, these photographs may make us see people of color differently but still do not make us understand ourselves, and our radical everyday interconnection with them. My

concern comes from reading an insightful text on globalization by Rebecca Todd Peters (2006).

13 On April 13, 1994 the *New York Times* ran a full-page advertisement in recognition of the three Pulitzer Prizes that it won in that year. In describing Carter's photo it read: "To *The New York Times* for Kevin Carter's photograph of a vulture perching near a little girl in the Sudan who had collapsed from hunger, a picture that became an icon of starvation." Quotation from Kleinman and Kleinman (1996, p.5).

14 A classic text giving the historical, liturgical, theological, and spiritual meaning of icons is Lossky and Ouspensky (1999).

15 Carter and three other white South Africans (Joao Sliva, Greg Marinovich, and Ken Oosterboek) were on a mission to use photojournalism to expose the brutality of apartheid. The four men became so well known in the townships for capturing the violence of apartheid that they became known as the "Bang-Bang Club."

16 See note 13.

17 Using Carter as an example, Harwood explores the positive contribution of photojournalists, while also giving a nuanced picture of their ethical dilemmas.

18 Dreze and Sen demonstrate the political causes of famine in sub-Saharan Africa.

19 See also Walter Slatoff (1985).

20 An example of this thinking is in C.S. Lewis's idea that at any one moment in the universe there is never more pain than one person experiences (C.S.Lewis, 1994, pp.103–4).

21 This volume demonstrates how the World Bank and International Monetary Fund impact on post-Cold War global conditions which adversely effect health care and social policies in sub-Saharan Africa, especially for women.

22 For another such example see the photo by Ruth Fremson of an unnamed Haitian woman, with the caption, "A woman in Fort Dimanche laying out biscuits to dry, biscuits made of butter, salt, water and *dirt*" (*New York Times* May 5, 2004: p.1; emphasis my own). I want to thank Anna Perkins, Ph.D. who commented that the perspective of the photo and caption's message implies that Caribbean peoples may be thought by Americans as destined to eat dirt.

23 One example is the photograph of a frightened Rwandan child entitled, "Helpless" on the cover of *The Economist* July 23, 1994. For more on this see Hall (1997, pp.225–77).

24 "Those thus rendered Other are sacrificed to the idealization, excluded from the being of personhood, from social benefits, and from political (self-)representation" (Goldberg 1993, p.151).

25 On the history and cultural (dis)function of this image see Marilyn Kern-Foxworth (1994) and Patricia Turner (1994).

26 Here it is important to note that I am not referring to "shared humanity" as a philosophical category, which can and has been usurped by whiteness. But rather, I refer to the living, concrete and embodied existence that all human beings vulnerably share together in breathing air and needing to drink water. Whiteness obfuscates the radical inter-dependence of our shared existence as humans on this earth. I am grateful to George Yancy for his astute observation regarding this point.

27 For the implications of this perspective for racism see Carter (2008).

28 See also Sobrino (1988, pp.117–24).

29 See West (1999).

30 I explore this idea at length in Cassidy (2007).

31 See Schillebeeckx (1980). In this text Schillebeeckx begins Chapter 1, "The authority of new experiences," by citing Adorno as his first source (p.30). The influence of Critical Theory is seen in many parts of this work but clearly in the section "A critical-rational 'utopia' in a value-free society: problems for planning the future" (pp.666–70).

32 Pineda-Madrid offers an insightful constructive theological response to the evil at work in social suffering, and declares that, as Christians, we must respond. However, as she clearly explains, no human plan or action that we have can eradicate evil. How we respond to suffering makes us cooperate with God's saving presence—or not.

33 This idea of objective and subjective notions of salvation comes from the work of Schillebeeckx (1980), pp.512–14.
34 I am grateful to Alex Mikulich, Ph.D. for this phrase "forks in the road" and insight regarding the privileges of choices at these junctures.
35 I want to thank Margie Pfeil (2007) for this insight.
36 Copeland 1997, p.112. Copeland makes this same point in Copeland (1996, p.11). See also Griffin (1982), pp.110–60; Rivers (1998, p.239).
37 For a profound treatment of how this dynamic of being "known" and invisible impacts on the understanding of domestic violence against Black women see West (1999, pp.57–59).
38 These ideas of uncertainty, critique, and listening are explained at length by Barbara Applebaum (2010, pp.186–95).
39 Walter Wink (1992) has been a leading voice in understanding the Christian practice of discernment as constitutive of the struggle for social justice. He argues for the development of a self-reflective capacity that honestly, humbly, and clearly acknowledges our racist, homophobic, sexist, spontaneous inner reactions. He suggests that we notice these reactions as a reverberation of the systems of injustice in which we live. Only through this honest acknowledgement and critical reflection will Christians understand the inner workings of the systems of oppression.
40 Here I am applying Barbara Applebaum's insight about the distancing strategies of white students in her description of "white complicity pedagogy" (2010, p.183.)
41 See also Holler (2002), p.171.
42 See *Economic Justice for All*, no. 28.
43 See *Economic Justice for All*, no. 28.
44 For more on this idea of the unconscious but very active images that condition perception and judgment, see Shankar Vedantam (2010).
45 This question is compiled from a series of questions suggested by Susan Sontag (2003, pp.116–17).

References

Applebaum, Barbara. (2010). *Being White, Being Good: White Complicity, White Moral Responsibility, and Social Justice Pedagogy*. New York: Lexington.
Carter, Cameron. (2008). *Race: A Theological Account*. New York: Oxford University Press.
Cassidy, Laurie. (2010). "Picturing Suffering: The Moral Dilemmas in Gazing at Photographs of Human Anguish," *Horizons* 37/2 (Fall): 195–223.
——(2007). "'Becoming Black with God': Toward an Understanding of the Vocation of the White Catholic Theologian in the United States," in L. Cassidy and A. Mikulich (Eds.) *Interrupting White Privilege: Catholic Theologians Break the Silence*. Maryknoll, NY: Orbis Books.
Chouliaraki, Lilie. (2006). *The Spectatorship of Suffering*. London; Sage Publications.
Collins, Patricia Hill. (1998). *Fighting Words: Black Women and the Search for Justice*. Minneapolis: University of Minnesota Press.
Copeland, M. Shawn. (1997). "Foundations for Catholic Theology in an African American Context," in Jamie T. Phelps (Ed.) *Black and Catholic: The Challenge and Gift of Black Folk*. Milwaukee: Marquette University Press, pp.107–48.
——(1996). "The Exercise of Black Catholic Theology in the United States," *Journal of Hispanic/Latino Theology*, 3 (3), 5–15.
Desjarlais, Robert et al. (1995). *World Mental Health: Problems and Priorities in Low-Income Countries*. New York: Oxford University Press.
Dreze, Jean and Sen, Amartya. (1991). *Hunger and Public Action*. New York: Oxford University Press.
Frederickson, George. (1987). *The Black Image in the White Mind*. Hanover, NH: Wesleyan University Press.

Goldberg, David. (1993). *Racist Culture: Philosophy and the Politics of Meaning*. Cambridge, MA: Blackwell.

Griffin, Susan. (1982). "Pornography and Silence," *Made From This Earth: An Anthology of Writings by Susan Griffin*. New York: Harper & Row.

Guider, Margaret E. (2002). "White Privilege and Racism," *Proceedings of the Catholic Theological Society of America* 57, 132.

Hall, Stuart. (1997). "The Spectacle of 'The Other,'" in Stuart Hall (Ed.) *Representation: Cultural Representations and Signifying Practices*. London: Sage Publications, pp.223–90.

Harwood, Richard. (1994). "Moral Motives," *Washington Post* (November 21), A25.

Hobgood, Mary. (2007). "White Economic and Erotic Disempowerment: A Theological Exploration in the Struggle Against Racism," in Laurie Cassidy and Alex Mikulich (Eds.) *Interrupting White Privilege: Catholic Theologians Break the Silence*. Maryknoll, NY: Orbis.

——(2000). *Dismantling Privilege: An Ethics of Accountability*. Cleveland, OH: The Pilgrim Press.

Holler, Linda. (2002). *Erotic Morality: The Role of Touch in Moral Agency*. New Brunswick, NJ: Rutgers University Press.

hooks, bell. (1992). *Black Looks: Race and Representation*. Boston: South End Press.

Keller, Bill. (1994). "Kevin Carter, a Pulitzer Winner for Sudan Photo, Is Dead at 33," *New York Times* (July 29), B8.

Kern-Foxworth, Marilyn. (1994). *Aunt Jemima, Uncle Ben, and Rastus: Blacks in Advertising Yesterday, Today, and Tomorrow*. Westport, CT: Praeger Publishers.

Kleinman, Arthur and Kleinman, Joan. (1996). "The Appeal of Experience; The Dismay of Images: Cultural Appropriations of Suffering in Our Times," *Daedalus*, 125 (1), *Social Suffering*: 1–23.

Lewis, C.S. (1994). *The Problem of Pain*. New York: Macmillan.

Lorch, Donatella. (1993). "Sudan Is Described as Trying to Placate the West," *New York Times* (March 26).

Lossky, Vladimir and Ouspensky, Leonid. (1999). *The Meaning of Icons*. New York: St. Vladimir's Seminary Press.

Massingale, Bryan. (2010). *Racial Justice and the Catholic Church*. Maryknoll, NY: Orbis.

MacLeod, Scott. (1994). "The Life and Death of Kevin Carter," *Time*, 144:11 (September 12) 70–73

Mark 10: 23–27. This translation from *The Jerusalem Bible: Reader's Edition* (1968). New York: Doubleday.

McIntyre, Alice. (1997). *Making Meaning of Whiteness: Exploring Racial Identity as White Teachers*. Albany: SUNY Press.

Mikulich, Alex. (2007) "(Un)Learning White Male Ignorance," in Laurie Cassidy and Alex Mikulich (Eds.) *Interrupting White Privilege*. Maryknoll: Orbis, pp.160–75.

Mills, Charles. (1997). *The Racial Contract*. Ithaca, New York: Cornell University Press.

Mitchell, W.J.T. in Margaret Dikovitskaya (2006). *Visual Culture: The Study of the Visual after the Cultural Turn*. Cambridge, MA: MIT Press.

Morris, David. (1997). "Voice, Genre, and Moral Community," in Arthur Kleinman, Veena Das and Margaret Lock (Eds.) *Social Suffering*. Berkeley: University of California Press.

National Conference of Catholic Bishop. (1986). *Economic Justice for All: Pastoral Letter on Catholic Social Teaching and the Economy*. Washington, DC: U.S. Catholic Conference.

Perkinson, James. (2004). *White Theology: Outing Supremacy in Modernity*. New York: Palgrave.

Peters, Rebecca Todd. (2006). *In Search of the Good Life: The Ethics of Globalization*. New York: Continuum.

Pfeil, Margie. (2007). "The Transformative Power of the Periphery: Can a White U.S. Catholic Opt for the Poor?" in Laurie Cassidy and Alex Mikulich (Eds.) *Interrupting White Privilege: Catholic Theologians Break the Silence*. Maryknoll: Orbis.

Pineda-Madrid, Nancy. (2011). *Suffering + Salvation in Ciudad Juarez*. Minneapolis: Fortress Press.

Rivers, Clarence Rufus J. (1998). "The Oral African American Tradition Versus the Ocular Western Tradition. The Spirit of Worship," in Diana Hayes and Cyprian Davis (Eds.) *Taking Down Our Harps, Black Catholics in the United States*. Maryknoll: Orbis.

Schillebeeckx, Edward. (1980). *Christ: The Experience of Jesus as Lord*, trans. John Bowden. New York: Seabury.

Sedgwick, Eve Kosofsky. (1980). *Epistemology of the Closet*. New York: Oxford University Press.

Shapiro, Michael. (1988). *The Politics of Representation: Writing Practices in Biography, Photography, and Policy Analysis*. Madison: The University of Wisconsin Press.

Slatoff, Walter. (1985). *The Look of Distance: Reflections on Suffering and Sympathy in Modern Literature – Auden to Agee, Whitman to Woolf*. Columbus, OH: Ohio State University Press.

Sobrino, Jon. (1988). *Spirituality of Liberation: Towards a Political Holiness*, trans. Robert Barr. Maryknoll, NY: Orbis.

Sontag, Susan. (2003). *Regarding the Pain of Others*. New York: Picador.

——(2001). "Preface," in *Don McCullin*. London: Jonathan Cape.

Szorenyi, Anna. (2009). "Distanced Suffering: Photographed Suffering and the Construction of White In/Vulnerability," *Social Semiotics* 19 (2): 93–109.

Townes, Emilie. (2006). *Womanist Ethics and the Cultural Production of Evil*. New York: Palgrave/Macmillan.

Turner, Patricia. (1994). *Ceramic Uncles and Celluloid Mammies: Black Images and Their Influence on Culture*. New York: Anchor Books.

Vedantam, Shankar (2010). *The Hidden Brain: How Our Unconscious Minds Elect Presidents, Control Markets, Wage Wars and Save Our Lives*. New York: Spiegel and Grau.

West, Traci. (1999). *Wounds of the Spirit: Black Women, Violence and Resistance Ethics*. New York: New York University Press.

Wink, Walter. (1992). *Engaging the Powers: Discernment and Resistance in a World of Domination*. Minneapolis: Augsburg Press.

Yancy, George. (2008). *Black Bodies, White Gazes: The Continuing Significance of Race*. Lanham, MD: Rowman & Littlefield.

3

JESUS MUST NEEDS GO THROUGH SAMARIA

Disestablishing the mountains of race and the hegemony of whiteness

Cheryl Townsend Gilkes

"The Samaritans were the spooks!" Jeremiah Wright declared, "There was a race problem in John 4!" Identified by EBONY Magazine in 1984 and 1993 as one of the fifteen greatest African American preachers, Wright, with an exegesis informed by black liberation theology, provided an iconoclastic, scholarly, and gritty approach to one of the most well-known, oft-preached biblical texts in black churches. His aim was to make the text live in such a way that his black middle-class congregation would realize Jesus's solidarity with them and their experiences in white America.[1] Both the African American preaching tradition and music tradition made this story of Jesus's encounter with the Samaritan woman a prominent feature of popular biblical consciousness. The preaching tradition often leaned on the rhetorical constructions of the King James Bible, a rhetorical construction that stressed that Jesus "must needs go through Samaria." In most black sermons, that phrase became "must *neeeeeds* go through Samaria!"[2] In spite of the patriarchal misreadings of this familiar story, black preaching always viewed Jesus's presence in Samaria as indicative of his determination to stand with the poor and the oppressed. In this story, Jesus represents a God who sides with the least, the lost, and the excluded.

When Wright called the Samaritans "spooks," he used a racial epithet that also served as a self-deprecating in-group nickname that older African Americans sometimes used. The term "spook" was made famous by Sam Greenlee in his 1969 novel, *The Spook Who Sat by the Door*. The novel pointed to the way in which it was possible for black people to use their marginality and invisibility in white America for revolutionary purposes. By viewing the Samaritans as "the spooks," Wright placed them in an analytical context that allowed his listeners to think of the problems of the Samaritans as parallel to the problems of black people in white America. If there was a problem of oppression, segregation, marginalization, and ghettoization in John 4, then Jesus's encounter with the Samaritan woman created a prophetic challenge to these arrangements. As a Judean, Jesus placed himself squarely as an ally to the Samaritans, including them fully among "the lost sheep of the house of Israel."

Current thinking about race relations and social justice focuses on the role of whiteness and white privilege in shaping a racialized society—a society whose structure is characterized by oppression, segregation, marginalization, and ghettoization (Bonilla-Silva, 1997). Taking the work of Jesus as a starting-point, this chapter uses two biblical stories to explore the problems of whiteness and privilege in moving the mountain of "race." Both stories connect with Samaria: the story of Elisha's servant, Gehazi, who becomes white as the result of a curse, and the story of Jesus's encounter with the Samaritan woman. The stories act as bookends for a particular prophetic stream in what biblical scholars call "salvation history." While Jesus is, for Christians, prophet, priest, and king, it is within the prophetic tradition that Jesus, the Son of Man, does his most visible work of human reconciliation. If Christianity is to be useful in the project of human liberation and reconciliation, it is important to grasp the ways in which Jesus's ministry provides models for us today.

In this chapter, not only do I examine the way in which Jesus engages the Samaritans, the *others*—the "spooks" of his day—but I also examine the way in which Samaria matters in Jesus's approach to healing the divided nation and, therefore, preparing a pathway or a highway for God's witness to go forward to the world.[3] The reconnection and healing of Samaria seem to fulfill the prophetic declaration that Jesus and John emphasize: "all flesh shall see the glory of the Lord together." Jesus identifies specific tasks that represent the fulfillment of God's will and some of that work is specific to Samaria. As a prologue to examining Jesus's ministry in Samaria, I examine the Hebrew Bible/Old Testament story of Elisha and Gehazi both to highlight the contradiction of "whiteness" in modern understandings of race and at the same time to underscore the significance of Samaria in salvation history and the tradition of the prophets of ancient Israel/Judah. As often as white racists in the United States appealed to the Bible to justify their views on racial hierarchy and to argue the inferiority of black people, the story of Elisha and Gehazi represents a glaring omission from these discussions. I then examine the story of Jesus's encounter with the Samaritan woman and the revolutionary implications of that story and its links to Jesus's ministry in Samaria. I examine the possible problems associated in making a direct comparison between contemporary North America and the biblical world. Jesus's encounters with "others" during his ministry provide important foundations for generating a Christological perspective on whiteness and racial privilege.

By using these stories I am able to explore two issues of difference in the biblical world so as to develop an extended reflection on whiteness and race—lepers and Samaritans. While the choice may seem arbitrary, leprosy and Samaria are linked both in the Hebrew Bible (or Old Testament) and in the Gospel accounts of Jesus's ministry. In both settings, the linkages between leprosy and Samaria foster prophetic work that disestablishes the hegemony and dominance of Mt. Zion and includes the oppressed and excluded as agents of salvation history. In both the Hebrew Bible (or Old Testament) and the New Testament Gospels, Samaria is the site of prophetic agency, first in the Elijah/Elisha cycle of stories and then in Jesus's own insistence, so vividly described in the King James Bible language of John 4:4, Jesus "must needs go through Samaria." Exploring selected aspects of God's prophetic dealings with lepers and Samaritans provides an interesting insight on whiteness that challenges the presumptuousness of contemporary notions of whiteness and highlights the selectivity required for using the Bible to construct race and justify racism—for imagining race in the Bible. Gehazi's story highlights biblical whiteness as a kind of divine punishment in the form of leprosy. The issue of leprosy as whiteness is an inverted strategy for deconstructing the racialized use of the Bible. The second story—the encounter at Jacob's well—highlights the way in which Jesus approaches the disestablishment of hegemony and privilege in a style that emphasizes relationship and revelation as pathways to transformation, social justice, and the beloved community.

"Art thou he that should come?": why Samaria matters

In the gospel of Luke (7:19–28), two disciples of John the Baptist come to Jesus asking "Art thou he that should come or look we for another?" Jesus responds at first by working and then describes the tasks that are central to his earthly ministry:

> And in that same hour [Jesus] cured many of their infirmities and plagues and of evil spirits; and unto many that were blind he gave sight. Then Jesus answering said unto them, Go your way, and tell John what things ye have seen and heard; how that the blind see, the lame walk, the lepers are cleansed, the deaf hear, the dead are raised, to the poor the gospel is preached.

Of Jesus's many accomplishments in this passage, one accomplishment is particularly significant for our purposes: "the lepers are cleansed." We often think of the leprosy connection in terms of healing and we think of healing as an issue of individual somatic problems. It is important, however, to think of the cleansing of lepers as an act of restoration and reconciliation. Lepers were outsiders who experienced the greatest exclusion and segregation from their communities. They were the ultimate strangers. Furthermore, lepers were compelled to participate in their own oppression by loudly advertising their situation. Obery Hendricks (2006: 165), in a discussion of Jesus's expression of anger during his healing of a leper, pointed out:

> [T]he anger that welled up within Jesus was not anger at the leprous man, but at the authorities' refusal to treat his needs as holy. But not only did the leper have to beg the religious authorities to be treated like a human being, he also had to give them an offering—that is, pay them—to be treated humanely again. ... Thus the system subjected the sick to a double oppression.

The gospel of Mark (1:40) depicted Jesus healing a leper at the very beginning of his ministry. In the gospel of Luke, after Jesus made a dramatic declaration of his prophetic role (Luke 4:17–21), Jesus healed a leper in "a certain city" (5:12–15). In both of these cases, Jesus sent the lepers to the priests so that they could be reinstated into the community. What followed from the physical healing was an act of social inclusion; lepers had to be affirmatively integrated into their communities.

On a particularly interesting occasion, Jesus encountered ten lepers in his travels through Galilee and Samaria:

> And it came to pass, as [Jesus] went to Jerusalem, that he passed through the midst of Samaria and Galilee. And as he entered into a certain village, there met him ten men that were lepers, which stood afar off: And they lifted up their voices, and said, Jesus, Master, have mercy on us. And when [Jesus] saw them, he said unto them, Go shew yourselves unto the priests. And it came to pass, that as they went, they were cleansed. And one of them, when he saw that he was healed, turned back, and with a loud voice glorified God. And fell down on his face at [Jesus's] feet, giving thanks: and he was a Samaritan. And Jesus answering said, Were there not ten cleansed? But where are the nine? There are not found that returned to give glory to God, save this stranger. And he said unto him, Arise, go thy way: thy faith hath made thee whole.
>
> *(Luke 17:11–19)*

First of all, the fact that Jesus was in "the midst of Samaria" is highly significant, since, as we shall see with Jesus's encounter with the woman at the well, "the [Judeans] have no dealings with the Samaritans" (John 4:9d).[4] In the midst of·Samaria, Jesus met ten lepers whom he healed. However, only one returns to thank Jesus directly and Jesus describes him as a "stranger" and a "Samaritan." To Jesus the Judean, the Samaritan was a stranger. The implication, of course, was that the other nine lepers were Judeans and, given what we know about Judeans and Samaritans, those lepers, upon discovering that they were cleansed, returned directly to Judea, and possibly to Jerusalem and, therefore, Mount Zion.

As we think about this passage, it is important to realize that Judeans did not know their way around Samaria all that well. I teach at a small liberal arts college where the student body is overwhelmingly white in a state (Maine) that the Census Bureau has labeled the whitest state in America. A group of my white students, when visiting Boston, made a wrong turn and found themselves in one of Boston's black neighborhoods. They were lost. They asked a young black man for directions to their destination and he informed them that he would be happy to give them directions "for ten dollars." The students paid him! At some point, I think, the Judeans found themselves in a situation similar to that of my students—they were privileged strangers in a ghetto and needed directions. The Judean lepers wanted to find Jesus in order to be healed and found themselves dependent on the Samaritan leper's insider knowledge to achieve that healing. By working in the midst of Samaria, Jesus challenged Judeans, the dominant privileged group in that context, to cross borders and boundaries so that healing and reconciliation could take place. Once healed, however, they did not come back to Samaria.

Samaria is highly significant. Samaria is the area where Elijah and Elisha served as prophets of God. In order for the Messiah to come, Elijah must come back.

According to Malachi 4:5, "Behold I will send you Elijah the prophet before the coming of the great and terrible day of the Lord. … " Elisha, as Elijah's successor, carried forward that ministry but, unlike Elijah, who was taken up to Heaven in a fiery chariot, Elisha actually died and was buried. However, for our purposes, it helps to view that Samaritan ministry as the first in a set of bookends involving Samaria and the relationship of Samaria to the healing of lepers. There are two significant stories involving lepers attached to the ministry of Elisha: one involving the healing of a Syrian captain named Naaman (2 Kings 5:1–27) and the other involving the prophetic role of lepers in the fulfillment of prophecy (2 Kings 7:3–10).[5]

The Elijah/Elisha ministry was located in Samaria, and Jesus insisted on working in Samaria. Along with other locations, Jesus's ministry drew people away from the environs of the Jerusalem elite and to places where people's ritual cleanliness did not matter. By working in Samaria, Jesus addressed a long-standing schism among the people of God and reintegrated the foundations of salvation history in Israel/Judah. In the gospel of John (4:4–42), Jesus is determined to go through Samaria, and in so doing extends the ministry of John the Baptist, whom Jesus himself recognizes as the Elijah-type forerunner identified by the prophet Malachi. As Jesus points out, after telling John's disciples to report back on Jesus's activities, "This is he, of whom it is written, Behold I send my messenger before thy face, which shall prepare the way before thee. … [T]here is not a greater prophet than John the Baptist … " (Luke 7:27–28). In the larger context of salvation history, Samaria mattered mightily.

"A leper white as snow": Gehazi and the silence about whiteness

Elisha conducted a particularly significant healing during his ministry in Samaria (2 Kings 5:1–27). A captain in the Syrian army, Naaman, contracted leprosy. One of his slaves, an Israelite (Samaritan), suggested that he visit "the prophet that is in Samaria" (2 Kings 5:3). Naaman brought substantial wealth with him as he set out to find the prophet. Elisha told Naaman to wash seven times in the Jordan river and, after being coaxed out of his reluctance by his Samaritan slave girl, Naaman washed and was healed. What is significant for salvation history is Naaman's confession in response to his healing: "Behold, now I know that there is no God in all the earth but in Israel" (2 Kings 5:15). Naaman then offered the money and clothing to Elisha: "Now therefore I pray thee, take a blessing of thy servant." Elisha refused Naaman's offer. However, Elisha's servant, Gehazi, decided to run after Naaman and tell a lie in order to secure some of Naaman's treasure. When Elisha discovered Gehazi's disobedience and duplicity, Elisha cursed Gehazi, saying, "The leprosy therefore of Naaman shall cleave unto thee, and unto thy seed for ever. And [Gehazi] went out from [Elijah's] presence a leper as white as snow."

In spite of all of their differences and the range of differences, all of the people in the biblical world would be considered to be some variety of beige or brown—with the darkest browns coming from Ethiopia (Cush). The people of the biblical world would find the modern attempt to distinguish who is white and non-white strange and possibly laughable. As Gehazi's situation demonstrates, visibly white people in the

Bible were lepers. The problem of whiteness in biblical times was a problem of uncleanness, ritual pollution, and rigid boundaries of separation. People described as white in the Bible were unclean and excluded and in those cases where we know about the beginnings of the leprosy—the cases of Miriam and Gehazi—the lepers were described as being white as snow. As I have told my students, if a person is white as snow, there is a serious medical problem involved. Such people are very, very, very ill. Although most cases of biblical leprosy involve characters who were already ill and who presented themselves to Jesus for healing or, as in the case of the Samaritan lepers, during a famine, the lepers were involved in a particular prophetic narrative.

These two major incidents where the onset of leprosy is divine punishment—the punishment of Miriam and the cursing of Gehazi—offer a challenge to the conceit of whiteness in contemporary times. In these two cases, leprosy occurs because of divine judgment. In the case of Miriam, she challenges her brother, Moses, because of his Cushite (African) wife. Miriam's prophetic office is so important to the people of Israel that Moses pleads her case to God and the people wait in the wilderness until she is healed and able to rejoin the community. In the case of Gehazi, not only does he become a leper but the leprosy that turns his skin white becomes a heritable curse for his children. Gehazi, cursed by God to be distinctively white, is cursed because he is a greedy, covetous, acquisitive liar. Property means more to him than the prophetic agency that moves the confession of God beyond the boundaries of Judea and Israel to the known world. Gehazi is punished because he cares more about treasure than the transformation of the enemies of God and God's people. Gehazi obstructed the growth of "a universalistic, spiritually oriented Judaism echoed by the great Hebrew prophets" (Solomon, 2001:151).

It is ironic that, although religion plays a central role in the construction of race and the perpetuation of racism (Gilkes, 2010), biblical apologies ignore the descriptions of whiteness in the Bible. The silence of white racists about the white-ness of Gehazi echoes the silence of modern society about whiteness as a dominant hegemonic frame. The central theme of explicit religious racism in America is the argument for black inferiority. White dominance and hegemony are evident in the ability of white racists to pick and choose among elements of the Bible, reading race where it does not exist and ignoring the paradox of biblical whiteness. The silence about Gehazi points to the tremendously complex problem of framing (Feagin, 2010). Although blackness and whiteness are modern inventions (Painter, 2010; Rothenberg, 2008), theories of race have grown alongside a tradition of white biblical interpretation that is totally silent about Gehazi, a man whose children inherit his whiteness.

"Neither in this mountain": the mountains of race and cult, Judea vs. Samaria

In his sermon about Jesus's encounter with the Samaritan woman, Wright, then pastor of the Trinity United Church of Christ in Chicago, took a somewhat revolu-tionary approach to this story. He focused on the historical schism between Judeans and Samaritans. Most sermons about Jesus's encounter with the "woman at the well" marveled that Jesus was talking to a woman. Furthermore, those sermons ritually destroyed the Samaritan woman in order to magnify the greatness of Jesus's encounter with her. She had, according to the story, five husbands, and, as the oral song tradition interpreted this encounter, Jesus told her, "the one that you have now is not your own!"

Contemporary biblical scholar A.J. Levine (2006:131–33) points out that the focus on the Samaritan woman's gender has been misdirected by what she calls the "misogynistic morass." That misdirection is fueled by presumptions stemming from male biblical interpreters' and preachers' reading contemporary patriarchy back into the biblical world. The truly revolutionary and revelational aspect of this story was Jesus's insistence upon going through Samaria and his willingness to ignore the boundaries that kept Samaritans and Judeans segregated from one another. Not only was speaking to this Samaritan person revolutionary, but Jesus also asked her for water, fully intending to use the dipper that she would offer. This boundary-breaking encounter was highly significant and, as Wright's sermon emphasized, smashed a nearly 800-year-old schism in order to advance the reach of God throughout the world.

In the discussion that Jesus carried on with the woman, she addressed the debate over the proper place of worship. After a discussion of her family situation, this unnamed Samaritan exclaims, "Sir, I perceive that thou art a prophet." It is at this point that she and Jesus get into a discussion over which mountain is the correct mountain for worship, Mount Zion or Mount Gerizim. She lays out the terms of this historic debate: "Our fathers worshipped in this mountain; and ye say, that in Jerusalem is the place where [people] ought to worship" (John 4:20). Jesus responds by stating that there will be, in effect, a turning-point in salvation history: "The hour cometh when ye shall neither in this mountain, nor yet at Jerusalem, worship the Father. ... God is a spirit: and they that worship him must worship him in spirit and in truth" (John 4:21, 24).

The symbolic importance of mountains has not been lost on African Americans in the United States. Langston Hughes (1926) utilized that symbolism when coming to terms with the way race matters in America. Mountains symbolized not only structures of exploitation and obstruction but also the established, seemingly eternal, nature of these structures. In Mark 11:23 (KJV), Jesus informed his disciples, "That whosoever shall say unto this mountain, Be thou removed, and be thou cast into the sea; and shall not doubt in his heart, but shall believe that those things which he saith shall come to pass; he shall have whatever he saith." Obery Hendricks (2006: 121–22) has argued that Jesus's reference is actually to the Temple mount, Mount Zion, as a representation of the religious establishment. This official religion was obstructing redemption, healing, and liberation. According to Hendricks's translation and interpretation, Jesus declares to the disciples:

> [T]hat if they were truly serious about transforming their situation, they had the power to throw "this mountain" into the sea, if that was their choice. It is not coincidental that out of every image available to him Jesus used the phrase "this mountain." When [Jesus's] statement is considered in context, there is little question that he was referring to ... Mount Zion. ... This then was the

meaning of Jesus's protest … a repudiation of the Temple and those who ran it, repudiation of their abuse of people's trust, their haughty dismissal of the people's worth, their turning the Temple of God into a profiteering enterprise, their exploitation of the people in the name of God and for the benefit of themselves and the Romans. It was a prophetic pronouncement to the priestly aristocracy that they must change or be judged by God.

Throwing down and disestablishing mountains of anti-human self-interest was central to Jesus's ministry. A contest over established mountains was at the heart of the tension between Judea and Samaria, eventually leading to the Samaritans' becoming, in Jeremiah Wright's words, "the spooks." The traditions about Israel/Samaria in the Hebrew Bible were an important component of the history of monarchy and prophecy in ancient Israel. The tension between Samaria and Judah actually began, according to I Kings 12, when Jeroboam rebelled against the oppressive rule of Rehoboam. In the ensuing conflict, one of the prophets discouraged all-out war between the northern the tribes (Israel) under Jeroboam and the southern two tribes (Judah and Benjamin) under Rehoboam. He preached, "Thus saith the Lord, ye shall not go up, nor fight against your brethren the children of Israel" (I Kings 12:24a). The result was that Israel, whose capital was Samaria, was the site of a parallel monarchy that rivaled the monarchy in Judah/Jerusalem. Until Israel's conquest in 722 B.C., worship in the South/Judah was centered in Jerusalem on Mount Zion while worship in the North/Israel took place at alternative sites, especially at Bethel on Mount Gerizim. As the result of warfare in 128 B.C., where Judeans gained control, Samaria, by the time of Jesus, was a marginalized area that Judeans avoided, so much so that travelers to areas north of Samaria went *around* rather than *through* Samaria (O'Day, 1992). The social geography was such that, as with modern ghetto areas, the dominant social groups avoided the area.

If Jesus worked to disestablish the mountains that separated God's people and to wipe away the cultic hegemony that fostered separation and oppression, then Jesus's ministry challenges us to action now to disestablish the mountain of race and to erase the hegemony of whiteness. Although race as we have known it in the modern era did not exist in the biblical world (Boring and Craddock, 2004: 300), the borders and boundaries engendered by nation and tribe functioned in the same way. In the Bible, nation was defined by the deity and the territory of those who served that deity. Nation operated in ways similar to the ways in which race operated in the Jim Crow South or apartheid South Africa. Once the tribal confederacy of Israelites became a monarchy—"a nation like all the other nations"—the first three kings, Saul, David, and Solomon, ruled over a nation ostensibly unified in its allegiance to the God of Abraham, Isaac, and Jacob—Yahweh—whose cultic center was on Mount Zion in Jerusalem. The transition from Solomon split the kingdom, and the northern ten tribes constituted the kingdom of Israel, while the southern two tribes became the kingdom of Judah. Judah's cultic center was Jerusalem; Israel's cultic center was Samaria. Over time the distinction between Judeans and Samaritans, especially in the era of the second temple, became as conflicted and separatist as the distinction between black and white people in the Jim Crow South. Although Judeans and Samaritans prayed to the same God, Judeans controlled the temple at Jerusalem and had the power to define the Samaritans' worship on Mount Gerizim as defective and inferior.

The ritual practices and the social geography of the biblical world paralleled those of contemporary race relations. Like the Samaritans and Judeans, black and white people in the United States lived lives governed by laws and customs that determined what social interaction was forbidden. The segregation that resulted also created ghettoes to be avoided.

Whiteness and the religion of Jesus

Thinking theologically about race and whiteness is necessary if our thinking is to contribute to a world of love and justice. For decades, sociologists thought about race as a problem of "minority groups" and "subordinate groups" and the problems they posed for social order and equilibrium. One of the consequences of the civil rights and black power movements was the "discovery" of racism by activists and social scientists. A transformed Malcolm X argued that the problem was not civil rights but human rights and that, in the face of growing black nationalism, an important task for white people of good will involved their addressing racism in their own communities (Knowles and Prewitt, 1970). Building on Malcolm X's argument that the problem in American society was white racism, Stokely Carmichael and Charles Hamilton (1967), in their landmark *Black Power: The Politics of Liberation in America*, distinguished between individual acts of racism and institutional racism—the consequences of historically structured inequality. Also taking Malcolm X seriously, a group of significant seminarians and graduate students examined the consequences of history and structure for racial inequality in American institutions—the economy, politics, health care, education, and law—producing *Institutional Racism in America* (1972). By 1968, through the efforts of Charles King, the Kerner Commission actually named "white racism" as a factor in causing the ghetto rebellions of the 1960s. Whiteness and racism became part of the lexicon of concern in the struggle for the beloved community.

The rise of the Black Power Movement coincided with religious transformations that gave rise to liberation theologies, including black theology (Wilmore, 1973). Black theologians asked questions about the meaning of Jesus Christ for black people in America (Cone, 1999). Following the lead of James H. Cone, black theologians affirmed that God's option is for the poor and oppressed, and Jesus Christ, particularly, lived a life that affirmed the allegiance of a liberating God. Authentic Christians were called to stand with the poor and the oppressed. In the quest for the beloved community, the oppressed and their allies raise questions about the role of Jesus. Much of liberation theology points to the commitment of Jesus to the poor and the oppressed—to the disinherited of this world.

Because of its role in the African American religious experience, the Bible is an important norm and source for black theology (Callahan, 2006; Kling, 2004; Wimbush, 2003). Translating the issues of social justice from the biblical world to the modern world and from the modern world to the biblical world is fraught with problems. Regardless, thinking people of faith want to know how Jesus would address the problem of whiteness. Jesus experienced a wide variety of encounters with people who were considered others and outsiders in his world. One can argue that the most prominent thread in Jesus's ministry was his breaking down of the barriers and boundaries—physical deformity, nationality, femaleness, and leprosy to name a few— that kept people alienated from God. In Jesus's time, that alienation took the form of barriers and boundaries limiting or prohibiting worship at the temple on Mount Zion.

Race, racism, whiteness, and durable inequalities in the Bible

Those concerned with social justice must address what Charles Tilly (1998) calls the durable inequalities of race, class, and gender. The problems associated with durable inequalities were also a part of the ancient world, especially the world of the Bible. The problems of class and gender were very much a part of the biblical stories. However, instead of the modern problem of race, the salient durable inequality of the Hebrew Bible was nation. People were very aware of their visible differences, but such differences were not so salient. People expressed their awareness of these differences, recognizing that the whole world consisted of those who looked as if they came from Africa and those who came from what are now the boundaries between Asia and Europe—in the words of the writer of the Book of Esther, "from India to Ethiop." Physical and cultural differences were real and remarkable, but they were not a necessary reason for constructing social hierarchies that oppressed and excluded. These physical and cultural differences did not constitute and construct race.

Long before people invented race, they invented ways of separating themselves from one another. And when they had the power, they denigrated those from whom they wished to be separate. In the biblical world, the principal argument for separation was nation, and the principal distinctions among nations were their deities. Those who loved and feared the God of Israel, the Lord, the One who was revealed to Moses in the burning bush, the One who sided with those who were strangers and slaves and made them a nation—those who loved the LORD were the good people, the in-crowd, the folks who were supposed to be dominant, and the Bible is written from that point of view. Good people from other nations were people like Rahab, Ruth, Uriah the Hittite, and Naaman—they were people who confessed the power and sovereignty of God and who acted on their confession by becoming part of the nation of Israel and sharing that nation's interests. These people were remarkable because of their faith and their actions as faithful members of ancient Israel, even though they started their lives in the wrong nations. Their actions and their faith became central threads in the complicated tapestry of salvation history.

The problem of whiteness in modern times is also a problem of uncleanness, ritual pollution, and rigid boundaries of separation. Those boundaries of separation are associated with the concept of race, a modern invention rooted in the Atlantic slave trade, slavery in the New World, domination, segregation, colonialism, the color curtain, and the color line—in the words of W.E.B. Du Bois (1961), "the relations of the lighter to the darker races of [people] in Africa, America, Asia, and the islands of the sea." According to Gossett (1997), the ideology and science of race emerged because Europeans and Americans of European descent needed to justify slavery, the slave trade, and domination in societies that benefited from these events. In the modern world whiteness is associated with the history of Europeans and their domination of two-thirds of the world. As Mann (2011) points out in his journalistic exploration of the "Columbian Exchange," Europeans moved out of Europe and came to dominate substantial portions of the world. Along with that economic and political domination, they constructed a set of ideas and ideologies now known as "race" and established whiteness as a hegemonic condition of the western world. Everyone else is "non-white" even though non-white peoples are the world's majority.

The ancient biblical world is not the modern world. The history of race in the modern world is the history of people who view themselves as white conquering and dominating people who, by the standards of those powerful white people, are not white. In places like the United States and South Africa, the categories of social life include an understanding of whiteness as the normative variety of humanity, with others beyond the boundaries of whiteness labeled black and non-white. Beyond hegemony, the United States established and enforced laws that structured a white-supremacist society and determined who was white and who was not. Those social structures were violently established and violently enforced.

The United States and South Africa are nations dominated by white Protestants. These nations consider themselves to be white and are also predominantly and historically Christian, with elaborate and well-developed images of Jesus and biblical characters. These images are overwhelmingly white. In the United States, religious approaches to whiteness reach their zenith in terrorist fraternal groups such as the Ku Klux Klan whose arguments for whiteness appealed to Bible arguments claiming that God created the races and placed them on separate continents. The Church of Jesus Christ of Latter Day Saints, another religious tradition with a history of explicit white supremacy, utilizes a scripture that explicitly distinguishes between black and white people and identifies blackness as a mark of God's disfavor. A tour through the Church's Salt Lake City Museum of Church History and Art provides a tour through a religious story that extends the Christian story to North America and inscribes that story with unrelieved whiteness.

Race and its companions, whiteness and blackness, are modern inventions. Race is an idea invented and constructed in modernity. Race, as it is understood in the United States and South Africa, does not exist in the Bible. Thomas Gossett, in his *Race: The History of an Idea in America* (1997), points out that theories and thinking about race in America, and by extension in the modern world, arose primarily to justify the enslavement of black people. Most constructions of race are historically specific, such that understandings of who is white and who is "of color" can vary widely from society to society in the New World. Regardless, whiteness exists at the zenith of most racialized societies, even in societies, such as Haiti, where the numerical majority is black. The historical development of race and whiteness was so consequential that European immigrant groups, when confronted with racialized ideas about whiteness, were quick to seize the identity of whiteness, regardless of their levels of disadvantage (Ignatiev, 1995; Jacobson, 1998; Painter, 2010; Roediger, 1991; Sacks, 1994).

Religious ideas have been central to the ideas of whiteness and racial hierarchy. For the United States, the racial battles have included Bible battles between resisting, rebellious black people and dominating, oppressive white people. Both white and black people claimed that the Bible supported their positions. Black people utilized Exodus, the Jubilee of Leviticus 25, and Psalm 68 to argue that a liberating God included them in the plan of universal salvation. White people insisted that the story of Noah and his curse of Ham justified the white-over-black racial hierarchy. The misreading of Genesis 11 persists, in spite of the fact that the biblical text says that Noah cursed Canaan and not Ham. Furthermore, white racists argued that slavery was present in the Bible and that the apostle Paul had sanctioned it with his admonitions to slaves to be obedient.

The biblical imagination of "race," however, actually requires certain mental gymnastics that, when examined closely, are highly problematic. Although race as we know it in modern America does not exist in the Bible, the Bible looms so large as an American cultural artifact that its contribution to discussions of whiteness and blackness must be explored. In the social construction of race and racism, the Bible has been a vital tool. The biblical imagination of race requires a biblical imagination of whiteness. Whiteness is largely, however, a default category. If people are not specifically identified as Ethiopians, Cushites, or "black and comely," then most American readers, until recently, assumed that all the characters were white. Furthermore, the body of art connected to western tradition reinforced and nurtured this imagination of whiteness.

Africans and their descendants in North America have always questioned the racial imagination of biblical whiteness. Even though the standard images of Jesus with long, blonde hair are in black people's Bibles and homes, black people have often challenged that notion directly. Pointing to the powerful images in the book of Revelation, they point to the hair like lamb's wool and the feet of burnished brass as direct evidence that Jesus would not be able to get into the churches where the segregation and oppression of black people were the norm.

As a consequence of the civil rights and black power movements, black theologians offered an understanding of God as being on the side of the oppressed. James Cone pointed out that in a society where black people were the oppressed, exploited, and excluded, the religion of Jesus placed Jesus on their side (Cone, 1975). Like other forms of liberation theology, black theology pointed to Jesus's option for the poor and the oppressed, who, in North America, were very clearly black people. Cone was not the first to make such an argument. A.M.E. Bishop Henry McNeal Turner, during the Civil War, raised the assertion that "God is a Negro." Later, when confronted with the contradiction of Christian white racism while traveling in India and Ceylon, Howard Thurman (1981) penned the book *Jesus and the Disinherited* to point to Jesus's own status as a marginalized Jew in a colonized Holy Land and the empathy with the oppressed that was central to his ministry.

Black people had historically identified with Jews because of their history as slaves liberated by a divinely appointed Exodus. That identification was amplified by the post-holocaust consciousness that governed the civil rights movement. Most black activists identified with the Jews as a people liberated from enslavement, and the direct involvement of Jews as activists and supporters, especially at the urgings of Abraham Joshua Heschel, reinforced the identification with Jesus as one of the oppressed. However, in the Bible, Jesus was actually someone whose identity was tied to a dominant group, at least in relation to the Samaritans.

In order to theorize about Jesus's response to whiteness and race, one has to explore the cleavages in the biblical world that function like race and that have become resources for people of faith as they struggle to disestablish race and to end racism. The ethnic or national cleavages in the Bible and biblical world were not about color or categorical notions of ancestry. Instead, the most salient cleavages were religious. They were about the deity to which one was committed. The stories of "others" like Ruth and Rahab have happy endings because Ruth and Rahab recognize that the God of Israel is the one true and living God. By the time we get to the end of the story of ancient Israel, there are stories of "otherness" that are resolved by the affirmation of the one-ness and only-ness of Yahweh.

When using the Bible as a tool for racial domination, white people in Europe, the United States, and South Africa assume that Jesus and the ancient Israelites are white. These readers have chosen and expanded upon selected portions of the Bible. Those selections sometimes refer to people of African descent, noted in English translations as Ethiopians or Cushites. The curse of Ham is actually non-existent. In Genesis 11, Noah's curse is placed upon Canaan, Ham's son. The other sons of Ham, who are the eponymous ancestors of Cush and Mizraim, are excluded from Noah's utterance. In order to argue that black people are cursed, white people have engaged in a massive misreading that reaches back to Ham in order to include Africans under that curse. Since the presumption of whiteness applies to everybody else in the Bible, whiteness is never specifically identified in biblical racial ideology—once again whiteness is silent. There is a problem with failing to acknowledge and identify whiteness in the Bible. Whenever white skin is specifically mentioned there is usually a terrible problem. Those biblical stories that could be construed to be about whiteness are about leprosy, usually as a curse from God.

There are many theories about leprosy in the Bible. It is not unreasonable to imagine that biblical leprosy may have included the auto-immune condition vitiligo, a condition where pigment-producing melanocytes die or simply fail to function. Both Moses's sister, Miriam, and Elisha's servant, Gehazi, became "white as snow." Miriam, whose brother pleads for her before God, is healed of her leprosy. Gehazi is not healed and is cursed to pass on his leprosy to his descendants.

Ironically, Gehazi's story is a biblical story that black people have never exploited and that white people never explore critically. It is, however, in light of the history of race and racism, a fascinating tale. In II Kings 5, the story of Naaman, "captain of the host of the king of Syria," illustrates the importance of humility. In spite of his tremendous military reputation, "he was a leper." Leprosy becomes his master status. Naaman's healing requires that he stand with the least. It is one of his wife's Israelite slaves who suggests that Naaman go to "the prophet that is in Samaria" for his healing. Naaman embarks on an odyssey that takes him from the royal courts of Israel to the humble abode of Elisha, the prophet of the LORD, the prophet who followed Elijah. Naaman is absolutely appalled at the instructions he receives in order to be healed: "Go and wash in the Jordan seven times." Once again, it is the least and the lowly in Naaman's household who convinces him to listen to Elisha. His eventual healing causes him to confess his faith in the God of Israel and to ask pre-emptive forgiveness for assisting his monarch in continued idolatry.

However, the story does not end with Naaman's healing and return to Syria. Naaman offers gifts to Elisha—lavish gifts. Elisha refuses these gifts and sends Naaman on his way. Elisha's servant, Gehazi, decides to pursue Naaman. Gehazi utilizes the ruse that two "sons of the prophets" who need silver and two changes of clothing have come to visit Elisha. Naaman gives not only two changes of clothing but double the amount of silver Gehazi requests. After Gehazi hides his booty, Elisha confronts him; Gehazi lies; Elisha reveals the lie and then pronounces a curse upon Gehazi: "The leprosy therefore of Naaman shall cleave unto thee, and unto thy seed forever. And he [Gehazi] went out from his [Elisha's] presence a leper as white as snow." Gehazi, like Miriam during Israel's trek in the wilderness (Numbers 12:10), became white, as a consequence of God's judgment. (Interestingly, Miriam's leprosy was the consequence of her conflict with Moses because he had married a Cushite/Ethiopian woman. Cushites, later known as Ethiopians, were people from sub-Saharan Africa—people from the land of burnt faces—decidedly darker than the brown people who constituted the cultures of the ancient Near East.) Not only does Gehazi become white, but it is a whiteness that his descendants are cursed to inherit – "unto thy seed forever." What happened to Gehazi's descendants? Where are the white people who are the descendants of a duplicitous, greedy white man? One has to wonder why there are no claims by angry peoples of color that white people are the descendants of a leprous, greedy liar.

Fortunately, the oppressed have been able to take seriously Jesus's ministry. That ministry cleanses lepers and restores and reintegrates community. Howard Thurman (1981) recognized that racial oppression was a breeding-ground for fear, deception, and hatred on the part of the oppressed. Jesus made a conscious decision to emphasize love and to act on that love. He grasped the significance of history and, like the prophets before him, used that history as a tool for transformation. Jesus acted to break down barriers and to cross borders to disestablish mountains of privilege and conflict; Jesus moved back and forth between both sides of the conflict in order to move both the Judeans and the Samaritans beyond their respective mountains. Most importantly, Jesus went to the places where the oppressed resided, and stood with them. Jesus insisted upon going through Samaria, engaging the Samaritan woman and ignoring the customary practices of separation and exclusion. By doing this, Jesus worked to heal a historic schism and challenge notions of supremacy on both sides of a nation.

Obery Hendricks (2006) described the ministry of Jesus as a political ministry. Hendricks argues that Jesus was a strategic tactician who offered models of challenge and change for us to follow. The needs of the poor and oppressed were holy. The workings of oppression needed to be exposed in order to be challenged. Jesus lifted up his own voice so as to give a voice to the voiceless. In his conflicts with the Temple elites, Jesus acted to demystify power. In addition to description and analysis, Jesus acted. He chose to be prophetic in word and in deed. Jesus's ministry included the excluded and erased barriers erected by war, disaster, exile, cultural disruption, economic dislocation, powerlessness, and the tradition of religious interpretation. We must go and do likewise.

Notes

Jayeon Kim and Jayde Bennett provided research and editorial assistance for this chapter.

1 This discussion of Wright's sermon is based on portions of the sermon contained in the PBS Frontline documentary titled "Keeping the Faith" (Washington Media Associates and Jones, 1989).
2 In honor of the rhetorical power of the King James Version of the Bible and the contribution of that rhetorical power to the black preaching tradition, I have chosen to utilize the King James Version of the Bible throughout this chapter. As I do this, I acknowledge the tremendous problems associated with this text, with its errors, its androcentric language, and its role in fostering racialized symbolism.
3 Isaiah 40:1–5.
4 I have chosen to use "Judeans" rather than the prevailing translations' usage of "the Jews." It has been argued that the English translation of "Ioudaioi" is a mistranslation—a mistranslation that has served to foster the tradition of Christian anti-Judaism. See, for instance, "The Myth of a Judeo-Christian Tradition" from *New Dawn Magazine* No. 23 February–March 1994 (www.informationclearinghouse.info/article4803.htm) for an extended discussion of this problem.
5 I have talked extensively about the prophetic and redemptive role of the lepers in 2 Kings 7 as a model for understanding and responding to HIV/AIDS. That reflection was published in *The Journal of Religious Thought* [47(2): 56–63 (Winter–Spring, 1990–91)].

References

Bonilla-Silva, Eduardo. 1997. "Rethinking Racism: Toward a Structural Interpretation." *American Sociological Review* 62(3): 465–80.
Boring, M. Eugene and Fred B. Craddock. 2004. *The People's New Testament Commentary.* Louisville, Kentucky: Westminster John Knox Press.
Brown, Raymond E. 2003. *An Introduction to the Gospel of John.* New York: Doubleday/Random House.
Bruteau, Beatrice, Editor. 2001. *Jesus through Jewish Eyes: Rabbis and Scholars Engage an Ancient Brother in a New Conversation.* Maryknoll, New York: Orbis Books.
Callahan, Allen Dwight. 2006. *The Talking Book: African Americans and the Bible.* New Haven: Yale University Press.
Camp, Claudia. 1992. "1 and 2 Kings." Pp. 96–110 in Carol H. Newsom and Sharon H. Ringe, Editors. *The Women's Bible Commentary.* Louisville, Kentucky: Westminster John Knox Press.
Carmichael, Stokely and Charles V. Hamilton. 1967. *Black Power: The Politics of Liberation in America.* New York: Random House.
Cone, James H. 1975. *God of the Oppressed.* New York: Seabury Press.
——1999. *Risks of Faith: The Emergence of a Black Theology of Liberation, 1968–98.* Boston: Beacon Press.
Du Bois, W.E.B. 1961 [1903,1953]. *The Souls of Black Folk.* Greenwich, Connecticut: Fawcett Publications, Inc.

Feagin, Joe R. 2000. *Racist America: Roots, Current Realities, and Future Reparations*. New York: Routledge.

——2010. *The White Racial Frame: Centuries of Racial Framing and Counter-Framing*. New York: Routledge.

Gilkes, Cheryl Townsend. 2010. "Still the Most Segregated Hour: Religion, Race, and the American Experience." Pp. 415–43 in Patricia Hill Collins and John Solomos, Editors. *The SAGE Handbook of Race and Ethnic Studies*. Los Angeles: Sage Publications.

Gossett, Thomas F. 1997. *Race: The History of an Idea in America* (New Edition). New York: Oxford University Press.

Greenlee, Sam. 1970 [1969]. *The Spook Who Sat by the Door*. New York: Bantam Books.

Halley, Jean, Amy Eshleman, and Ramya Mahadevan Vijaya. 2011. *Seeing White: An Introduction to White Privilege and Race*. Lanham, Maryland: Rowman & Littlefield Publishers, Inc.

Hendricks, Obery M. 2003. *Living Water*. San Francisco: HarperSanFrancisco.

——2006. *The Politics of Jesus: Rediscovering the Truly Revolutionary Nature of Jesus' Teachings and how They Have Been Corrupted*. New York: Three Leaves Press (Doubleday).

Hughes, Langston. 1926. "The Negro Artist and the Racial Mountain." Poetry Foundation. www.poetryfoundation.org/learning/essay/237858.

Ignatiev, Noel. 1995. *How the Irish Became White*. New York: Routledge.

Jacobson, Matthew Frye. 1998. *Whiteness of a Different Color: European Immigrants and the Alchemy of Race*. Cambridge, Massachusetts: Harvard University Press.

Kling, David W. 2004. *The Bible in History: How the Texts Have Shaped the Times*. New York: Oxford University Press.

Knowles, Louis and Kenneth Prewitt, Editors. 1970. *Institutional Racism in America*. Englewood Cliffs, New Jersey: Prentice Hall.

Levine, Amy-Jill (A.J.). 2006. *The Misunderstood Jew: The Church and the Scandal of the Jewish Jesus*. San Francisco: HarperSanFrancisco.

Mann, Charles C. 2011. *1493: Uncovering the New World Columbus Created*. New York: Alfred A. Knopf/Random House.

O'Day, Gail R. 1992. "John." Pp. 305–13 in Carol H. Newsom and Sharon H. Ringe, Editors. *The Women's Bible Commentary*. Louisville, Kentucky: Westminster John Knox Press.

Painter, Nell Irvin. 2010. *The History of White People*. New York: W.W. Norton & Company.

Roediger, David R. 1991. *The Wages of Whiteness: Race and the Making of the American Working Class*. London: Verso.

Rothenberg, Paula S. 2008. *White Privilege: Essential Readings on the Other Side of Racism*. New York: Worth Publishers.

Sacks, Karen Brodkin. 1994. "How Did Jews Become White Folks?" Pp. 78–102 in Steven Gregory and Roger Sanjek, Editors. *Race*. New Brunswick, New Jersey: Rutgers University Press.

Solomon, Lewis D. 2001. "Jesus: A Prophet of Universal Judaism." Pp. 151–67 in Beatrice Bruteau, Editor. *Jesus Through Jewish Eyes: Rabbis and Scholars Engage an Ancient Brother in a New Conversation*. Maryknoll, New York: Orbis Books

Thurman, Howard. 1981 [1949]. *Jesus and the Disinherited*. Richmond, Indiana: Friends United Press.

Tilly, Charles. 1998. *Durable Inequality*. Berkeley: University of California Press.

Washington Media Associates and Sherry Jones. 1989. *Keeping the Faith*. Alexandria, Virginia: PBS Video.

Wilmore, Gayraud S. 1973. *Black Religion and Black Radicalism: An Examination of the Black Experience in Religion*. Garden City, New York: Doubleday and Company.

Wimbush, Vincent L., Editor. 2003. *African Americans and the Bible: Sacred Texts and Sacred Textures*. New York: Continuum.

4

THE BLACK CHURCH AND WHITENESS

Looking for Jesus in strange places

Moni McIntyre

> Beloved, let us love one another, because love is from God;
> everyone who loves is born of God and knows God.
> Whoever does not love does not know God, for God is love.
>
> (1 John 7–8[1])

Likely it comes as no surprise to anyone that churches are sometimes the last places in which one would expect to find evidence of a loving God. If by "love" one means a welcoming, inclusive, open environment in which each person is valued and respected, then persons of all stripes on occasion may have to look beyond churches to find Jesus, the human face of God. This is not a new phenomenon. Indeed, it would appear that even Jesus the Christ may have been hard pressed to find evidence of love when Blacks and whites came together to worship in these United States all down the centuries. A quick survey of both nondenominational and mainline churches confirms the impression that classism, racism, and/or sexism prevail. The marginalized who sometimes come to the usual places to experience Jesus know that they must at times look for him in some other place, in an unexpected place perhaps of their own making, unknown to those who believe in and cater to whiteness.

The Black Church

"The Black Church" is a well-known phenomenon in the United States, despite the fact that at least one scholar has declared it obsolete.[2] What cannot be disputed is that Black churches have in the past exercised a major influence upon the lives of most African Americans. Beginning long before their life on plantations, Black ministers of many sorts cultivated local leadership and provided strength and consolation to those who desperately needed them. By the time that the phenomenon known as the

Black Church emerged in the nineteenth century, slaves and their descendants had been conducting their own services for centuries.

Although one could cite many examples of successful Black churches throughout the centuries in North America, perhaps the most obvious example of the power and magnitude of the Black Church in the United States is found in the story of the civil rights movement and the Rev. Dr. Martin Luther King, Jr. Standing before a packed church congregation in December, 1955, King launched the Montgomery, Alabama bus boycott that not only honored the courage of Rosa Parks and united the African Americans of the city and the nation, but it also finally forced the U.S. Supreme Court in 1956 to do something about the evils of unchecked segregation. For the rest of his short life, King continued to exemplify the power and efficacy of the Black Church as few others have done. Black churches formed the nucleus of the civil rights movement, even as the latter incorporated other institutions. These churches have never been mere houses of worship. Rather, the churches were groups of activists who wished to "lift ev'ry voice and sing, Till earth and heaven ring, Ring with the harmonies of liberty" (Johnson, 1900).

Long before King, however, independent Black churches in the United States were created in colonial times and were widespread by the 1740s.[3] Once evangelical revivals were introduced into the lives of slaves, the number of converts to Christianity soared. One did not need a sophisticated command of theology in order to preach and pray. Faith expressed in emotional fervor often was enough to get African American men licensed to preach by Baptists and Methodists. In an atmosphere of "sola scriptura," a Bible and a place to proclaim it were sufficient to form a church. Black antebellum churches in the South grew slowly, despite white harassment. An independent body of Black worshippers emerged in substantial numbers, often without the consent of their owners. Prohibited from attending white churches, in many cases, the slaves fashioned their own. Not surprisingly, a distinctive style of preaching and music developed that expressed the plight of the slave. Reflection upon the scriptures convinced the slaves that God is on the side of the poor and marginalized. As far as they knew, there were no more poor and marginalized persons in the country than they were. It was a short step to connect their plight with those closest to God in the Bible. Aside from such obvious stories as the Exodus, as well as David and Goliath, and Jesus, there were the plight of Tamar and Ishmael, Susanna, and the unnamed woman in Judges 19 to help them find meaning in their own sufferings. The absence of academic degrees or even literacy could not conceal a compassionate God yearning to free their captive souls.

Depicting themselves as God's chosen people, African Americans longed for their own exodus from the bondage of chattel slavery. During the century following the 1863 Emancipation Proclamation, many freed slaves maintained their religious independence in Black churches, aware that genuine freedom was still a dream.[4] As the decades went by in their segregated world, Black churches provided safe spaces for their members. In addition to functioning as worship sites, church buildings evolved into community centers that fostered a spirit of solidarity and safety not often experienced in white churches.[5] W.E.B. DuBois (2003) observed this phenomenon in 1903:

The Negro church of to-day is the social centre of Negro life in the United States. ... Take a typical church in a small Virginian town. ... This building is the central club-house of a community of a thousand or more Negroes. Various organizations meet here—the church proper, the Sunday-school, two or three insurance societies, women's societies, secret societies, and mass meetings of various kinds. Entertainments, suppers, and lectures are held beside the five or six regular weekly religious services. Considerable sums of money are collected and expended here, employment is found for the idle, strangers are introduced, news is disseminated and charity distributed. At the same time this social, intellectual, and economic centre is a religious centre of great power.

(p. 137)

While most African Americans remained in their own segregated churches, some Blacks became members of white-dominated churches. People of color, however, were almost never accepted as equals, and dissatisfaction often ran high. Perhaps the most treasured story of rupture occurred when African Americans in Philadelphia founded two churches in 1794: Bethel African American Methodist by Richard Allen and St. Thomas African Episcopal Church by Absalom Jones, who later became the first Black priest in the Episcopal Church, and the first Black ordained minister in any denomination. Allen later formed the first African American denomination, the African Methodist Episcopal (AME) Church. Other denominations subsequently arose, including the African Methodist Episcopal Zion Church, the Church of God in Christ, Inc., the National Baptist Convention, USA, Inc., the National Baptist Convention of America, Inc., Christian Methodist Episcopal Church, and the Full Gospel Church Fellowship. There can be no doubt that these groups, as well as the thousands of nondenominational Black churches, have had a significant impact on the life and times of African Americans.[6]

What prompted white Christians to exclude their darker sisters and brothers from the very act of worshiping the God who made them both? The answer lies in *whiteness*, the insidious reality upon which this book is focused. Whiteness has been variously described and defined; indeed, John H. McClendon III (2004) attests to the difficulty of characterizing the notion of whiteness. He states that "whiteness cannot be confined to any particular area of social relations and institutions, especially when viewed in light of its ascribed character-instantiated forms of harmful, oppressive and exploitive social practices" (p.219). These "oppressive and exploitive social practices" are what gave birth to and have necessitated the continuance of the Black Church. African Americans have never been able to worship freely in an atmosphere in which racism prevails. Black churches function as safe havens where, at least on Sunday mornings, the otherwise ostracized can feel at home in the presence of God and one another. The effects of whiteness are at least mitigated in the all-Black Church setting.

That the reach of whiteness extended even to the churches whose sacred scriptures proclaimed that "God is love, and those who abide in love abide in God, and God abides in them" (1 John 4:16b) is scandalous yet all too familiar. Whiteness is the antithesis of biblical love. There is no room for oppressive and exploitive social practices among those who claim to follow the living God. Still, these practices prevail and exclusivity is often proclaimed as God's will. Whiteness embodies the raw power that proclaims and implies that "I, who am white (and male), am better than you because you are not white (and male)." Whiteness infected the attitudes of slave-holders—indeed whiteness made slavery possible. Whiteness held, and in too many cases still holds, white pastors and their congregations in its grip. Preachers preaching universal divine love while imbued in a prevailing culture of whiteness made the development of segregated churches inevitable. Separate and unequal, therefore, was certain, whether in independent Black churches or integrated denominations.

One cannot help but wonder why a people so marginalized by Christians saturated in whiteness would choose to belong to "their" religion. Two logical responses present themselves: (a) one was born into the Christian faith and saw no reason to change; (b) the marginalized believers could look beyond the erroneous and distorted claims of the majority and thereby discover there a message of liberation for themselves. Contemporary scholar Kelly Brown Douglas (2005) has no difficulty arguing for the faith of African Americans. She notes that the liberative message of Jesus, and not merely the simple accident of birth into a particular religion, accounts for her profession of the Christian faith.[7]

The creator God of the Hebrew scriptures as well as the compelling person of Jesus the Christ speak to a violated people. Not even rampant racism could obscure the power of biblical stories of God's love for the underclass, especially the quintessential story of God's love poured out in the blood of Jesus. Enslaved Christians and their descendants grasped a depth of meaning in the Christian story that they would not forsake. They developed a relationship with the risen Christ, because the depth of his suffering and the ignominy of his death mirrored their own. Powerful New Testament statements such as Galatians 3:28 underscored their favor before God: "There is no longer Jew or Greek, there is no longer slave or free, there is no longer male and female; for all of you are one in Christ Jesus." Slaves and their Christian descendants discerned that if this is true, then whiteness in any guise, time, or place must be false and could not be of God. Clearly, whiteness spawned a society in which Blacks and whites could not worship the God of liberation in the same space. From the beginning, separate churches and even separate denominations led to the oft-repeated statement that 11:00 on Sunday morning is and was the most segregated hour of the week.

Although not all denominations excluded African Americans, those that did often refused to recognize the full humanity of all their members. Mainline denominations admitted African Americans into their churches while confining them to a separate place either in the church building or in a separate mission or parish. Because white clergy often did not want to serve African American congregations, Black clergy structures arose that roughly paralleled their white counterparts. There were indeed benefits to attending an all-Black Church, as Henry Louis Gates, Jr. (1995) has noted about his growing up in a segregated town in West Virginia in the 1950s.[8] The young Gates and his friends had fewer people pressing them to believe that they were lesser beings in an alien world. Separate and unequal could indeed be a mixed blessing. African Americans in segregated parishes within a denomination retained a measure of autonomy in these settings, despite their second-class status and accommodations.

The Episcopal Church

One denomination that included and segregated African Americans was the Episcopal Church (see Prichard, 1991). Riddled with racism in polity and practice since its inception, the Episcopal Church mirrored the society in which it was born and began to thrive. From Philadelphia to Detroit and from Key West to Boston, Black Episcopalians were forced and then encouraged to worship in segregated spaces long after slavery ended.

Kit Konolige and Frederica Konolige (1978) point out that "Episcopalians [identified] with the first American settlers [and] with the original growth of the corporate elite ... " (p.27). Not surprisingly, then, both upper-class whites and Blacks gravitated to the Episcopal Church. Willard Gatewood (1990) has noted that "The ranks of the Black Episcopalians included a disproportionately large number of the most respected 'old families,' professional people, and others whose education and affluence often set them apart from other Blacks. The small number of Black Episcopalians (amounting to only 15,000 by 1903) also contributed to an image of exclusiveness ... " (p.276). Interestingly, then, the racism that characterized white America spilled over to the wealthy Blacks. Indeed, according to Lawrence Otis Graham (2000), "the Black elite have often selected the more formal high Episcopal Church or Congregational Church." Moreover, he writes, "The Episcopal faith was attractive because of its formality, and both faiths were appealing because they were known for having well-educated clergy and a small number of members. ... And for some of the most cynical and status-conscious members of the Black elite, the two denominations were particularly appealing simply because most Blacks were not of that faith" (p.13).

Harold T. Lewis (1996), mindful of the centuries of abuse heaped upon African Americans in the Episcopal Church, maintains that the catholicity of the Episcopal Church, and not merely its potential for greater social status, is the reason why some African Americans have chosen to become and remain Episcopalian. Lewis argues compellingly for the religious choices that African Americans make in spite of their suffering at the hands of the controlling majority culture. He writes, "Blacks have remained in the Episcopal Church because they have distinguished the essential message of the Gospel from its original packaging" (p.175).[9] Indeed, Lewis's arguments reveal the evils inherent in whiteness and the power of the minority to resist and challenge the power brokers to be who they claim to be: "The Gospel has been understood by Black Episcopalians as empowering, not subjugating; as liberating, not controlling. The Christian faith, and more particularly the Anglican expression of it, was not dismissed simply because it was deemed a 'white man's religion'" (Lewis, 1996, p.176). Indeed, "Blacks have remained in the Episcopal Church, moreover, not only because they believe in their inherent right to be in it, but because they believe they have unique gifts to offer the Church which will accrue to its benefit" (Lewis,

1996, p.176). In sum, African Americans recognize the liberative message of Jesus as the heart of human existence, and some of them choose to express their faith in mainline denominations that have often failed to recognize their unique gifts for the whole community.

The Church of the Holy Cross (Episcopal), Pittsburgh, Pennsylvania

When a group of Episcopalians wishes to start a new church, it is called a "mission" until it can become a "parish," i.e., self-supporting and pay its annual assessment (i.e., dues or taxes) to the diocese, which is the regional headquarters of the national church. Although the journey from mission to parish is seldom easy and each parish has its own history, the story of the Church of the Holy Cross in Pittsburgh, Pennsylvania is illustrative of the plight of African Americans in the Episcopal Church.

As Leon L. Haley (1995) explained in the Holy Cross 120th Anniversary Celebration souvenir book,

> Prior to the formation of an organized and separate place of worship, Black Episcopalians in Pittsburgh belonged to the local church. In the late 1800s, several Blacks, concerned about the social isolation of their children and seg-regated religious setting they experienced, began to push for the establishment of a separate mission to serve their needs. ... In response to this request, in 1875, Bishop Kerfoot of the Diocese of Pittsburgh brought the Reverend W.F. Floyd to Pittsburgh to establish a mission among the "colored people" of this community. As a result of this effort, St. Cyprian's Mission was established and met in Trinity Church parish house.
>
> *(p.2)*

Bishop Kerfoot's successor closed the mission in 1879, although the people had moved their congregation into a building in the historic Hill District. Refusing to give up, however, the people did the best they could by conducting lay-led worship services at various locations with the help of clergy from time to time.

In 1905, with diocesan approval, the gathering was renamed St. Augustine Mission. A wealthy businessman gave money to William Tibbs, a member of the mission, so that they could rent space in an Odd Fellows Hall just north of the city, near the white Episcopal church in which they had been worshiping. Subsequently, the members of St. Augustine's were able to purchase their own building in the same vicinity.

Another mission, St. Phillip's, was formed in the Hill District a few years later. Both St. Augustine's and St. Phillip's functioned as separate missions until 1917, when they were united in the Hill District building. The new name was the Church of the Holy Cross. The church experienced extraordinary growth during the early Holy Cross years. The church finally achieved parish status shortly after the two missions united.

Doris Brevard, granddaughter of William Tibbs, describes the expense and incon-venience realized by young African American Episcopalians living on the north side of the city of Pittsburgh during the 1930s and 1940s: "I grew up in an integrated neighborhood. The white children could go anywhere to church and close to their home. We had to walk two long blocks, take two streetcars each way, and pass the white Episcopal Church to get to Holy Cross, the only church we could go to. My mother had to have carfare for my sister and me each Sunday. My father worked seven days a week" (Brevard, 2011). Ironically, when Grandfather Tibbs retired to join his wife's family in another city, African Americans were not welcome in the Episcopal Church there. Brevard noted that he never went to church again. Tibbs had come to Pittsburgh shortly after the end of the Civil War to escape the racism in Virginia, where he had lived as a child.

Continued growth and crowded conditions prompted another move for Holy Cross. The early 1950s saw the parish gain space and lose members, as the shift was made a few miles away to the Homewood section of Pittsburgh. Still, as new African American Episcopalians came to town, their only place to worship was Holy Cross. All that changed in the 1960s with the civil rights movement. Other Episcopal churches in the city were opening their doors to African Americans, and some chose to attend more affluent parishes. African Americans new to the city suddenly had several choices. No longer limited by the color of their skin, potential members of Holy Cross saw the parish as one choice among many. Consequently, the church suffered a decline in membership. Most of the older members chose to remain, while their children often went elsewhere.

Today, Holy Cross can be seen as a remnant of days gone by, or it can be viewed with the enthusiasm of its membership. Younger and older persons of various colors have recently chosen Holy Cross as their church home. The warmth of the people is contagious, and visitors sense that here is a house of God worthy of the name. Although signs of whiteness are evident everywhere in the now crime-riddled neighborhood of Homewood, the God of love breathes through the generosity of the parishioners. Thriving Baptist and nondenominational Black churches dot the regional map of Pittsburgh. Holy Cross could be seen, in some ways, as a relic of the past. Current members, however, are hopeful that a new Holy Cross is being born and will become an ever-brighter beacon of hope in Homewood and the City of Pittsburgh through their outreach programs and commitment to love one another as God has loved them.

Conclusion

Black churches in the United States came into being when men and women of courage saw a need to worship God in an unencumbered fashion. Despite overwhelming obstacles, and over time, the original small gatherings grew into flourishing communities that met many of the social, political, and economic needs of their members as well as others beyond the church membership. Despite the whiteness that pervaded and controlled their lives, some African Americans found meaning in established mainline denominations, while others followed a more evangelical bent and became Baptists, Methodists, or members of nondenominational churches. Some forsook Christianity altogether. Those who chose to join established denominations faced almost insurmountable odds. The story of Blacks in the Episcopal Church illustrates the amazing depth of their faith, the magnitude of their commitment, and their astounding initiative. The Church of the Holy Cross in Pittsburgh, Pennsylvania is one such Episcopal Church that epitomizes the hope and persistence of generations seemingly born to struggle. Through it all, they found a resilient Jesus in many strange places, a God who yearns to breathe freely through them.

Notes

1 All biblical quotations in this chapter are from the New Revised Standard Version of the Bible.
2 Professor of Religion and Chair of the Center for African American Studies at Princeton University Eddie Glaude, Jr. emphatically pressed that point in an online post entitled "The Black Church Is Dead." Glaude points out that, although the majority of African Americans strongly identify with religion, "the idea of this venerable institution as central to black life and as a repository for the social and moral conscience of the nation has all but disappeared" (Glaude, 2010).
3 For a comprehensive history of the Black Church, see *The Black Church in the African American Experience* by C. Eric Lincoln and Lawrence H. Mamiya (1990).
4 See *Slavery by Another Name: The Re-Enslavement of Black Americans from the Civil War to World War II* by Douglas A. Blackmon (2009) for examples of egregious behavior that illustrate this point. Blackmon describes widespread collusion between local Southern government officials and commercial firms to lease African American convicts who had been arrested on petty or trumped-up charges. The net effect was, in many cases, worse than the conditions of enslavement endured by their ancestors.
5 A notable exception was the ethnic Roman Catholic churches that existed to accommodate the needs of recent immigrants.
6 Lincoln and Mamiya (1990) explore this in great detail.
7 Kelly Brown Douglas addresses this issue in *What's Faith Got to Do with It?: Black Bodies/ Christian Souls* (2005). Because Douglas is able to distill the essence of God as expressed in genuine Christian faith from the practice of it by many of its members, she concludes that she can remain a Christian; it is the faith of her grandmother, who knew the person of Jesus the Christ in her daily life and struggles and knew the power of prayer.
8 See Gates's autobiography entitled *Colored People* (New York: Vintage, 1995) in which he describes his life as a young student in West Virginia at the time of Brown v. Board of Education in 1954.
9 See Harold T. Lewis, *Yet with a Steady Beat: The African American Struggle for Recognition in the Episcopal Church* (1996). In this volume, Lewis traces the story of Black Episcopalians from 1623 through 1968 and offers an impressive analysis of racism in the Episcopal Church throughout its history.

References

Blackmon, Douglas A. (2009). *Slavery by Another Name: The Re-Enslavement of Black Americans from the Civil War to World War II*. New York: Anchor.
Brevard, Doris Garrett. Interview with author, Pittsburgh, PA, 2 May 2011.
Douglas, Kelly Brown. (2005). *What's Faith Got to Do with It?: Black Bodies/Christian Souls*. Maryknoll, NY: Orbis.
DuBois, W.E.B. (2003). *The Souls of Black Folk*, 1903. New York: Barnes & Noble Classics.
Gates, Henry Louis, Jr. (1995). *Colored People*. New York: Vintage.
Gatewood, Willard. (1990). *Aristocrats of Color: The Black Elite, 1880–1920*. Bloomington: University of Indiana Press.

Glaude, Eddie. Jr. (2010). "The Black Church Is Dead." www.huffingtonpost.com/eddie-glaude-jr-phd/the-Black-church-is-dead_b_473815.html. Posted February 24.

Graham, Lawrence Otis. (2000). *Our Kind of People: Inside America's Black Upper Class.* New York: HarperPerennial.

Haley, Leon L. (1995). "History of The Church of the Holy Cross," in the 120th Anniversary Celebration souvenir book.

Johnson, James Weldon. (1900). "Lift Every Voice and Sing."

Konolige, Kit and Konolige, Frederica. (1978). *The Power of Their Glory—America's Ruling Class: The Episcopalians.* New York: Wyden Books.

Lewis, Harold T. (1996). *Yet with a Steady Beat: The African American Struggle for Recognition in the Episcopal Church.* Valley Forge, PA: Trinity Press International.

Lincoln, C. Eric and Mamiya, Lawrence H. (1990). *The Black Church in the African American Experience.* Durham, NC: Duke University Press.

McClendon, John H., III (2004). "On the Nature of Whiteness and the Ontology of Race," in *What White Looks Like: African-American Philosophers on the Whiteness Question*, ed. by George Yancy (New York: Routledge).

Prichard, Robert. (1991). *A History of the Episcopal Church.* Harrisburg: Morehouse.

5

WHAT WOULD ZACCHAEUS DO?

The case for *dis*identifying with Jesus

Jennifer Harvey

I first noticed "WWJD?" bracelets on my students at Drake University. Many of these were students involved with our campus chapter of Intervarsity Christian Fellowship. The assertion that the appropriate question for Christians to be asking is "What Would Jesus Do?" is popular beyond merely this one evangelical community, however. Moreover, such an assertion can be made by persons engaging WWJD? from a variety of theological perspectives.

To ask, as this volume does, "What Would Jesus Do?" is typically intended to provoke a type of reflection that invites the reflector to identify with Jesus. The question contains both historical and Christological dimensions. It purports to look to the past, making an interpretive claim about who Jesus was in his particular time and place. It also presumes that who Jesus was matters at a level beyond mere intellectual curiosity. WWJD? asserts that there is something prescriptive about the historical event of Jesus for the person or community asking the question. In most cases, the prescriptive nature of that event is linked to Jesus' status as a Christ figure—thus, the Christological dimension of the question.

Before exploring the question of WWJD? in relation to whiteness, I must identify a few assumptions that are salient in my understanding of whiteness itself. Whiteness is a complex and hydra-headed phenomenon intrinsically related to white supremacy. It pervades the U.S. landscape, normalizing and making normative the collective dominance of persons racialized as "white." But, whiteness is more than a phenomenon "out there" in the social landscape. Because race is a social construction and social processes are the scaffolding on which racial identities become meaningful and recognizable, whiteness is deeply intertwined with the actual bodyselves of those of us who are white.

This tangled relationship between white supremacy and white racial identity can be best illustrated by way of two examples that capture the construction of race in relation to systems of power. Example one: Imagine someone walking down the street late at night. If that person has physical features generally recognized as white, a passing police officer might slow down and make sure the person is not lost. If that same person has features recognized as Latino/a or Black, that same officer might instead slow down and ask for identification. Example two: Noel Ignatiev and John Garvey argue that whiteness works like a club in which those who look white are given membership in exchange for complying with certain rules. Take the case of racial profiling (and its bedfellow, police brutality). Racial profiling depends on police officers' being able to assume that passers-by who look white will not interfere when they observe a person of color being harassed. Light skin tone signifies that one can be relied upon to look away and a system that disparately harms people of color functions smoothly because skin tone indeed accurately predicts behavior (Ignatiev and Garvey, 1996).[1]

Race is actually constructed in the moments these examples capture. Race comes into existence in the relationships between institutional power, physical characteristics, and behavioral choices. Individuals are racialized in these moments as well: we see here the light-skinned person literally becoming white. As such, these two examples reveal at least three important things about whiteness and race on which the argument made in this chapter hinges.

First, those of us racialized as white have a fundamentally different relationship to whiteness than do persons racialized as "of color." While people of color are targeted, rendered invisible and generally harmed by whiteness, white people tend to be privileged by it; of course, the heterosexual, male, and economically secure among us are privileged more than others. While people of color are profiled for harassment in the preceding examples, white people are profiled for protection.

Second, white supremacy's smooth functioning depends on the knowing and unknowing complicity of white people. In contrast, it could be significantly disrupted if many white people found strategic and active ways by which to resist it on a sustained basis. As illustrated in example two, if a police officer could not assume that someone who looks white will passively walk by, racial profiling would be much more risky and its prevalence would thereby be reduced.

Third, the social processes by which race is constructed give actual content and meaning to racial identities. Our racial identities are not neutral phenomena, nor are they best understood as only, or primarily, cultural. They have political meaning and material content as they come to be recognizable and meaningful in relationship to white-supremacist construction processes. Thus, systems of racial injustice are repeatedly inscribed on our very bodies as we move through such landscapes as racialized selves. These inscriptions deeply shape and form (and malform) the self at psychological and spiritual levels. Psychologists have been able to document stages of white racial identity development characterized by certain perceptions and relatively predictable behaviors because of the shared experience of being white in the context of white supremacist systems, for example. Moreover, because the nature of the processes in which we are racialized is so nefarious and unjustly privileges the light-skinned at the direct expense of the darker-skinned, to "be white" is to exist in nothing less than a state of acute moral crisis. The white people in these examples are given police protection in exchange for the willingness to look the other way while their fellow citizens are targeted. To the extent that such unjust exchanges racialize the white person, being white becomes an inherently compromised racial identity.

Given my understanding of how whiteness operates and of its complex entanglements with our actual bodyselves, the project of asking WWJD? has different implications for the white Christian than it does for the Black Christian, the Latina Christian, the Christian who is Asian American or for any Christian whose racial identity locates them outside the presumed normativity of whiteness. Thus, in this chapter, I explore WWJD? with the racial particularity of the white Christian in mind. I argue that the affects of whiteness on and the relationship of whiteness to white bodyselves mean that for the white Christian to ask what Jesus would do as a means of identifying with Jesus is a problematic enterprise that might actually reinscribe whiteness. In making this claim, I do not suggest that Jesus should be unimportant to white Christians, nor that WWJD? is an intrinsically flawed question. However, the pitfalls created by the move to identify with Jesus lead me to conclude that a better question for the white Christian seeking an anti-racist, anti-white supremacist practice would be WWZD?: What would Zacchaeus do?

I locate this argument in the context of two theological phenomena that make claims about both historical and Christological dimensions of the Jesus figure, and which lend themselves to considering WWJD? in relation to whiteness: WWJD? projects visible in contemporary evangelical contexts, and the theology of the Black Christ. In what follows I argue that, for white practitioners of Christianity, reflection on WWJD? should lead to a recognition of the need for a radical disidentification with Jesus; that taking seriously the historical and Christological possibilities implied in the Jesus query reveals a demand to turn away from the divine and to attempt to identify, instead, with the human.

WWJD?: Identifying with the social justice Jesus

Since the mid-1990s the WWJD? moniker has become something of a cultural icon. It may be most easily recognized in its bracelet version, and in some sense has become a commodified, marketable brand.[2] One can buy shirts, hats, rings and bumper stickers. An article on the emergence of the WWJD? phenomenon describes it as having caught on in part because high school students recognized it as a "cool" trend and in part because Paul Harvey mentioned it every day for a week on his radio broadcast in 1997. Bracelets created by the Michigan youth group credited with first exploring WWJD? as part of a Sunday school lesson in 1989 sold like wildfire and soon there was a market for products with the "WWJD?" inscription; an inscription that quickly became recognizable in the broader culture.[3]

WWJD? has other religious significations that run in a more authentic direction than its more commodified expression. One major signification is a devotional one. Among some groups, WWJD? is a way of articulating a spiritual formation that focuses upon developing one's character in line with the character ascribed to Jesus the Christ. As one Intervarsity devotional curriculum puts it:

As we cultivate intimacy with the Father, we seek to develop Christ-like qualities and to live as he would. Our goal of becoming "conformed to the likeness of his Son" (Romans 8:29) leads to wholeness and integrity in our own lives.[4]

This manifestation of WWJD? represents a kind of virtue ethic fueled by meditation upon the person of Jesus. The concerns by which it tends to be marked have to do with issues of personal morality—among college students, for example, sexual purity or abstinence from alcohol. These are the sorts of moral codes with which evangelical Christians are most often associated.

For the purposes of this inquiry, I am more interested in the ways WWJD? manifests in projects in which Christianity is articulated as a tradition calling adherents to engage issues of social justice based on some claim about what the historical Jesus was up to. Drake's campus chapter of Intervarsity is a good example. I became familiar with this group when its leaders invited me to speak at one of its major events in the spring of 2006. The event was a week-long exploration of the theme "Jesus, Justice and Poverty." Because I am a lesbian who is quite out on campus, I was surprised by the invitation. I was equally surprised to learn that when these students ask what Jesus would do they envision a figure who calls Christians today to engage racism, poverty, environmental degradation and other pressing social justice matters. These students seek to identify with Jesus in a manner that is powerful and life changing. Most importantly, they seek to identify in a manner that translates into action that impacts the civic body for the good.

My students are not unique. Among many evangelical young people today there is an increasingly visible claim that the significance of Jesus was not only as a spiritual savior, but also as a socially engaged figure—a social justice Jesus.[5] One prominent example here is a loosely affiliated network of young evangelical Christians who call themselves New Monastics. New Monastics have established a number of communities in impoverished urban neighborhoods throughout the United States. They practice radical hospitality, communal living and civic participation in local and global contexts.[6] Some of the leaders describe themselves as following in the tradition of the desert fathers. Instead of retreating to the wilderness, however, "our deserts are the inner city and the places that empire has abandoned" (Greenfield, n.d.).

Writings coming out of the New Monastic movement capture an attempt to live a life today that looks like the one (their interpretation of) Jesus lived. In *Jesus for President: Politics for Ordinary Radicals*, Shane Claiborne (2008) critiques today's church for placing its trust in the state, the military and markets (p.20). In *Irresistible Revolution: Living as an Ordinary Radical*, he describes going to Calcutta and there tending the wounds of lepers. Claiborne (2003) and other New Monastics went to Baghdad on the eve of the U.S. bombing to literally stand with the people of Iraq. More pertinent here, another New Monastic, Jonathan Wilson-Hartgrove (2008), writes of his journey as a white southerner to come to terms with racism and to understand racial reconciliation as central to the meaning of Christian discipleship in contemporary U.S. contexts. There is nothing abstract about Wilson-Hartgrove's perspective. In *Free to Be Bound*, he describes how he and his wife, who is also white, started Rutba community in the Black part of a deeply segregated Durham, North Carolina. He also recounts the humbling lessons he received in the process of becoming associate minister at the historically Black St. John's Missionary Baptist Church.

Like my students, New Monastics seek to live practices that resonate with those modeled by a social justice Jesus. These WWJD? projects claim a Jesus who cuts against the grain of a church culture that is relatively non-distinguishable from the white-supremacist, capitalist, imperial contexts in which it is embedded.[7] In so doing they are in keeping with the origins of the Jesus question as it first emerged more than one hundred years ago. The opening crisis of Charles Sheldon's 1896 classic *In His Steps* takes place when a pastor is confronted by a man who is homeless. The man says to the pastor:

> But what would Jesus do? … It seems to me as if the people in the big churches had [sic] good clothes and nice houses to live in, and money to spend for luxuries, and could go away on summer vacations and all that, while the people outside the churches, thousands of them, I mean, die in tenements, and walk the streets for jobs, and never have a piano or a picture in the house, and grow up in misery and drunkenness and sin.
>
> *(1973, p.9)*

Convicted by this encounter, the pastor challenges his parish for an entire year to ask what Jesus would do before engaging in even the most mundane daily activity.

Because the opening foil is a crisis engendered by a pastor's encounter with the homeless, Sheldon's novel suggests that a life identified with Jesus is one engaged in practices that are responsive to contemporary social ills. While Sheldon's imagined parishioners are also personally transformed by their practice—along the lines of "becoming conformed in his likeness"—a central concern of this original WWJD? project is that of being relevant to the well-being of society.

Scholarship on the historical Jesus supports the claim to a social justice Jesus. This is the Jesus described by William Herzog (1994) in *Parables as Subversive Speech*, whose parables were intended to conscientize the oppressed masses of his day. In his parable of the talents (pp.150–68), for example, a master going on a journey gives three servants funds to invest during his absence (Matthew 25:14–30 and Luke 19:11–27). Upon his return, he violently rebukes the servant who buried his talent in the ground rather than investing and multiplying it. According to Herzog, traditional biblical scholarship and many a Sunday morning sermon has spiritualized, and thereby misinterpreted, this parable by assuming the master figure to represent God, and the parable a lesson about faithful obedience or the call to use one's "talents" in God's service. For Herzog (1994), to so easily identify as God a figure who is described as a harsh man who instills such fear (not the most flattering picture) reveals a profound interpretive bias (p.154). He conducts a rigorous historical-critical analysis to offer a very different interpretation. In Herzog's reading, the master is an archetype of the ruling elite, an oppressive figure whom Jesus' audience would have recognized from their own experience of subjugation. Jesus' original parable lifted up the third servant as a whistleblower whose act of burying the talent was a means of protesting the exploitative investment practices of the day. In Herzog's analysis it is this servant with whom Jesus' listeners were to identify, and the moral is a political and material one.

Any number of biblical scholars might be cited here to fill out the description of the social justice Jesus. The point is that scholarship like Herzog's makes available a figure who was allied with the outcasts of the day, and whose ministry challenged the many ways in which social structures systemically harmed people's lives. This is a Jesus who was executed by the state because of the threat he posed to the powers that be. It is this Jesus who is being remembered and emulated in WWJD? projects calling their adherents to social justice. A commitment to this historical Jesus as the Christ might include a theological understanding of him as a savior from personal sin. But it also prioritizes a recognition of the significance of social sin and the political call Jesus makes to today's follower who lives in a society in which people's lives are harmed by racism, poverty and other social ills. Surely the social justice Jesus would have something important to say about whiteness.

WWJD?: Identifying with the Black Christ

To assume the relevance of both history and Christology and to ask WWJD? in relation to whiteness requires that the question of Jesus' race be raised. Yet, almost nowhere in the WWJD? projects described above is a conscious attempt made to racialize either the historical Jesus or the present-day Christ with whom identification is being sought. *Free to Be Bound* is a partial exception, in that Wilson-Hartgrove (2008) explicitly identifies Jesus as Black at one point and briefly engages the work of theologian James Cone (pp.86, 91). Wilson-Hartgrove does not let white people off the hook for racism, nor downplay the evil in which white Christians are implicated. However, his ultimate conclusion is that race is, at its essence, a divider beyond which a relationship with the Christ calls us all. Thus, in my reading, Wilson-Hartgrove's Jesus ultimately becomes race-less, at best (calling us to unity beyond race), and not Black.

Given the extent to which Christianity has been tied up with the white-supremacist constitution of the United States, the default political and cultural image of Jesus is that of a blonde-haired, blue-eyed white guy. One might begin with U.S. origins as a slave-holding nation-state formed on land that was stolen from persons against whom genocide was committed, activities fueled and sanctioned by Christian interpretation, practice and, of course, practitioners. One might move to the horrors of U.S. lynching history, events at which Christian pastors often presided and hymns were sung in something resembling a (white) church service (Patterson, 1998, p.217). One might continue to the contemporary moment in which the backlash erupting after the election of our first Black president has been articulated through endless entanglements of race and religion, led by a "Tea Party" claiming Christian sanction as it questions simultaneously President Obama's religious and national identity. In U.S. contexts, if Jesus' race is not overtly re-envisioned, Jesus is white. This remains true even in the case of the social justice Jesus.

No one has pointed out the pervasiveness of the white Jesus more powerfully than Cone. In Cone's work, history and Christology come together to make a powerful case for the existence of the Black Christ. Cone's argument is disarmingly simple: Jesus is who he was. Jesus was a Jew living in occupied Palestine. He was one of the oppressed. His life's ministry was the annunciation of liberation for the oppressed and his resurrection was evidence of the ultimate victory and ongoing realization of such liberation (Cone, 1990, pp.110–28).

Cone (1990) argues that there must be continuity between the historical Jesus and the kerygmatic Christ. If there is not, then any community might interpret "the kerygma according to its own existential situation" and make Jesus into its own image (p.113). Traditional Christianity has committed this sin in its invention of the white Jesus. Instead, the historical Jesus' membership among the oppressed must be theologically significant. Continuity between Jesus' divine and human natures means that Christ is present today literally with and as the oppressed, realizing liberation as God's salvation in human-history. Cone (1990) writes: "The importance of the concept of the Black Christ is that it expresses the *concreteness* of Jesus' continued presence today" (p.123). Jesus is who he was.

In *Black Theology of Liberation*, Cone (1990) argued that blackness is the appropriate ontological symbol for the divine because the "white American inability to recognize humanity in persons of color" means that any racially oppressed community has to affirm its identity in terms of an anti-white reality. "Blackness, then, stands for all victims of oppression who realize that the survival of their humanity is bound up with liberation from whiteness" (p.7). Important critiques might be made of Cone's use of Black as a sufficiently representative symbol. However, in his subsequent theological career, while Cone has continued to write from and for his community and in regard to the salience of blackness, he has also encouraged diverse theological voices articulating claims in regard to the identity of the Christ made in response to their own discrete cultural and political contexts.[8] (In other words, the blackness of Christ is neither the only nor the final symbol.) By engaging the Black Christ rather than ontological symbols for God from other liberation theologies, I risk reaffirming the problematic tendency in racial discussions in the U.S. to present race on a Black/white binary. It is the oppressed Jesus, who might meaningfully be racialized in any number of ways, that is actually relevant to my argument. But Cone's use of blackness and his articulation of the reality of the Black Christ are particularly relevant to this discussion of Jesus and whiteness, and to U.S. racial history. Moreover, his theology directly racializes Jesus more than any other theological framework in a manner that is particularly helpful for this discussion.

Biblical scholarship buttresses Cone's indictment of the pervasiveness of the white Jesus. Cain Felder (1993), for example, writes in regard to the literal "color" of Jesus and the way in which traditional biblical scholarship has whitewashed him (pp.184–95). Felder argues that the European academy created the geographical designation of the Middle East as "an effort to avoid talking about Africa!" This designation falsely separated the African continent from the sacred story of the biblical text (Felder, 1993, p.194). Felder (1993) demonstrates how the African presence in the Bible has been erased, while the European presence, which is actually minimal, has been magnified (open the back of almost any Bible and the maps that show as much as possible of Europe and Eurasia, and as little of Africa) (p.189). Felder (1993) points out that Canaan was an extension of the African land mass, and that frequent migration from the African continent through Canaan toward Asia makes "'Afro-Asiatic' … probably the most accurate way to identify the mixed stock of people who populated the so-called ancient Near East" (p.189). Add to this the question of how a light-skinned Jesus could have hidden in Egypt, and an Afro-Asiatic Jesus is almost a certainty, argues Felder (1993, p.192).

Given the symbolic nature of Cone's use of blackness, Cone's theological claims do not stand or fall on the strength of Felder's arguments.[9] However, Felder's engagement of the texts and with what traditional biblical scholarship has done with those texts makes clear just how much the actual Jesus has been a victim of white supremacy utilized in the service of whiteness—a claim roundly endorsed by Cone's indictment of white Christianity. Beyond the claim that Jesus as oppressed means that Christ is Black, the depths of Christianity's allegiance with white supremacy render imperative the articulation of a Black Christ or a Christ who is otherwise racialized outside the normativity of white racial identity.

I am not suggesting here that Cone's theology is appropriately understood as a WWJD? project. Indeed, it should be noted that the WWJD? projects described above seem to be largely, demographically white (a dynamic that itself invites inquiry relative to the question of whiteness). However, to the extent that asking WWJD? in relation to whiteness requires seriously contending with who the historical Jesus actually was, it has to take seriously the endless entanglements of U.S. Christianity with whiteness in general. In particular, it has to take seriously the reality of the Black Christ. If it does not, it cannot have any credibility.

The historical Jesus was not an unmarked figure announcing the kingdom of God as a reign of justice to be pursued in the here and now. He was marked by his particularity; an oppressed figure making such an announcement with and on behalf of his fellow oppressed human beings, his people. As one of the oppressed, his position was more vulnerable, more constrained, and that much more radical. Thus, while the social justice Jesus would obviously have something to say about the problem of whiteness, the Black Christ's denouncement of it would resonate in a more powerful key because his social critique would put him in much greater peril. The Black Christ would encounter the power of whiteness not as an outsider, unaffected by the death-dealing designs of the United States, but as one already despised and vilified by the state and the dominant tradition that has helped to legitimate it. If the social justice Jesus would denounce whiteness, the Black Christ would be its mortal enemy.

Dangerous moves: reiterating whiteness and evading race

As a student at an evangelical Christian college I did not understand how my peers could see Christianity as a tradition obsessed with the sin of premarital sex but apathetic about their willingness to drive BMWs down streets teeming with men, women and children who were homeless. My distress soon turned into an intellectual and spiritual search for theological articulations that seemed more truthful. I quickly discovered and fell in love with liberation theology, in which I found an indictment of my religious and social contexts that resonated acutely. Cone in particular provided me with a theological framework through which to respond to the contradictions that I encountered at my relatively wealthy, predominantly white Christian college and a vocabulary that allowed me to critique a Christian culture that was complacent in the face of human suffering directly caused by injustice. Proclaiming my allegiance to the Black Christ made perfect sense to me.

My love of theology led me to undertake graduate work at Union Theological Seminary. There I expected to ground myself more deeply in Black and Womanist Theologies. I arrived at Union earnestly committed to the Black Christ. However, in the vibrant multi-racial community in which I found myself, this identification suddenly became vexed. While my peers appreciated my apparent intellectual and spiritual commitments, they pushed me hard in response to something they saw as a significant problem that I needed to face: I wasn't Black.

What did it mean for a white woman to claim to identify with the Black Christ? Did I understand that my white racial identity made my struggle against racism fundamentally different than the struggle in which my peers of color were engaged? That I was privileged at every turn by the very systems, processes and ideologies I claimed to disavow? That my racial identity itself was actually produced by those systems? In short, what did it mean to me to be white? I realized that I had few answers to these questions.

My dilemma was brought home further by another Union experience: the student caucus system. Students at Union regularly form caucuses for the purposes of community building, and organizing and strategizing around justice issues. The most prominent of these included the Black Caucus, the Black Women's Caucus, the Latina/o Caucus and the LGBT Caucus. During my graduate work, other students formed a Social Justice Caucus. Predictably, the membership of this caucus was completely white. This struck me as illustrative of a very serious problem—as perhaps related to the problem to which my peers' questions pointed.

As earnest as was my desire to respond to Cone's call to conversion, my experience in a multi-racial seminary community revealed to me that my white racial identity complicated this desire. My being racialized as white rendered my claim to identify with the Black Christ deeply problematic. Instead, it began to be clear to me that I needed to contend in a serious way with what psychologist Beverly Daniel Tatum (1997) describes as "the reality of [my] own Whiteness" (p.107).

When Tatum calls for white people to contend with their own whiteness, she is not asking white people to engage in an apolitical round of navel-gazing. Rather, she is pointing to the reality that our social contexts shape us in profound ways that cannot be ignored as we attempt to act in response to those contexts. Whiteness is not just "out there" in the social landscape. The need to contend with one's own whiteness refers to recognizing the realities about race and racial identity articulated in the opening pages of this chapter: that my white racial identity is not somehow removed from the white-supremacist contexts through which it is formed; that an intellectual commitment against racism does not, in and of itself, disrupt the ways that the social construction of race inscribes supremacist ideologies and processes on my bodyself; that I cannot engage in anti-racist struggle as a non-racial human, nor as a person of color, but must face the profound dilemmas that my white racial location creates.

Janet Helms (1992) writes: "For racism to disappear in the United States, White people must take responsibility for ending it ... " (p.i). But, like Tatum, Helms has identified several stages of white racial identity development that seriously impede the ability of white people to do so. Upon coming to the painful recognition that racial equality and justice are not realized in our society, which Helms calls the disintegra-tion stage, one white response—reintegration—is to accept such inequity as evidence of the innate superiority and inferiority of white people and people of color, respectively. A better response is to conclude that social structures generate inequity, but from here the white person still faces many challenges. In this pseudo-independent stage of development the white person questions assumptions of superiority and inferiority, and acknowledges that racism is perpetuated by white people.[10] But, having rejected what Tatum and Helms both call a "negative white identity" without having moved into a "positive white identity," the white person might experience isolation, become paralyzed by guilt, romanticize people of color or continue to see the self as race-less in the attempt to distance the self from white perpetration (Tatum, 1997, 105–8; Helms, 1992, 88). Each of these responses subverts the white person's attempt to act in liberative ways in response to white supremacy.

Analyses such as Helm's and Tatum's make clear that a challenge to whiteness must have at least two foci simultaneously: the social landscape and the self. Given the hydra-headed nature of white supremacy, this is no surprise. Both Helms and Tatum make clear that the social processes of racialization have real psychological effects, and create significant developmental challenges and moral conundrums for white people. Coming to terms with one's own whiteness by facing such affects and conundrums is challenging. But it is an essential part of the journey of being able to be a true ally in the public and political struggle against white supremacy.

I want to suggest that to ask WWJD? in relation to either the social justice Jesus or the Black Christ invites the white Christian to identify with Jesus without seriously engaging his or her own whiteness. The ways in which whiteness is avoided in rela-tion to each are different, but identifying uncritically with either of these Jesuses risks reiterating and reaffirming whiteness itself.

It is not difficult to imagine what the social justice Jesus would do in response to white supremacy. If white supremacy is an evil social structure that has acquired a normative status within the political, economic, and cultural forces of the day, this Jesus would target it as a social sin that needs to be directly challenged. He would obviously take a rigorous anti-whiteness stance and engage in a radical critique of the structures within which all of our lives are embedded. Perhaps he would angrily denounce churches that support the white-supremacist constitution of the United States by way of their easy acquiescence to U.S. culture; much like he turned over the money-changing tables in the Temple to protest the ways in which religious practice had become entangled with economic gain (Matthew 21:11–13; Mark

11:15–16; John 2:14–16). Perhaps he would question whether the individual follower who has failed to renounce white privilege can access eternal life; much like he disappointed the rich young ruler when he told him that in failing to give away all his possessions he impeded his own salvation (Matthew 19:16–26; Mark 10:17–27; Luke 18:18–25).

We might imagine many scenarios in which Jesus' challenge to the social structures of his day could be translated into contemporary contexts. Clearly, social justice Jesus would stand with those most harmed and marginalized by whiteness. Moreover, whatever the particular actions he would undertake, this Jesus would engage in activity that was radical, public and political enough to get him into real trouble.

I am deeply sympathetic to the social justice Jesus figure claimed in the WWJD? projects described above. I am even intellectually persuaded that it is plausible that the Jesus being described is historically accurate. Indeed, it's a deceptively simple case to make: those inclined to ask WWJD? are called to take action against racist structures in prophetic and courageous ways as part of the journey of Christian discipleship.

However, it is at precisely this point that problems with WWJD? emerge in relation to the white Christian. One of the many effects of whiteness is that it always already locates white people at the center of most narratives and structures. Such positioning is mitigated by class, gender and sexual orientation, but when racial difference is present white people tend to be positioned as primary actors in whatever location we find ourselves.

People of color have long critiqued the white liberal in regard to precisely this phenomenon, and many a multi-racial coalition against racism has fallen apart because the justice-committed white people in the room behaved in ways inconsistent with the work of forging true solidarity across lines of racial difference.[11] In the case of the Black struggle for civil rights, for example, it was not the existence of overtly racist white people that spawned the call for separatism and Black power. It was the presence of well-intentioned white people who were inclined to dominate agenda-setting, take on racism in paternalistic postures and otherwise behave in ways that failed to take seriously the reality that white people are compromised by their privileged locations in white supremacy and that actually reiterated the very white dominance characteristic of white supremacy.

Such behaviors are part and parcel of the effects of structures on the bodyself. Those of us who are white always risk acting out of the brokenness that racialization in white-supremacist contexts has generated in our development as *white* people. This risk haunts even the most anti-white supremacy-committed among us. It follows us into our justice work, making truly subversive and justice-creating action on the part of white people deeply challenging.

It just so happens that identifying with or as the central agent in the narratives we embody is one of the broken ways of being toward which white people are prone. It just so happens that being inclined to do "for" in postures that are paternalistic is another damaged side-effect of white racialization. And it just so happens that these tendencies are valorized in the social justice Jesus who is the central power-agent in his saga. Social justice Jesus is like a superhero standing up to evil forces around him and attempting to inveigh on behalf of suffering others. And, thus, while it is laudable that he stands with or works on behalf of the marginalized, it, therefore, just so happens that the broken ways of being toward which white people are already inclined are likely to be triggered, maybe even amplified, by identifying with such a figure. This likelihood is particularly dangerous when the figure is one being elevated as a power-agent in what is ultimately a triumphant story. It is even more dangerous when he is a figure not racialized as Black. It is most dangerous when he is assumed to be divine!

Theological narratives have incredible power. Ethicist Traci West (2006) writes provocatively of the danger of prayer in churches that are predominantly white and middle-to-upper class. She argues that when prayers of thanksgiving are given for "blessings"—which, given our white-supremacist, capitalist structures, come by way of race and class privileges—unjust enrichments are accepted as nothing less than gifts from God (p.121). Similarly, many feminist theologians have written of the dangers that invoking the maleness of God can have, regardless of how symbolic they are claimed to be. To repeatedly call God "he" in contexts in which male dominance is pandemic is to risk divinizing human maleness in ways that sanction various manifestations of misogyny.

A similar danger resides here to that described by West. As has already been suggested, applying the insights acquired by an interpretation of Jesus' life to the present day involves more than disinterested speculation about what the historical Jesus would do were he with us today. WWJD? involves the asker in an identification with this Jesus; it involves a second gesture of making Jesus' actions, as a Christ figure, in some way normative for the self. In this move by the white Christian to identify with Jesus, the centrality and power of the white actor is reiterated and reaffirmed. Simply put, identifying with the divine is about the last thing that a white person whose life is embedded in white-supremacist structures should be doing.

Identification with the Black Christ raises a different but equally problematic set of issues. On the one hand, the invocation of the Black Christ as part of WWJD? offers the important possibility of de-centering white racial identity (even when such identity has remained centered simply because it has gone unmarked). This is a significant step forward from the social justice Jesus. On the other hand, in seeking to identify with the Black Christ, the white Christian runs the risk of actually avoiding their own race and power.

In her landmark text *White Women, Race Matters*, Ruth Frankenberg interviews white women in order to explore the conundrum of being positioned in a posture of dominance even while being committed to justice. Specifically, Frankenberg (1993) is interested in how white women who articulate a genuine commitment to racial justice might simultaneously help to maintain whiteness. She finds that some women participate in maintaining whiteness because they are without "language with which to analyze in sufficiently complex fashion the relationship between the white self and racism as a system of domination" (p.169). Some feel overdetermined by whiteness and become too paralyzed to act against racism because of being laden with guilt and/or negative self-perceptions (Frankenberg, 1993, p.171). Others engage in what

Frankenberg identifies as race and power evasion. Failing to find ways to simultaneously hold a rigorous anti-whiteness stance while acknowledging their own "white" skin, these women in a sense felt "underdetermined" (my word, not Frankenberg's) by their racial identity, and simply ignored or denied the actual power and privilege with which their light skin imbues their lives. Such denial did not enable behaviors that could genuinely aid in the struggle against the power of whiteness, even among those who went out of their way to establish relationships with people of color. Rather race- and power-evasion kept their own whiteness transparent (to themselves, if not to others) and ignored the actual material and political conditions through which relationships of solidarity are forged (Frankenberg, 1993, pp.14, 15).

The dilemma that these women experienced is a real one generated by a need for a racial identity in a social landscape in which everyone is racialized, and yet in which white supremacy is primary in giving white racial identity meaning. I often ask my students to consider their reaction were they to see African American students walking through Drake's commons carrying signs that read "Black is beautiful," for example. Their response to this is to assume a positive invocation and to support such a demonstration. Their response shifts radically when I ask how they would view white students similarly carrying signs that read "White is beautiful." This thought exercise captures the dilemma with which Frankenberg's race- and power-evasive interviewees are contending. These two images do not elicit the same response because white racial identity and Black racial identity are not parallels. While people of color have collectively articulated unique and creative identities that subvert and challenge the meanings white supremacy would ascribe to their racial locations, white people have overwhelmingly failed to do so. These social identifications simply do not signify in the same manner.

So what is a white person to do? To join the Social Justice Caucus is a response that unwittingly but powerfully reiterates whiteness by allowing white racial identity to remain transparent. To join the Black Caucus—even if one were allowed to do so—is equally evasive of race and power, differently ignoring the real material and political content of white racial identity that renders "being white" problematic in ways that "being Black" is not.

The white Christian cannot claim an easy identification with the Black Christ any less problematically than he or she joins the Black Caucus. In the move to do so the white Christian risks engaging in precisely such race- and power-evasion. This was the reason my peers at Union pressed me so hard. The desire to skip over one's own whiteness and join with the Black Christ is an understandable response to the real problem of not having a positive racial identity from which to stand and oppose racist structures. It is a seductive position to proclaim oneself opposed to evil social structures (like the Black Christ) and as standing with the marginalized. Yet, if such denunciations are not accompanied by a serious coming to terms with the ways in which one's life is itself invested with, embedded in and even given material and political meaning by the very powers one is seeking to denounce, one risks ignoring or denying one's actual location. For white people, that location is at the other end of the finger as the Black Christ points and denounces.

Becoming race-cognizant, becoming human: what would Zacchaeus do?

WWJD? is not a meaningless or inherently flawed question. Nor is it the case that white Christians should have no interest in what Jesus would have done vis-à-vis whiteness. Rather, the preceding analysis demonstrates the danger of the move to identify with Jesus. If we take the social justice Jesus and the Black Christ seriously, the white Christian discovers that he or she stands among the accused when Jesus as the Christ calls out deadly and dangerous systems of oppression and subjugation. We find ourselves among powers that be. Our task then becomes that of figuring out just what it would mean to respond to Jesus' indictment.

To be complicit in injustice is to participate in one's own dehumanization. The reality is that collective and sustained complicity with white supremacy over centuries in the United States has malformed our very humanity as white people. To the extent that we have been identified with whiteness and to the extent that white supremacy itself has had a determinative say in what it means to be white, white people have lost our humanity. To that end, rather than understanding the goal of identification with the divine—race-less, white, or Black—as the goal for the white Christian, the goal is to figure out how to seek authentic identification with humanity—to attempt to become human. By this, I do not mean, however, to become human as somehow above and beyond race—our humanness is always particular. Rather, for white people, the only way forward to humanness is to go back through our whiteness and become traitors to it. Ignatiev and Garvey (1996) have helpfully captured this process in the phrase "treason to whiteness is loyalty to humanity." Race treason is a way of conceptualizing the kind of action needed that might simultaneously keep both the social and the self in view.

Tatum and Helms both argue that white people need to journey developmentally to a place in which they can embrace a "positive white identity"—a stage of development that Helms calls autonomy. In this stage the white person has moved out of guilt or romanticization. Neither over- nor underdetermined by whiteness, the white person asks "who am I racially?"; "who do I want to be?" Developing an increasingly complex analysis of racism, he or she seeks to learn from others who are different, but does so without denigrating or idealizing people on the basis of their racial identities. Nor does this white person denigrate or idealize him- or herself.

The realization of these kinds of behaviors and understandings indeed is key for coming into an anti-racist practice. Yet, the language of a "positive white identity" is problematic. As long as the social structures through which white people are racialized are supremacist, "white" cannot be a positive racial identity.[12] Yet, as has already been argued, evacuating racial identity somehow is simply not an option.

A better way to articulate the needed response to the conundrum of being justice seeking in a context in which one's race is literally formed by supremacy is to acknowledge the conundrum and the paradox that it creates: white people need to continually acknowledge that we "be white" even while we attempt to refuse to "be white." The challenge is to identify and strategically disrupt those very social processes and systems that produce our white identities. Such action, repeated sufficiently, collectively and over a sustained period of time might actually have the power to reconstitute white identity in very different terms (to the extent that it successfully inveighs against white supremacy).

One of my white students shared an experience that captures the kind of activities I have in mind. She explained that over spring break she had gone to a club to see a band in which the musicians were Mexican. The club had heavy security, and most of the patrons were also Mexican. On the way in to the club, people were being frisked by the white bouncers. As this student entered, the bouncers waved her through. She stopped and put her arms in the air and said very loudly, "if you are looking for weapons on everyone else here, you better frisk me too." Her response created quite a ruckus, and while the guards tried to collect themselves, other patrons in the line started yelling "solidaridad." This is a small, but significant, example of action that, even if only for a fragile and elusive moment, challenged the very processes through which whiteness was being constituted, and did so in a race- and power-cognizant manner. It is also worth noting that while she had no illusion that this act radically changed the world and brought down white supremacy, the student did have a sense that for a moment she had disrupted whiteness and that she would be more empowered to do it again in the future.

White people committed to justice must figure out ways to become race- and power-cognizant race traitors. Jesus, therefore, who cannot be envisioned today as a race traitor, since he was historically among the oppressed, is simply not our model. I would argue instead that the figure of Zacchaeus offers a better figure with whom the white Christian should seek identification. What we know about Zacchaeus is that when he encountered Jesus he did so as someone who had been utterly complicit with the powers that be. Just like white people in the United States, he had forsaken brotherhood and sisterhood, and been seduced into allegiance with death-dealing power structures. He had been massively and unjustly enriched by way of this allegiance. Despite sharing a religious-ethnic heritage with Jesus, he was Jesus' structural enemy. When Jesus challenged him, however, Zacchaeus did not remain over-determined by his oppressor location. In response, Zacchaeus chose radical conversion. Evidence of this conversion was not his mere verbal declaration of belief in Jesus' divine mission or social vision. Nor was it a declaration that he would become Jesus' disciple. Rather, the evidence of Zacchaeus' conversion came when he determined to give half of his wealth to the poor and to repay anyone whom he had defrauded with four times what he had taken (Luke 19:8).

Mark Lomax (2001) writes that Jesus only recognized the authenticity of Zacchaeus' repentance and affirmed his salvation in response to his words and behavior together. It was only then that Jesus affirmed his salvation. Poignantly, Lomax (2001) notes that the crowd likely waited to accept the authenticity of Zacchaeus' repentance until the promised behavior was implemented (p.19).

The task of white Christians is not to ask what Jesus would do in order to identify with or imitate Jesus—at least not yet. As long as whiteness is the norm and white supremacy that which constitutes our identity, we must ever acknowledge the real hurdles that exist, creating distance between ourselves and the Black Christ. Our task is to recognize that what Jesus did and said, taken seriously, means that the white Christian is instead called to identify with and imitate Zacchaeus. WWZD? enables us to avoid the dangers of race- and power-evasion. WWZD? enables us to avoid the risk of reaffirming the privilege of being the central actor in the story and presuming ourselves to be doing for others. Perhaps most importantly, WWZD? models what humility and repentance look like—both of which begin by taking seriously one's morally compromised identity—and provide an example of what is required to turn away from complicity.

What would Jesus do? He would ask the white Christian to begin *disidentifying* with him or with any other divine figure. Instead, he would ask us to ask "What would Zacchaeus do?" And, to the extent that we can strategically and creatively figure out how to identify with Zacchaeus by engaging in public and political acts of race treason as myriad and multiple as whiteness itself, we will have begun the journey to an authentic identification with humanity.

Notes

1 See also the now defunct journal *Race Traitor: A Journal of the New Abolitionism.* Ignatiev and Garvey regularly use the club metaphor and racial profiling example to illustrate their notion of race treason.

2 See, for example, http://www.whatwouldjesusdo.com.

3 The church was Calvary Reformed Church in Holland, Michigan. Sheppard (1998).

4 www.intervarsity.org/news/spiritual-formation.

5 The emergence of this claim looks a good deal like the vision of Jesus and Christianity articulated by Jim Wallis and Sojourners.

6 In 2004, New Monastics gathered to identify twelve "distinctives" of their movement: "living with the poor and outcast, living near community members, hospitality, submission to the larger church, nurturing common community life and a shared economy, peacemaking, reconciliation, care for creation and contemplation." For a brief history of the emergence of the New Monastics, see Greenfield (n.d.).

7 On the same website where they market WWJD? items, Agape Enterprises sells "God Bless America" and "Support our troops" paraphernalia.

8 See Cone's "Preface" to the 1986 edition of *Black Theology of Liberation* for a discussion of his theological growth over the course of his career.

9 "But some whites will ask, 'Does black theology believe that Jesus was *really* black?' It seems to me that the *literal* color of Jesus is irrelevant, as are the different shades of blackness in America. Generally speaking, blacks are not oppressed on the basis of the depths of their blackness ... But as it happens, *Jesus was not white* in any sense of the word, literally or theologically" (Cone, 1990, 123).

10 Here I am drawing on an unpublished work, Mary Foulke's "White Racial Identity Development Chart," based upon Janet E. Helms, ed. *Black and White Racial Identity: Theory, Research and Practice* (Praeger Paperback, 1993). These stages are also summarized in Helms (1992).

11 For a particularly excellent history of the breaking down of solidarity between white and Black anti-racist activists in response to these particular problems, see Becky Thompson (2001).

12 Ian Haney López makes the same point, but articulated slightly different reasons for it in *White By Law: the Legal Construction of Race* (1996). For Haney López, the call for a positive white identity, which critical race theorists have also been known to make (he

cites Barbara Flagg, for example) when "white" continues to be assumed as a superior identity, cannot reinscribe discourses of superiority.

References

Claiborne, Shane. *Jesus for President: Politics for Ordinary Radicals* (Zondervan, 2008), 20.
Cone, James H. *A Black Theology of Liberation*, 20th Anniversary Edition (Orbis Books, 1990).
Felder, Cain Hope. "Cultural Ideology, Afrocentrism and Biblical Interpretation," in *Black Theology: A Documentary History*, Volume II 1980–92 edited by James H. Cone and Gayraud S. Wilmore (Orbis Books, 1993), 184–95.
Foulke, Mary. "White Racial Identity Development Chart," based upon Janet E. Helms, ed. *Black and White Racial Identity: Theory, Research and Practice* (Praeger Paperback, 1993).
Frankenberg, Ruth. *White Women, Race Matters: The Social Construction of Whiteness* (University of Minnesota, 1993).
Helms, Janet. *A Race is a Nice Thing to Have: A Guide to Being a White Person or Understanding the White Persons in Your Life* (Content Communications, 1992).
Herzog, II, William R. *Parables as Subversive Speech: Jesus as Pedagogue of the Oppressed* (Westminster/John Knox Press, 1994).
Ignatiev, Noel and John Garvey, *Race Traitor* (New York: Routledge, 1996).
Lomax, Mark A. "Reparations: Getting to the Ground Level," *Horizons* (November/December 2001): 19–23.
López, Ian Haney. *White by Law: the Legal Construction of Race* (New York University Press, 1996).
Patterson, Orlando. *Rituals of Blood: Consequences of Slavery in Two American Centuries* (Civitas Counterpoint, 1998).
Sheldon, Charles. *In His Steps* (New York: Grosset and Dunlap Publishers, 1973; original version 1896).
Tatum, Beverly Daniel. *"Why Are All the Black Kids Sitting Together in the Cafeteria? And Other Conversations about Race* (Basic Books, 1997).
Thompson, Becky. *A Promise and a Way of Life: White Antiracist Activism* (University of Minnesota, 2001).
West, Traci C. *Disruptive Christian Ethics: When Racism and Women's Lives Matter* (Westminster John Knox, 2006).
Wilson-Hartgrove, Jonathan. *Free to Be Bound: Church beyond the Color Line* (NavPress, 2008).

Web Sources

Claiborne, Shane. "Glimpses of Life in Baghdad: Nomadic Solidarity," March 20, 2003. See www.counterpunch.org/claiborne03202003.html.
Greenfield, Craig. "New Monasticism is now in Your Backyard" (n.d.). Available at miketodd.typepad.com/files/new-monasticism—craigs-article.doc.
Sheppard, Sandy. "What Would Jesus Do?" *Christianity Today International* (1998). Available at www.christianity.com/Christian%20Living/Features/11622298/.

Websites

www.intervarsity.org/news/spiritual-formation
www.whatwouldjesusdo.com

6

IS CHRIST WHITE?

Racism and Christology

Rosemary Radford Ruether

A fundamental tenet of Christian faith has been the universality of Christ. Christ is said to transcend all nations and to redeem all people, regardless of gender, race, ethnicity or political, economic or legal status. This is expressed in the oft-quoted Pauline text of Galatians 3:28: "There is no longer Jew or Greek, there is no longer slave or free; there is no longer male or female, for all of you are one in Christ Jesus." Yet Christian practice and teaching has frequently undermined this claimed inclusivity.

The most obvious of these exclusions has been gender. Although women are said to be redeemed by Christ, much of Western Christian tradition has said that they cannot represent Christ as priest. This view was elaborated by thirteenth-century theologian Thomas Aquinas, basing his view on the biological anthropology of Aristotle.

According to Thomistic anthropology, women lack the fullness of human nature. They are defective in bodily, volitional and intellectual capacities. In procreation, the male seed provides the active formative power, while the female provides only the "matter" that is formed. Normatively, every male seed would produce another male. So the female is produced only when there is a deficiency in the process of formation of the female matter, producing an incomplete or defective human or female. This means that the male must dominate and rule over the female in all social relations and the female can never represent the human community as ruler or leader.

This view of women's defective or incomplete nature shaped Thomas' Christology and view of priesthood. Christ has to be a male in order to represent the headship of the New Adam of regenerated humanity because only the male possesses "perfect" or complete humanness of mind and body. It follows, then, that women cannot be ordained or represent Christ as priest, since, as defective humans, they cannot image Christ's fullness of humanity. This exclusion of women from ordination is not only juridical. By nature, they cannot validly receive the sacrament of ordination (Aquinas, I.1.92, ad. 1; also I.99.2. ad 2).[1]

Unlike gender exclusion, Christian teaching has never explicitly said that Christ was literally "white" or a member of the Caucasian "race" and that therefore only "whites" or Europeans can be ordained or represent Christ in ordained leadership. Yet, in European and American art, from the Middle Ages to the present, Christ (as well as God, Mary and the disciples) have been depicted as light-skinned Europeans. This is evident in any Western book of art depicting Christ. Take, for example, Neil MacGregor's 2000 volume, *Seeing Salvation: Images of Christ in Art*.

As we peruse the images in MacGregor's book, we see that, as a baby, as a child, as a young man preaching and teaching and as the crucified, Christ is typically seen as looking like a Western European, as having light skin, often with light-colored hair and even blue eyes. As resurrected, Christ can be seen as luminously pure white, with light-yellow hair and beard (MacGregor, 2000, p.187).[2] This convention is so typical as not to be noticed by most European Christians. Yet, if he were depicted as a brown-skinned, dark-haired, semitic-looking person, undoubtedly closer to what Jesus actually looked like, this would be noticed by most Western Christians, and probably be seen as demeaning.

But the whiteness of Christ in Western Christian culture is more than an artistic convention, depicting Jesus as "like us," as Christian art in Africa or Asia might depict Jesus as looking like an African or Asian. It reflects certain assumptions in Western culture about the superiority of whiteness and the inferiority of "non-whites," or people of "color". This was a viewpoint particularly shaped in the sixteenth to twentieth centuries in Europe and the United States in the context of the enslavement of Africans and the conquest of indigenous peoples of the Americas. In order to claim that such forms of conquest and enslavement were appropriate, Spanish, English, Americans and other people colonizing and enslaving Africans and "Indians" began to differentiate themselves as "white," while styling the others as "red" or "black," although these colors were hardly literally the skin tone of any of these humans. In other words, the use of these "color" terms for different groups both exaggerates skin-color difference and shapes the way European and American people see these "others."

Scholars of the concept of "whiteness," like Jacqueline Battalora of the Department of Sociology and Criminal Justice of Xavier University in Chicago, have traced the use of the term "white" in American law in order to define and enforce the separation and subordination of darker-skinned people from Africa and the Americas from lighter-skinned people from northwestern Europe, or, to be more exact, to differentiate the conquerors–settlers from northwestern Europe from conquered people of the Americas and the captured peoples being shipped as slaves from Africa (Battalora, 1999).

This differentiation came to be seen as urgent, so as to prevent the legitimation of inter-marriage between these two groups, even though the use of "Indian" and African women as concubines was not forbidden to European males, who were, thereby, from the beginning of colonization, engaged in producing interracial offspring. In the English colonies and the United States, in contrast to somewhat different patterns among the French in North America and the Spanish in Latin America, there was also a concern to prevent these "mixed" offspring from inheriting the status of the "white" father and ascending into the free, privileged class. So the offspring were defined in terms of the enslaved or marginalized status of the "Indian" or African mother.

In the United States this view was canonized by the legal ruling that "one drop" of "black" blood made a person "black." In other words, if it was known that a person had any African ancestors, then they were to be defined as Black, to prevent those "mixed" people who looked "white" from "passing" (Davis, 2001).[3]

The definition of "white" people versus non-whites evolved over time in American law. In the sixteenth and seventeenth centuries, distinctions were often unclear. "Indians" were being Christianized and settling into European-style life. The distinction between enslaved Africans and indentured labor from England or other European areas, who served for a limited time and then could be free, was vague. Some Africans arrived in North America as free or became free after some service and were acquiring land and employment and marrying Europeans.

Colonial law at first defined the identity of the European settlers as "English" or "Christian." But Africans or "Indians" could become Christians. And the settlers from northwestern Europe soon included French, Scandinavians, Dutch, Germans and Irish. So these two terms were seen as inadequate to differentiate the would-be privileged settlers from the enslaved or marginalized others. By the late seventeenth century, the term "white" replaces "Christian" and "English" to define the European settlers and differentiate them from "others." At the same time, there was an effort to differentiate Africans from European indentured servants, defining Africans as permanent slaves and forbidding legal intermarriage of "whites" (particularly women) and "Blacks" (Battalora, unpublished manuscript, ch. 1).

From that point on, in American law and culture "white" becomes the collective definition of the privileged group in the United States, differentiating it especially from "Blacks," descendants of Africans, and also from "Indians" and from any "mixed" people with African or "Indian" ancestors. This was further confirmed in law following the American Revolution. In 1790, the newly formed American Congress ruled that in order to become a naturalized citizen one had to be white (Act of Congress of March 26, 1790 ch. 3, stat. 103). Enslaved Blacks were excluded as citizens, although defined in the Constitution as three-quarters of a person for the purpose of electing whites to Congress on the basis of population figures of the states. "Indians" were also excluded as citizens, defined in hostile terms by the Declaration of Independence of 1776 as "inhabitants of our Frontiers, the merciless Indian Savages. Whose known rule of Warfare is undistinguished destruction of all Ages, Sexes and Conditions."

But subsequent law and practice found it difficult to maintain this line of "white" against people of various mixtures. One of these challenges was occasioned by the Mexican–American War of 1845–47, which incorporated into the southwest of the United States a third of Mexico, with its mixed Spanish and other European, "Indian" and African populations. In the treaty of Guadalupe-Hildago, which concluded the war, the American Congress agreed that the Mexican population of these territories would be defined as "white" and given United States citizenship, if they so chose and did not opt for Mexican citizenship within a year.

However, unlike the United States, Mexico had abolished slavery in 1824 and given citizenship to all, regardless of race. Many Mexicans in the territories taken over by the U.S., which included what would become the states of Texas, Arizona, New Mexico and California and parts of Utah, Nevada, Wyoming and Colorado, were of mixed race, particularly European and "Indian," but some had African ancestry as well. These included some of the leading Mexican landowners. For example, Pio de Jesus Pico, the last Spanish governor of California and a wealthy rancher and businessman, was of African, "Indian" and European (Italian and Spanish) ancestry.

The California Constitutional Convention, meeting in Monterey, the former capital of Mexican California, from 1 September to 13 October, 1849, to define the state constitution, sought to exclude non-whites from citizenship. This directly excluded former Black slaves and Indians, but left in doubt the citizenship of Mexican landowners of mixed ancestry, several of whom were actually delegates of the convention. Although most of these were included in U.S. citizenship, in practice, Californian whites, who rushed into the state, particularly with the Gold Rush, regarded Mexicans as people of a degraded mixed race (and religion) and set about depriving them of their land (Ruether, 2007, pp.85–91).

To this day, Mexicans continue to be viewed by "whites" in the United States, especially in the former Mexican areas (reinforced by recent laws in Arizona[4]), as second-class citizens and as people likely to be present as illegal "aliens," despite the fact that some are descended from people present in these areas before the advent of "whites." Their earlier presence is manifest through the Spanish names of many of the regions, cities and streets.

In discussing the meaning of "whiteness" in American law and culture, it is important to be clear that, from the beginning of the use of this term, it meant more than just a collective ethnic name for light-skinned people from Europe. Rather, it carried certain religious and cosmological connotations. "Whiteness" is not so much an ethnic identity as it is an identity marker that places under erasure the diversity of cultures, classes and experiences of the peoples of northwestern Europe and their descendants. To be "white" is to forget that your ancestors in England were Welsh or Scottish, or came from France, Austria or Norway. It is to become members of the privileged group without ethnic, historical or cultural particularity.

This group has permeable borders which allows light-to-medium tan people to assimilate into it culturally and economically. Thus the Irish, initially regarded as belonging to a non-English inferior race of "Celts," became "white" in the United States by adopting the cultural identity of the American dominant group and setting themselves against free Blacks in American cities with whom they often competed for jobs (Ignatiev, 1995). By a similar process, American Jews, Arabs and light-skinned Latin Americans become "white," although their status continues to be vulnerable if their "difference" of language, ethnicity or religion becomes singled out.

Significantly, "white" in American culture is not a "color" among other colors, but is defined as "colorless." Thus all "non-white" people, Africans, "Indians," Asians, Latin Americans of mixed ancestry, can be defined as "people of color," while by implication whites are outside of any "color." They are a people who lack "color."

This also reflects the fact that "white" is not seen as one particular group within a diversity of groups. It is not one particularity among others. Rather, it is one side of a dualism, defined normatively as "white" to be differentiated from "Black." Although other "colors" may be seen as inferior to "white," those called "black" play the central role in this terminology. The purpose of being defined as "white" is to differentiate one as the opposite of "black," to be one side of the dualism of "white" versus "black."

The dualism "white/black" evokes a set of religious and cosmological dualisms in Western thought set in opposition to each other in a hierarchical relationship: light versus darkness, heaven versus earth, godly versus ungodly, good versus evil, beautiful versus ugly, being versus non-being, pure versus polluted. Thus, to be "white" is to claim a good, beautiful, true and pure moral and cosmological nature against the opposites of evil, impure, unclean, unredeemed reality (see Winthrop, 1968). It is in the context of this implied godly, moral and redeemed higher nature that "whiteness" implies a connection to Christ, the epitome of goodness, godliness and redeemed and redemptive being over against its opposites. That Christ must "look" and "be" white in Christian thought and art, although perhaps beginning as an ethnic convention, takes on a theological meaning.

To elucidate further this theological connotation of "whiteness" and its normative association with Christ as "white," I will examine some examples of the conflict of Western Christian evangelization of "non-white" people in which a concept of a "white" or "European" Christ is explicitly identified and repudiated as false or idolatrous. This form of repudiation is done in order to define a Black, "Indian," African or Asian Christ as the authentic nature of Christ and as truly redemptive for non-whites. In these contexts Christ is named as "white" in order to repudiate such a Christ as anti-Christ, as the opposite of the authentic Christ.

An example of this is the public liturgical action of Archbishop Augustus Stalling of the Imani Temple, an African American congregation in Washington D.C., who, in full vestments on Easter of 1993, took some images of a white Christ with a typically insipid "sweet" face, pale skin and light hair, and tore them up at the altar, thus ceremonially repudiating the "white Christ" as idolatrous and oppressive to all authentic Christians, particularly people of "color." He called on Black churches to burn their "white" Christs.[5]

Many Black churches were slow to take offense at images of a white Christ. In the summer of 1965, I volunteered for the Delta Ministry in Mississippi on issues of racial justice, including campaigning for the passage of the Civil Right Act. On one occasion, a Black colleague and I traveled across the state border to visit Bogalusa, Louisiana, where a tense standoff between the Black community and the regional Ku Klux Klan (KKK) was taking place. The Black churches had organized a round-the-clock vigil, led by the Deacons for Defense, against the KKK, which had surrounded the town.

My colleague and I attended a vibrant evening service of prayer and preaching in a Black church. The preaching was militant and the atmosphere was electric. In the midst of the service, my eye was suddenly caught by a fresco down one side of the church depicting life-sized images of Christ and the disciples all as white European males. The contradiction between what was happening in the church and these images was so startling to me that I wondered why the people of the church didn't fall on these pictures and tear them down. But the church community appeared oblivious to them.

In the following part of this chapter, I turn to exploring liberation Christologies which, in one way or another, seek socially transformative understandings of Christ as alternatives to Christologies that implicitly or explicitly validate an identification of Christ with white European domination and/or define redemption in an asocial way that supports passivity in the face of oppression and injustice.

I start with Black American Christologies that use the black–white symbolism to distinguish liberating from pacifying views of Christ. I then turn to African, Latin American and Asian views of Christ that also seek culturally indigenous and liberating views of Christ against those that validate colonial domination, but usually without using black–white symbolism.

The U.S. civil rights movement in the 1960s, particularly with the Black Power movement that embraced the term "Black" as a liberating symbol against the historical use of whiteness as racial superiority, unleashed several versions of Black theology which defined the authentic Christ as Black against a white Christ. A range of views of the meaning of Christ's blackness emerged in these theologies, specifically the views of Albert Cleage, James Cone, and J. Deotis Roberts.

Cleage's 1968 text *The Black Messiah* is the most literally ethnic or biological of these views. For Cleage, Jesus was racially African. "The intermingling of the races in Africa and the Mediterranean is an established fact. The Nation Israel was a mixture of Chaldeans, Egyptians, Midianites, Ethiopians, Kushites, Babylonians and other dark peoples, all of them were already mixed with the Black people of Central Africa" (Cleage, 1968, p.3). Cleage (1968) identified Jesus as an explicit Black nationalist. "Jesus was the non-white leader of a non-white people struggling for national liberation against the rule of a white nation, Rome" (p.3). Jesus's liberating work was not only political and military, as an armed Zealot seeking the overthrow of the Roman Empire. It was on behalf of the Black elect people of Israel, and, by extension, all Black people today who are engaged in a struggle to liberate themselves from white imperial domination. It is not about "all nations," but a liberation exclusively for and about Black people.

James Cone's understanding of the Black Christ departs from this racial literalism and exclusivism to a more symbolic view. For Cone, Jesus was a Middle Eastern Jew. Although doubtless this meant he was brown and Semitic looking, for Cone the important thing is that his context was one of struggle for the liberation of a people oppressed by Rome. It is his stance on the side of the oppressed that is decisive. Thus, in every generation and context Christ stands for liberation from oppressive conditions. In America, and in much of the world since the advent of European imperialism and slavery, this has meant particularly Black people, Africans, who are the primary oppressed people of the world. Christ is Black in this sense of being historically on the side of the oppressed (see Cone, 1986, 82–109; Cone, 1997, pp.99–126).

Whites are included in the liberation offered by Christ by ceasing to be "whites" culturally and politically and joining in the struggle against racist domination on the side of Blacks. Cone demands a rigorous cultural and political dismantling of the racist system and a radical conversion from racist consciousness and identity by those who have been privileged by the white system. But this also allows an element of universalism in his view of the redemptive work of the Black Christ. By Euro-Americans' rejecting white privilege and joining with Blacks in the struggle against racist oppression, a new, liberated society can emerge for both groups.

In the context of this struggle against white racism, Blackness can be understood as symbolic of the very nature, not only of Christ, but of God as the divine power of liberation.

> The Blackness of Christ clarifies the definition of him as the *Incarnate One*. In him God becomes oppressed humanity and thus reveals that the achievement of full humanity is consistent with divine being. The human being was not created to be a slave, and the appearance of God in Christ gives us the possibility of freedom. By becoming a black person, God discloses that blackness is not what the world says it is. Blackness is the manifestation of the being of God in that it reveals that neither divinity nor humanity reside in white definitions but in liberation from captivity.
>
> *(Cone, 1986, p.121)*

J. Deotis Roberts' (1974) *A Black Political Theology* takes this implied universalism of Cone another step. Roberts argues that Christ represents the liberation of all humanity. In order to be liberating of all people, Christ must also be identified with all groups of people. Thus Christ can be imaged as African, Asian, indigenous or European. Christ must be understood as universal through being multi-particular, existing in the context of each people's cultural and social particularity. Christ embodies full liberation of all people.

Christ is not neutral toward social contexts of justice and injustice. Christ cannot be "white" in the sense of sanctifying oppression, but Christ could be seen as European in the sense of a European person's struggle for liberation in his (or her) context. Christ is Black, in the American context, as the embodiment of liberation for Blacks involved in the struggle against white racism. This, for Roberts, should be seen as political, but also as including the dimensions of intellectual, psychological and spiritual liberation. Full liberation is the promise of Christ, which each group of people experiences in their own context (Roberts, 1974).[6]

The African context is different from the American struggle for racial equality of peoples of diverse races and cultures all claiming equal humanity as citizens of the United States. Africa was christianized in the nineteenth and twentieth centuries in the context of European colonialization by the English, French, Germans, Portuguese, Belgians, Spanish and Italians. Colonization was political and economic; it meant Europeans taking over the land, appropriating the best land for themselves, reducing Africans to dependent serf labor, and creating a political-economic system to give the lion's share of profits to European settlers and their sponsoring nations. It was also cultural and psychological. It meant treating Africans as personally and culturally "primitive," their culture as backward if not demonic, thus seeking to strip Africans of their African cultural identity and to impose a Christianity and European language and culture seen as normatively human.

Thus, liberation from European colonialism has many dimensions for Africans. First, it meant political or national liberation, removing white rule for national rule by African peoples themselves. This resulted in a multiplicity of African nations emerging, particularly in the 1950s and 1960s. In some cases, such as Zimbabwe, the struggle extended to 1980. South Africa is a special case, since it represents a takeover of rule by settler whites who then sought to construct an apartheid state where Africans were separated into dependent groups of people theoretically of different "nations." This was overcome only with the collapse of apartheid in 1990–97 (Ruether, 2009, pp.213–25).

Political liberation, however, left Africans still economically dominated by white settlers and European nations, with many African nations still using as their "official languages" the colonial tongues of Afrikaans (Dutch), English, French or Portuguese and still dominated by their cultures. Thus, liberation for Africans takes on many dimensions of struggle. African Christologies reflect these different dimensions. Theologies from Africa have been differentiated between theologies of inculturation into African culture and Black theologies of political liberation from white racism, expressed particularly in the struggle against apartheid in South Africa.

African theologies of inculturation, expressed particularly by John Mbiti (1969) and E. Bojaji Idowu (1962) among others, sought to put Christ into an African cultural context, and to reveal the similarity between African contexts and those of the Hebrews shaping the Biblical worldview. Thus, Christ could be imaged in African cultural terms as an "ancestor," "victor," "chief" or "healer" (see Wessels, 1986, pp.109–14). Christianity was reshaped to reflect African rituals and cultural practices.

By contrast, in the South African anti-apartheid struggle based on the division of white and black, Black theology from the United States, with its sharp contrast of white as oppressive and black as liberative, found greater receptivity. This language was reflected in the Black theology of the anti-apartheid struggle by theologians such as Allan Boesak (1993) and Itumeleng Mosala (1986). As a post-apartheid South Africa has emerged, where all are citizens, but a great division between white wealth and black poverty persists, a new synthesis that integrates liberation and inculturation becomes appropriate (Martey, 1993).

In Latin America, the struggle against colonialism reflects a much longer history going back to the end of the fifteenth century, with Columbus' arrival in the Caribbean in 1492. Colonial rule by Spain and Portugal lasted more than three hundred years, until the nineteenth century. This was followed by national liberation movements and new nation-states led by Creole (American-born European) elites that gave little power to subjugated "Indians" and slaves or former slaves. Thus, the domination by Europeans, the marginalization of indigenous peoples, the arrival of Black slaves, the mixtures of "Indian," Black and European people, and their assimilation into and rule by a creole elite had much more time to shape itself in Latin America than in Africa, where white rule averaged only about a century.

A Christology shaped by European Catholic missionaries and reflecting and validating colonial domination was deeply entrenched in Latin American Catholic Christian culture for more than 470 years, when liberation theologies began to critique this religious culture and shape an alternative to it in the late 1960s to 1980s. As an illustration of this development of liberation Christology I will discuss Jon Sobrino's *Jesus the Liberator*, published in Spanish in 1991 and dedicated to the six Jesuits and two women assassinated in the Jesuit house at the Latin American University in El Salvador in November of 1989 by El Salvadoran military death squads funded by the United States. This was the second major book by Sobrino on Christology, the first being titled *Christologia desde America Latina* (*Christology from Latin America*) in 1976 (translated as *Christology at the Crossroads* in 1978).

In the first chapter of his 1991 book, titled "A New Image and a New Faith in Christ," Sobrino (1993) talks about the image of Christ as liberator as a correction to the classical Christology in Latin America, which was based on "dogmatic formulas" which stressed "the divinity of Christ rather than his real and lived humanity" (p.11). In addition to this abstract and dogmatic Christ there was the image of the suffering Jesus on the cross "with which the poor identified and which they associated with their own specific suffering—massive, cruel, imposed and unjust—which has accompanied them from the moment Christ was first preached to them until today ... of the Christ brought by the conquerors they [the Indians] adopted precisely what made them most like him, a Christ that had himself been annihilated and conquered" (Sobrino, 1993, p.11). This suffering Christ, although comforting, did not allow the indigenous people to name the suffering as unjust and to resist it.

With liberation theology there was a recovery of the historical Christ and a formulation of the image of Christ as liberator, which evoked criticism and opposition from those in power. This was a break with the previous alienating images of Christ. Those "traditional Christologies made possible and even encouraged an image of Christ that could be used by the powerful and in such a way that the poor had no alternative but to cling to the one-sided suffering image." This traditional Christ allowed the believers among the powerful to see themselves as redeemed by Christ in such a way that no critique of oppression was necessary and no need to become involved in "Jesus' mission in support of the oppressed" (Sobrino, 1993, p.14).

This traditional image of Christ spoke of him abstractly. It talked about his love, and work of reconciliation of humanity with God, but in no way that touched on real historical circumstances of oppression and injustice. It particularly stressed Christ's power, but in a way that buttressed the power of the powerful, sanctifying "in Christ's name, all sorts of authoritarianism and despotism in state and church." Relation to Christ was reduced to the purely personal, "abandoning the historical world to its wretchedness." One should love Christ "alone" in a way that excluded rather than directed the believer to care for others, particularly the wretched of the earth. As a result of these types of preaching of Christ, "we are left with the consequences: centuries of faith in Christ have not been able to respond to the distress of the continent, nor even suspect that there was something scandalous about the coexistence of unjust poverty and Christian faith" (Sobrino, 1993, pp.15, 16, 17).

Although Sobrino doesn't call this view of Christ a "white Christ," he clearly means much the same as African-Americans and Africans mean when they denounce the "white" Christ brought by the European missionaries or given to the slaves in America that sanctions "white" power and domination. By contrast, a liberator Christ who sides with the oppressed, who calls for the denunciation of oppression, who awakens the poor to resist injustice and calls the rich and powerful to repent and give up unjust power is not only an "unexpected and welcome novelty, but also an unmasking and abandonment of the un-Christian or anti-Christian aspects of the earlier images." This is why it is also seen by the powerful as unwelcome and dangerous, a challenge to their established power (Sobrino, 1993, p.17).

Having briefly discussed Sobrino's contrast between alienating and liberating understandings of Christ in Latin America, I turn to Asia and mention the Indian Renaissance or renewal of Indian culture that lay behind the Indian struggle against British colonialism in the nineteenth and twentieth centuries. This Indian Renaissance rejected the British view of Indian culture as corrupt and debased and as needing to be replaced by superior British culture. Indians engaged in a critique of their own culture in order to discard its debilitating elements and renew its best qualities. In this process, several appreciated and took over some elements of Christianity, but so as to revive the best of Hinduism, not to discard it for Christianity (Thomas, 1970).

I mention here particularly the thought of Mahatma Gandhi, a leader of the liberation struggle against the British Empire and the "father of the nation." Gandhi, as a young man studying in England, read the Bible carefully, finding little of help in the Old Testament, but delighting in the New Testament. He particularly loved the image of Jesus in the Sermon on the Mount. For Gandhi, Jesus was one of the great prophets and teachers of true religion in human history, alongside the best in Hinduism (Thomas, 1970, pp.199–245).

Jesus, for Gandhi, exemplifies the true religious quest for God as Truth (or, as he preferred to put it, "truth as God"). The way to this truth is *Ahimsa*, or non-violent love, which Gandhi made the central path of his own spiritual development and the way to resistance to and the eventual overthrow of British colonialism and the liberation of India. *Satyagrahi* or truth-power through *ahimsa* was the spiritual basis of the Indian struggle, as Gandhi saw it, and Jesus was one of the great exemplars of *satyagrahi* and *ahimsa*.

Although Jesus was a great teacher of the true path of religious truth and life, this hardly made most of historical Christianity exemplary. For Gandhi, Christianity was a great faith that had been little practiced by Christians. Gandhi sees Christianity as having been corrupted when it turned to support by the Roman emperor, distorting it into an "imperialistic faith" and "incorporated into a system based on might." Indians, including Indian Christians, must dissociate themselves from "Western civilization, which is based on 'violence and materialism,' where moral progress is measured by their material possessions" (Thomas, 1970, p.215). Gandhi too perceives a true Christ in the heart of the New Testament account of Jesus, in contrast to a false Christ shaped by imperialism and sanctifying violence and oppression. His views parallel those of African-Americans, Africans and Latin Americans, with their quest for a "black" or "liberator" Christ, against a "white" or "alienated" Christ of Western oppression.

However, as African-American feminist theologian Kelly Brown Douglas (1994) has made clear in her book, *The Black Christ*, simply to image Christ as a Black person on the side of the liberation of Black people is insufficient if this simply means a Black male Christ uncritical of the oppression of Black women within Black culture and in the larger white society (pp.97–117)—and, one might add, by the Christian church and its patriarchal theology that made women secondary and unable to image or represent Christ. Black theology must embrace a critique of sexist oppression, the oppression of women and also of homosexuals. The Black church must liberate itself from sexism and homophobia.

African women, particularly through the Circle of Concerned African Women theologians, have also given attention to this sexism of the white Christ brought by the European conquerors, as well as the sexism of traditional African cultures. Mercy Amba Oduyoye, a leading African woman theologian and founder of the Circle, has lifted up legendary African women redemptive figures. One of these is Anowa, ancestress of all Africans. This African woman chief, whose story is popular in the Mankessim and Saltpond areas of Ghana, led the people of Africa south from the Sahara to escape patriarchal domination by Islam and slavery. She took them on a search for a fruitful land where they could flourish.

In another story, when the Akan, children of Anowa, progressed south they became thirsty. They came upon a lake but were frightened to drink for fear it might be poisoned. The priestess Eku who was with them allowed her dog to drink and then she too tasted it to be sure that it was pure, and then allowed her people to partake of it (Oduyoye, 1995, p.6, note).

Anowa exemplifies the true identity of African people, the promise of a fruitful land where they can flourish, while Eku exemplifies sacrificial service by a priestess who risks tasting the water first to see if it is potable for her people. These female figures from African traditions can be seen as Christ figures. That Christ might be not only black, but an African woman, becomes thinkable, liberating Christology from both white and male dominance.

In conclusion, we can say that the "whiteness" of Christ has been both a way in which Western Christians of Europe and North America have imaged Christ in their art, and, more importantly, expresses their assumption that Christ should be represented as "white" because only "whites" possess the fullness of human nature and the image of God. Evangelized by white Europeans, Africans brought to the Americas as slaves, Africans, indigenous peoples of the Americas and Asians colonized by Europeans, have also been given a Christology which not only looks "white" but validates the dominating power of Western imperialism and colonialism.

African-Americans, Africans, Latin Americans and Asians have been engaged, parti-cularly in the twentieth to twenty-first centuries, in decolonizing this "white" Christ, recovering Christ as liberator against oppression, by imaging him (and sometimes even her) in terms of their own visions of liberation and authentic humanness. It is a project which "white" people of Europe and America need to join, standing with oppressed people for a world of true justice and mutuality of all cultures and, in the process, liberating themselves from bondage to the false privilege of "whiteness."

Whether it is white supremacy or male dominance, claims of hegemony that oppress and marginalize other human beings are antithetical to a Christology predicated upon Christ as liberator. We need a form of Christology where Christ is identified with those who continue to suffer because of various political, social and economic injustices. This means taking Christ's liberation message seriously: to free people of color from the multiple ways in which whiteness/white supremacy destroys their lives and unmasking and freeing whites from the idolatry of contemporary expressions of whiteness that imprison the spirit and militate against Christ's message of love and justice.

Notes

1 See Borresen (1981), pp. 141–334. See also Aristotle, *Generation of Animals*, 729b, 737a, 738b, 775a and *Politics*, 1254 a-b.
2 Mathis Grünewald, from the Isenheim Altarpiece (1510–16).
3 For the "one-drop" rule, see Davis (2001), pp.4–6, 13–16, 54–58, 113–17 and 189–200. On the difference of the United States from other countries where different status is defined according to the percentage of white ancestry, see ibid., pp.81–113.
4 Arizona's immigration law was signed by Arizona Governor Jan Brewer, April 23, 2010. It is considered the most rigid in the nation and has been challenged by civil rights groups across the nation and the Federal Government.
5 A photograph of Stallings in full vestments tearing up an image of the white Christ is found in Margon and Promey (2001), p.21.
6 For an evaluation of Roberts' Christology, see Douglas (1994), pp.60–63.

References

Act of Congress of March 26, 1790 ch. 3, stat. 103.
Aquinas, Thomas. *Summa Theologiae.*
Aristotle. *Generation of Animals*, 729b, 737a, 738b, 775a.
———. *Politics*, 1254 a–b.
Battalora, Jacqueline. (1999). "Toward a Critical White Ethics: Construction of White in Anti-Miscegenation Law" (Ph.D. Dissertation, Northwestern University).
Battalora, Jacqueline. "The Invention of White People: Whiteness as History, Biography and Transformation" (manuscript under review for publication).
Boesak, Allan (1993). *Farewell to Innocence: A Socio-Ethical Study of Black Theology and Power.* Maryknoll, NY: Orbis Press.
Borresen, Kari. (1981). *Subordination and Equivalence: The Nature and Role of Women in Augustine and Thomas Aquinas.* Washington, D.C.: University Press.
Cleage, Albert B. Jr. (1968). *The Black Messiah.* New York: Sheed and Ward.
Cone, James H. (1986). *A Black Theology of Liberation.* Maryknoll, NY: Orbis Press (2nd edition).
———(1997). *God of the Oppressed.* Maryknoll, NY: Orbis Press (2nd edition).
Davis, F. James. (2001). *Who Is Black: One Nation's Definition.* University Park, PA: Pennsylvania State University Press.
Douglas, Kelly Brown. (1994). *The Black Christ.* Maryknoll, NY: Orbis Press.
Idowu, E. Bojaji. (1962). *Olodumare: God in Yoruba Belief.* London: Longmans.
Ignatiev, Noel. (1995). *How the Irish Became White.* New York: Routledge.
MacGregor, Neil. (2000). *Seeing Salvation: Images of Christ in Art.* New Haven, CT: Yale University Press.

Margon, David and Promey, Sally. (Eds.) (2001). *Visual Culture of American Religions.* Berkeley, CA: University of California Press.

Martey, Emmanuel. (1993). *African Theology: Inculturation and Liberation.* Maryknoll, NY: Orbis Press.

Mbiti, John. (1969). *African Religion and Philosophy.* London: Heinemann.

Mosala, Itumeleng (1986). *The Unquestionable Right to be Free: Black Theology from South Africa.* Maryknoll, NY: Orbis Press.

Oduyoye, Mercy Amba. (1995). *Daughters of Anowa: African Women and Patriarchy.* Maryknoll, NY: Orbis Press.

Roberts, J. Deotis. (1974). *A Black Political Theology.* Philadelphia: Westminster Press.

Ruether, Rosemary. (2007). *America, Amerikkka: Elect Nation and Imperial Violence.* London: Equinox.

——(2009). *The Church and Social Systems: Historical Constructions and Ethical Challenges.* Lanham, MD: Rowman and Littlefield.

Sobrino, Jon. (1978). *Christology at the Crossroads.* Maryknoll, NY: Orbis Press.

——(1993). *Jesus the Liberator. A Historical-Theological Reading of Jesus of Nazareth.* Maryknoll, NY: Orbis Press. Spanish edition, 1991.

Thomas, M. M. (1970). *The Acknowledged Christ of the Indian Renaissance.* Bangalore, India: The Christian Institute for the Study of Religion and Society.

Wessels, Anton. (1986). *Images of Jesus: How Jesus is Perceived and Portrayed in Non-European Cultures.* Grand Rapids, MI: William B. Eerdmans Publishing Company.

Winthrop, Jordan D. (1968). *White over Black: American Attitudes toward the Negro, 1550–1812.* Chapel Hill, NC: University of North Carolina Press.

7

WHEN A WHITE MAN-GOD IS THE TRUTH AND THE WAY FOR BLACK CHRISTIANS

Traci C. West

For Christians of African descent in the United States, certain teachings about Jesus can advance their acceptance of white-supremacist ideas about their own black humanity. Critical discussions of white supremacy sometimes totter on a conceptual precipice. Their primary focus on the actions and psyches of whites can create a danger of inadvertently crafting a variation on the exclusivist racial patterns they intend to critique. As one way to ensure a dynamic concern with black subjectivity when exploring the topic of whiteness and Christology, I locate the question of "What would Jesus do?" within a consideration of how anti-black, white racism can impact on the actions and psyches of black Christians. If black Christians want to avert a white-supremacist Christology, what kind of everyday Jesus-ethic would they have to practice?

The ease with which white-supremacist ideas fuse with Christological beliefs in contemporary Christianity is rooted in the history of Christian theology. For much of the first and second millennia CE, Catholic and Protestant theology was sewn from the fabric of European cultural biases, including phenotypic, anti-black racism. This cultural fusion of ideas was given concrete expression in brutal socioeconomic practices, namely, Christian leadership in the Atlantic slave trade that brought millions of kidnapped Africans to the Americas and in centuries of European colonization of black and brown peoples. The magnitude and influence of this history is quite daunting. It makes the task of sorting out truthful understandings of Jesus Christ—of what Jesus would *really* do—from impostors that normalize the cultural superiority of (European and Euro-American) whiteness, at best, a formidable challenge for all western Christians. In particular, for twenty-first century black American Christians, faithful commitment to certain Christological traditions can perpetually reenact self-abnegation unless there is some kind of intentional, anti-racist resistance. Adopting a theology about a man-God Jesus who is supposed to honor their black humanity can, contrary to their intentions, instill a warped, devalued sense of their human worth and instruct them in the righteousness of devaluing others.

When teachings about the nature of Jesus' truth and transformative power reflect norms of white dominance, human well-being, imagination, and potential are held captive. Because of the particular historical patterns that the melding of western European and Christian cultural dominance have assumed, when breathing-in the sacredness of Jesus as her or his divine mentor, the believer inhales notions of whiteness in the amalgam of cultural definitions for Jesus. This cultural amalgam includes notions of whiteness as the classical form of western art, science, philosophy, literature, and economics. Whiteness is supposedly the progenitor of all important markers of civilization. Sacralized racist norms that result inhere in the believer's personhood, limiting her or his vision of human moral capacity and can, therefore, surreptitiously teach black Christians a Christocentric belief in white superiority and black inferiority.

A related, similarly contorted, moral and spiritual posture is required by hierarchical Christology supporting male and heterosexual superiority. In this Christology, particular gospel narratives, such as Jesus' calling of exclusively male disciples or favorable references to patriarchal, heterosexual marriage are proscriptively interpreted[1] while a broadly accessible, universal, savior—the man-God Jesus—is supposedly maintained. White-racist hierarchies readily cooperate with sex/gender hierarchies within western Christianities and other cultural relations. Because of its reliance on the opportunistic stigmatizing of selected group identities, a Christology that commends the virtuousness of obedience to white-racist hierarchies helps to make obedience to sexist and heterosexist hierarchies also appear virtuous. For some black Christians, faithful obedience to the latter hierarchies can remain even after white-racist hierarchies are supposedly rejected. Is it possible to locate contemporary Christological ethics that can comprehensively replace the tethers with freedom from these hierarchical cultural patterns? In the Christological ethics that I seek, Jesus is understood as a Christ who mirrors human moral worth, rather than one who confers human moral worth after certain conditions are met.

When missionaries who converted enslaved blacks in the Americas or colonized blacks in Africa taught a Christology informed by white dominance–black inferiority mythology, their evangelism confused truth with lies. How did such Christologically rooted confusion teach anti-black devaluation of embodied, human worth? Currently, what kinds of theo-ethical understandings of Jesus as Christ might assist Christians in disrupting racialized (and kindred heteropatriarchal) paradigms of human subjugation that continue to exist within Christian-dominated societies? In a contemporary liberationist Christian ethics that foments such anti-racist intervention, the varied permutations of anti-black racism interwoven for centuries into the Christology initially introduced to black converts would need to have been discarded—right?

Problematizing competing truths: notes on method

To discuss black Christianity without the distortion of oversimplifications, especially when garnering lessons from historical examples of white-racist Christology, several sets of competing, sometimes contradictory, truths about religion and racism must be acknowledged. Acknowledgements of competing truths are tricky to communicate.

Such acknowledgements can appear to be apologetics that dilute the validity of the competing claims. But this is not my intention. My method for developing liberationist Christological ethics requires conceptualization of robust, coexisting aspects of black Christianity linked to the influence of white racism that are both emancipatory and oppressive. In the history of U.S.-American theology, contradictory, dueling moral messages about Christ's salvation of black people resemble the fluctuating responses of an abusive intimate partner. Similarly, Ghanaian theologian Mercy Amba Oduyoye (2002) points out subjugating and liberating dialectics in early missionary Christianity in Africa. She asserts: "Jesus of missionary praxis was an ambiguous Christ. Thus it is that he has acquired many faces on the continent" (p.157). Yet, possibilities for imaginative, anti-racist theo-ethics can also be found in the cultural adaptability of Christological messages.

In the global history of black Christians of African descent, the moral calculus introduced to the earliest converts held the capacity to affirm as well as demean black humanity. The indoctrination of a Janus-faced Christian theology that incorporated deeply embedded, anti-black white racism began with the language and ritual practices surrounding baptism and reveals broader political and economic functions of conversion to Christ. These functions are usefully analyzed in thematically related theological and historical scholarship. Examples from both American and African historical contexts offer evidence of the consistent texture of anti-blackness. A comparative approach fosters deeper appreciation of the variations in white-racist interpretations of Jesus as Christ that were communicated in multiple locations.

In a contemporary liberationist Christology, historical awareness of this multiplicity may enable resistance practices for black Christians. An appreciation of contrasting versions of anti-black white racism and the divergent black cultural groups targeted historically can have strategic significance for self-scrutiny now. It can, for instance, contribute to fending off the potential for black U.S.-American Christians' claims about the singularity of their experiences of group victimization, such as chattel slavery. Positing the exceptionalism of their ethnic-group identity, due to heinous experiences of victimization, can militate against self-criticism of destructive internal group processes, such as black heteropatriarchal practices. However, taking account of the consistencies of anti-black Christology must not occlude awareness of the vastly different socio-historical contexts and local cultures that shaped both its delivery and reception in the Americas and Africa. Equally important, racist Christological formulas appropriated Jesus' own ancient, Jewish, socio-historical context, which, admittedly, I neglect here.

For a liberative Christology, historical references serve as a catalyst for crafting contemporary theo-ethics, but must do so without endorsing a trans-historical transmission of static, Christological ideas. White-racist theology taught by eighteenth- and nineteenth-century white missionaries[2] and slave masters has not survived centuries of political and cultural change in some unaltered form within the faith of present-day black Christians. Nonetheless, ideas from critical, historical studies of white missionary Christianity and black converts can offer a moral map of specific messages about "What Jesus would do?" for blacks who were willing to be saved by him. Those contorting and ambiguous moral messages can carve out historical consciousness. It is, perhaps, the kind of historical consciousness needed by contemporary black Christians to ferret out politically repressive notions of Christ's salvation and truth that many mistakenly identify as essential to Christian faith. In his study of race and colonial theological narratives, theologian Willie James Jennings (2010) challenges scholars in Christian religious studies to examine "the deeper realities of Western Christian sensibilities, identities, and habits of mind which continue to channel patterns of colonialist dominance" (p.8).

My call for the preservation of a liberationist Jesus-ethic has to confront the church's endemic conservative nature that has served white-racist interests so well. That is, conserving historical traditions of moral ideas and faith practices through the paradigm of Jesus-as-model is the church's primary cultural mission. There must be some type of ongoing intervention in the church's process of conserving historical–traditional claims about Jesus' power. Simply replacing one set of claims about Jesus with another set is an inadequate liberationist strategy.

Furthermore, an insistence upon the combined universality and particularity of Jesus perpetually complicates the conservation of historical claims about Jesus. The life and ministry of Jesus is historically located in a particular, first-century Jewish community described in Christian scriptures. At the same time, Jesus transcends historical notions of past, present, and future. For most Christians, Jesus is understood as a particular, unique, fully human, and fully divine being. In a standard, universalizing understanding of him, Jesus is claimed as someone in whom all Christian believers can find a reflection of their own humanity. Because a foundational Christological tenet of Christian theology locates the truth about God in the person of Jesus, he is moral exemplar. Both the believer's acceptance of Jesus' divine authority and emulation of Jesus' teachings constitute essential moral impulses for Christian behavior. Poisonous consequences for black Christian self-worth can rest in this moral formula when obedience to white dominance helps to define the particularities of appropriate Christian behavior needed to earn the universal benefits of salvation, as it has too often been taught in the past.

A liberationist Jesus-ethic should engage interlinked, multiple sites of cultural knowledge about anti-black white racism, but eschew any definition of white racism that is limited to binary, black–white relationships. In the United States, markers of anti-black whiteness in Christological–cultural traditions constitute a problem for more than just black Christians. The moral imaginations and self-understandings of white Euro-American Christians are also likely to be diminished. But besides whites and blacks, the faith and social identities of Christians who are Asian American, Latino/a American, and Indigenous/Native American are just as likely to be negatively impacted upon by anti-black, white-racist Christological ideas.

The potential for damaging relationships amongst all such groups can be intensified, as well. White-racist Christology may be a site of cultural meaning-making that feeds competition over claims of white-racist victimization with queries such as: was the land theft from and genocide of Indigenous/Native peoples or the enslavement of black peoples worse? This kind of racial/ethnic-group competition can combine with competition for the sacred moral worth conferred by a white man-God Jesus and form an amalgam of toxic Christological–cultural dynamics as they seek recognition from whites of racist wrongs committed against them and recognition from Jesus of socially denied moral worthiness. In addition, Christians across racial groups might be impacted by new, anti-Muslim versions of white racist, Christological ideas that have sprouted in recent decades about an increased urgency for aggressive propagation of Christian salvation rooted in white Euro-American/European cultural values.[3]

In short, a vast agenda awaits Christians and their non-Christian dialogue partners, who earnestly want to address the impact of a hydra-headed, Christ-centered white racism within Christian-dominated western cultures. Attention to what a liberationist Jesus-ethic could do when employed by black U.S.-American Christians represents only one discrete focus on that agenda. As it urges them to find ways to turn down the cultural rewards in deifying the whiteness of the white man-God Jesus, a liberationist Jesus-ethic also urges interdependence. Its efficacy requires solidarity work among peoples of multiple racial and religious backgrounds who are committed to similar disruptive practices.

The malleability of truth claims: historical examples

Rudimentary Christian claims about Jesus include his capacity to: speak only truth, embody divine truth, and lead anyone who believes in him to recognize truth. When understood as exclusive characteristics of their God, these claims have been some of the most troubling for Christian encounters with non-Christians.[4] This problem was apparent in much of the history of white missionary conversion of enslaved black Americans and colonized Africans. Christian scriptures such as the gospel of John exemplify this emphasis on Christocentric truth claims.[5] Jesus says "I am the way, and the truth, and the life. No one comes to the Father except through me" (John 4:16). Christian evangelists who introduce Jesus Christ to non-Christians frequently understand themselves as literally bringing truth to the converts. Anti-black white racism can flourish in missionary assumptions about an absence of truth in the cultural and spiritual traditions of black converts prior to or independent of Christian conversion. In addition, eighteenth- and nineteenth-century white evangelists frequently utilized racially encoded imagery to represent truths and falsehoods about their mission to enslaved or colonized blacks. The bright, white light of Christ's truth was juxtaposed with the black darkness of evil and barbarism.[6]

As I have already noted, the Christological messages that Euro-American and European Christians introduced were quite varied and often rife with contradictions. In equal measure, the responses by black converts also ranged in their outward expressions of acceptance and inward reinterpretations of the theology taught by whites. Similar to other scholars in Christian religious studies who analyze slave religion, womanist theologian Kelly Brown Douglas emphasizes a sharp distinction between a slaveholder's Christianity justifying chattel slavery and slave Christianity.[7] In slave Christianity, Brown Douglas (1994) stipulates, blacks understood that enslaving and brutalizing "others betrays the example that Jesus set and contradicts what it means to be Christian"(pp.28–29). Among the Christian beliefs embraced by enslaved black converts, however, there were undoubtedly many Christianities, each with differing degrees of acceptance of the fusion of white supremacy and Christology. When slave converts transformed pro-slavery Christian theology into a resource that helped them to both reject a Divine sanctioning of slavery and cope with its brutalities, the challenges of reinterpretation became a routine aspect of their faith. Belief in Christ offered an outlet in the midst of suffering and simultaneously added emotional and spiritual hurdles requiring self-defense against the religion's white-racist presuppositions. In a discussion of the distortions of white-racist Christology that contemporary black Christians must surmount, Brown Douglas (1994) queries: "[i]f Christianity can produce a white Christ ... is there not something inherently wrong with Christianity and its Jesus?" (p.47). But Christianity's Jesus always reflects specific cultural interests.

Details of the theology taught by white Christian slave masters and missionaries to black converts highlight a Christological–cultural fusion where Jesus is comfortably positioned within the mores of a racist, Christianized political economy. The individualistic focus on Jesus' response to the body and the soul of the black convert was especially serviceable to the political and economic aims of slave masters. In his study *Dark Symbols, Obscure Signs: God, Self and Community in the Slave Mind*, Christian ethicist and theologian Riggins R. Earl, Jr. (1993) describes the resourceful responses of black slave psyches to the racist Christianity that white slave masters taught. In an article based on this study, Earl points to a dichotomized approach to the souls of black slave converts by some white Christian supporters of slavery. Whites relied upon their "white Jesus' soul whitening power," he explains, in order to lift "the African from zero value status as a heathen to a subhuman level" (Earl, 2004, p.252). In this white evangelical approach that Earl describes, redemption for the slave was found in being washed in the blood of Jesus. In *Dark Symbols, Obscure Signs*, Earl (1993) further clarifies the viewpoint of white slaveholders: "[i]t was conceded that while the blood of Jesus could not change the blackness of the slave's body, it would transform the status of the slave's soul. This alone, it was thought, would improve the slave's market value" (p.16). This interpretation of the power of Jesus Christ justified chattel slavery as a crucial component in the project of civilizing supposed heathens from Africa. Also by design, Christianity was a tool of the U.S. slave economy that helped to sustain the disciplined subservience of the slaves to their white masters.

Earl (1993) offers several examples of the pedagogical practices of white missionaries aimed at producing docile behavior, such as one missionary's story about how the elderly Friday was a model black slave convert to Christianity (p.36). Friday, according to the missionary, "was a genuine African, not so long from his native wilds and greegree worship" (Harrison, 1893, p. 252).[8] But he was intensely grateful for the "clear peaceful light of the gospel that had come upon him" and thus "a living example of the power of Jesus to tame and make as new creatures his savage race" (pp.251–52). Moreover, the preface to the volume containing this missionary's description of Friday boastfully informs the reader that "two millions [*sic*] of dollars were contributed by the slave holders and their friends to forward the missions to the slaves" conducted by the Methodist Church from 1829 to 1864 (p.3).

The Christology in this account asserts the power of one particular body that was male and white, Jesus, to create something from "zero" (as Earl phrases it). Said differently, the theology offers a warped sense of hope to the converts by teaching them that the supposed nothingness inherent in their black bodily selves did not indicate a moral inevitability. Supposedly, they could find hope in also possessing black souls that could be transformed by the blood perpetually flowing from the body of the white, male Jesus. The symbolic humanization of God in a way that reflected those with so much actual power over the daily lives of the black slaves reinforced the truth of their assumed nothingness and of the theology that those powerful (white) people taught, asserting Jesus' power to transform their moral status.

During the eighteenth through the early twentieth centuries of the colonial period in Africa, many black African converts were similarly required to declare their nothingness before God. Practices surrounding baptism frequently demanded stripping away aspects of their African communal and cultural ties. In his study *Rediscovering the Human: The Quest for a Christo-Theological Anthropology in Africa*, Tanzanian theologian Andrea Ng'weshemi (2002) comments on the requisite disorientation caused by this mandatory, baptismal performance. To become Christian, Ng'weshemi asserts, meant "abandoning what made one African and human … abandoning one's self, one's culture, one's family, clan, and community or society as a whole" (p.44). As Ng'weshemi demonstrates, this aspect of the Protestant missionary strategy for converting black Africans was coercive and morally assaultive. For example, he explains how the candidate for baptism had to proclaim that he or she knew that the cultural practices "that made one African" were "evil and unwanted" (p.44). The evidence of readiness for baptism, Ng'weshemi contends, was the extent to which the missionary's lifestyle and conduct were assimilated. In making a commitment to Jesus Christ, the convert's prior sense of his or her own human worth was attacked in a comprehensive manner.

Kenyan Christian ethicist Teresa Hinga (1995) deepens our understanding of the problematic nature of this colonial missionary practice in Africa by adding needed sex/ gender analysis. In her article "Jesus Christ and the Liberation of Women in Africa," Hinga (1995) cites the dire economic consequences for some of the women in polygamous marital relationships when missionaries asked men to discard all but one of their wives as a condition of baptism (p.188). Under the auspices of teaching the superiority of Christian morality in marital relationships, missionaries seem to have been guided, at least in part, by the patriarchal perspectives nestled within their Euro-Christianity. In order to coercively create the cultural changes they sought, evangelists relied upon local African traditions granting men patriarchal entitlement to choose their wives. In this instance, missionary Christianity taught the disposability of women and children who were socioeconomically dependent upon patriarchal marital customs. The abandoned black African women and children learned their nothingness before the patriarchal Christian God in a profoundly costly manner. The male husband/father convert learned that the only avenue for gaining meaningful (read: non-African) human worth through baptism in Christ was by sacrificing the well-being of selected women and children in his family.

For U.S. black slave converts, rejection of cultural ties to black Africans usually signaled an authentic embrace of Christ. In her study of United States enslaved black women, African American religious scholar Renee K. Harrison (2009) stresses the destructiveness to selfhood—what she terms "self-violence" of slave women. She gives multiple examples of how subjugating conditions of chattel slavery helped to produce self-hatred as well as resistance. In Christian religious scholarship on U.S. slavery, Harrison's work stands out for its sustained attention to the self-deprecating views and anti-black antagonisms among black slaves that were nurtured by white-racist Christianity.[9] She cites one enslaved woman's gratitude for her liberation from the godless "black ignoramuses in Africa" when whites taught her that God's "son redeem you and save you wid his blood ... You got to believe on Him if it tek bondage to bring you to your knees" (Harrison, 2009, p.127). Her faith in salvation by Jesus Christ offered a comforting justification of her plight as a slave in the United States.

The symbiotic relationship between Christology and the political economy generated multifaceted moral contortions for black slave converts. Individual repentance was required of the slave in order to transform her or his supposedly savage nature. Yet the individual carried an immutable connection to her or his "savage race" that was perpetually in need of Jesus' salvation. Group identity, in this case, the racial group identity of blacks, marked their permanent moral inadequacy. While religious conversion and faith may appear to involve individual decision making, broader social forces were operative. The mutually reinforcing relationship between religion and the political economy of slavery was always at issue in the conversions. For a black slave such as the one Harrison cited, salvation by Jesus required an instrumentalized self-understanding that handily fit with her exploited position in the capitalist economic relations of the society. Pro-slavery white churches and white slave owners were conjointly invested (literally, with millions of dollars in the case of the Methodists) in the political-economic endeavor named Christian salvation.

In nineteenth-century African missionary Christianity, the link between salvation by Christ and black servitude to whites could sometimes be found within the internal political economy of the church itself. Ghanaian religion scholar Ebenezer Oberi Addo (1999) analyzes educational institutions that Christian missionaries set up to train African church leaders on the "Gold Coast"—as British Christian colonizers named the region. Addo explains that a "master-servant syndrome" emerged as standard within missionary church culture and "yielded the concept obooni or houseboy" (p.129). The selection of black male converts to become houseboys for missionaries was commonly practiced. For example, he cites the gratitude of Frederick France, a black Methodist product of a European missionary school that trained African converts to become church leaders. In an 1859 letter, Frederick France expressed his joy over how "the blood of Christ had cleansed me from my past sins ... my attention was then turned from all worldly business and I only wished to be a house-servant to the missionaries" (Addo, 1999, pp.128–29). In the theology expressed here, Christ's cleansing power created the opportunity for the black convert's servanthood to white missionaries. This practice nurtured a paternalism, Addo (1999) asserts, that African church leaders imbibed and reproduced "in their attitudes towards their own people and culture" (p.129).[10]

Encapsulating one significant element in the bond between missionary Christology and the political economy of European colonialism in Africa, ethicist Teresa Hinga (1995) asserts: "[t]he Christ of the missionaries was a conquering Christ. Conversely, winning Africa for Christ was a major motivating factor in missionary zeal. Africa was the booty to be looted for Christ." (p.187). On the continent of Africa, the commodification of black African converts in Christological–cultural mission work frequently enfolded opportunistic attitudes about controlling the psychic, bodily, and physical land space of Africans. One well-meaning white U.S. missionary, Louise Chapman (1945), illustrates the language of missionary zeal when she describes a Divine vision she received in the 1920s. She was called to go help "more than one hundred and fifty million black people who today stagger on in the dark without the light of Christ to guide them" (p.30).

Inasmuch as it reeked of colonialist paternalism, ideas about the guidance that Jesus Christ offers were distorted by Chapman, the teachers of Frederick France, and many others from Europe who participated in the colonization of Africa for centuries. I am also certain that white slaveholder evangelists taught a false understanding of Jesus Christ's salvation to enslaved blacks. Beneath impassioned assertions of this view by some Christian theologians, preachers, and ethicists such as myself, what is the basis for this judgment? It is tempting to rely upon a *sui generis*[11] understanding of religion to identify the wrongheadedness of the salvation taught by slaveholders and colonists which must be distinguished from the truth of the liberating, anti-racist Jesus. In this *sui generis* understanding, Christian religion (what Jesus would *really* do) becomes a trans-historical phenomenon that can be divorced from the subjugating material conditions in which it was located. But to make such a distinction between Christianity and slavery or Christianity and colonialism grossly misrepresents the history. It is also tempting to declare the morally self-affirming reinterpretations of Jesus by black slaves as the truth, in opposition to the pro-slavery teachings about him. However, this simple dichotomy denies Christianity's deep complicity in maintaining black enslavement, regardless of its simultaneous palliative capacity for slaves. Any view that minimizes how Christological–cultural values can be thoroughly enmeshed within the material realities of subjugation is unsatisfactory for my liberationist project.

Perhaps my very desire to reveal truthful representations of Jesus Christ by countering what was false about the pro-enslavement Jesus of white Christian slaveholders or the paternalistic, supposedly civilizing Jesus of colonizing Christians signals my own conceptual entrapment. I might be stuck in a reiteration of the exact light/dark, good/bad dualisms that I want to jettison because of their serviceability to white racism. Could I be, unwittingly, demonstrating a resilient hope, also plaguing some other black Christians, that revealing the falseness of white-racist Christianity's Jesus lends credibility to the idea of a true Jesus who *really* validates the moral worth of black humanity? Anti-black white racism can feast upon the insecurities about one's moral worthiness that Christian longing for Jesus's salvation generates.

Birthing a Countercultural Jesus Ethic

The need is urgent for a critical historical consciousness of the Christ-centered, anti-black white racism that the earliest black converts were taught. As a catalyst for self-scrutiny and transformative practices, this awareness can help to address a range of destructive legacies bequeathed to contemporary black Christians.

Christian theology that represents Jesus-as-model for moral life in a vertical relation-ship to humanity coheres with the logic of white racism, but, if acknowledged, couldn't it be interrupted? In these cohering moral economies, superior moral capital and status are attached to the identity of a unique man-God as well as the idealized cultural habits of a select racial/ethnic group identity (whiteness). In both cases, imitation of the superior identity is required of those below, seeking similar moral capital and status. Some black Christians uphold this same logic when asserting the righteousness of stigmatizing their own or another black Christian's gay, lesbian, bisexual, or transgender identity. In a capitalist U.S. economy, it is no accident that some of the most intransigent claims of moral superiority by heterosexist Christians have focused on marriage. Christian salvation that validates heterosexual superiority also, supposedly by happenstance as they may disingenuously claim, maintains their exclusive political hold on the considerable socioeconomic benefits of marriage granted by law.[12]

Similarly, the internal church leadership practices of some black churches (and many others) can replicate another version of this Christological–cultural logic of hierarchy. Maleness is commonly regarded as a non-negotiable aspect of what constitutes an appropriate head pastor, with its attendant salary, benefits, and status. The head male leader's public moral guidance and critique in sermons, for example, holds sway as arbiter of the moral status of his congregants, a majority of whom are usually women. The anthropomorphism of Christianity's man-God savior helps to reinforce the appropriateness of this concentration of power and authority in a male head leader.

Christological rationalizations of hierarchical social relations can also prompt innova-tive possibilities for resistance. Themes used by white Christian slaveholders for religious conversion of blacks, such as salvific bleeding, could be re-envisioned in relevant ways for contemporary theo-ethics. What if theology about the blood of a suffering Jesus that perpetually flows for the sake of human salvation were reimagined to inspire an ethic of opposition to hierarchical human relations that cause so much suffering? Christians could reject the fraudulence in theological claims about Jesus' blood as symbolizing salvific, trans-historical suffering that can be divorced from particular, sociopolitical interests. Instead of theology that annuls its significance, Christians could recognize the political reality of Jesus' execution. Crucifixion was a death penalty regularly imposed by the Roman state against slaves and rebellious Jews like Jesus. It reinforced very specific hierarchical social relations in the Roman Empire. Accordingly, current Christian references to Jesus' blood should invoke current political realities involving the subjuga-tion of peoples through policies that maintain their poverty and criminalization, as well as state violence against them. For inspiration, Christians could focus on their (horizontal) commonality with Jesus' human blood that pumped through him as he taught, healed, fed, organized, and listened to people in his ancient Jewish community.

Moreover, even symbolic language of the church could counter heteropatriarchal legacies, for example, by interpreting the blood of Christ as being like menstrual blood.[13] Similar to how menstrual bleeding neither signifies nor brings death, the divine power of Christ's bleeding is found in its generative potential to inspire salvific defiance of customs that treat peoples, cultural identities, and any aspect of intrinsic human dignity as disposable or as sacrificeable.[14] What if Christians envisioned the living body of Christ as neither male nor female but a multiply sexed/gendered, menstruating body comprised of many believers joined together by a common, richly dark blood with divine potential cycling through all of them? Instead of deference to a singular, unique, salvific identity located above us, it is the capaciousness of that egalitarian (horizontal), generative flow that saves. This capaciousness or grace offers divinized, darkening, moral potential only realizable in the birthing of a lived, Christological ethic with material, socioeconomic impacts. Christian commitment to such an ethic would have to evidence ongoing forms of doing and being that salvifically defy cultural assertions of one group's moral right to be known as innately superior. Unmasking these Christian hypocrisies would mean continuously destabilizing Christian assertions of truths and falsehoods about how to recognize human righteousness. Returning again and again to the history of how anti-black white racism has been embedded in Christian messages about Jesus' transformative power can be a source of more innovation.

What would Jesus do? I have located this question in a discussion of how anti-black white racism can be transmitted through Christological theology, focusing on the impact of that transmission for black Christian self-definitions. I have insisted on attention to the cultural adaptability of Christian moral assertions about what Jesus would do as well as the socioeconomic implications attached to those assertions. Contextually rooted sociopolitical interests are always embedded in Christological teaching. I have pointed to historical examples where the kind of moral behavior Jesus requires and the kind of moral worthiness Jesus recognizes was posited as necessitating black people's acceptance of their racially inscribed nothingness that only Jesus' blood could transform. This transformation that Jesus bestows could only be evidenced by black servile dedication to the socioeconomic interests of the white elites who were also the Christian teachers who taught them about Jesus' salvific blood. This history of how Christological–cultural truth was taught helpfully demonstrates the need for continuously destabilized notions of Christian truth and falsehood. Because of its reliance on the opportunistic stigmatizing of selected group identities, a Christology that commends the virtuousness of obedience to white-racist hierarchies also helps to make obedience to sexist and heterosexist hierarchies appear virtuous, which some black Christians retain even after rejecting white-racist Christology. Therefore, I want to replace concern with the question of what would a solo man-God tell us we should do with concern with how a destabilizing Jesus ethic could be lived out interdependently. I commend a Christological–cultural ethic where the body of Christ is constituted by multi-gendered, multi-cultured peoples practicing an everyday Jesus ethic of disrupting social hierarchies: engaging in concrete daily practices of undermining socioeconomic exploitation. This Jesus ethic could, perhaps, be imagined as a blackening process that healthfully bleeds justice.

Notes

1 For example, in Matthew 19, Jesus discusses divorce by citing a passage from the Torah (Genesis 2:24) about "man" joined to "his wife" upon leaving the homes of their parents, and then he says: "So there are no longer two, but one flesh. Therefore what God has joined together, let no one separate" (Matthew 19:6).

2 Throughout the late nineteenth and twentieth centuries there were African American missionaries to Africa who brought the same paternalistic Christianity as white missionaries. For example, see Moses (1989). In this chapter I have chosen to focus on studies that reference the theology of white European and Euro-American missionaries to Africa, who comprised the overwhelming majority during the centuries of colonial rule.

3 For an example of an extremist white hate-group of Christian crusaders against Muslims, see Southern Poverty Law Center's Intelligence Report, www.splcenter.org/get-informed/intelligence-report/browse-all-issues/2011/fall/christian-crusader (accessed September 1, 2011). For a discussion of anti-Muslim white racism in the United States since September 11, 2001 attacks, see Tehranian (2009).

4 For reflections on Christian truth claims from differing religious perspectives, see Shama (1993).

5 For a discussion of how witness to, judgment and trial of truth are motifs in the gospel of John, see Lincoln (2000).

6 For a discussion of how religion understood as Christian truth was historically propagated as the antithesis of barbarity and falsehood while functioning as an essential aspect of European and Euro-American capitalism and colonialism, see Fitzgerald (2010); Also see Yancy (2008). In one example, Yancy discusses the nineteenth-century white European exploitation and sexual violation of Sara Baartmann, which regarded her body as evidence of African primitiveness in contrast with the evolved, superior European. Yancy comments that "[t]he 'truth' of the Black body is not outside of the domain of white colonial *power*" (p.99) and then he wonders about Baartman's ability "to keep herself from being torn asunder" (p.99) as she contemplated her soul through the French, white-colonialist gaze imposed upon her.

7 See: Douglas (1994); Douglas (2005), especially Chapter 5. Also see Hopkins (2000); Martin (2000). Martin describes a "dynamic adaptation of Christianity by the enslaved," (p.42); Raboteau (1978). In this pioneering study, Raboteau notes that, on the one hand, "[s]laves distinguished the hypocritical religion of their masters from true Christianity and rejected the slaveholder's gospel of obedience to master and mistress" (p.294). But on the other hand, he gives several examples of how "the religion of the slaves could support accommodation to the system of slavery" (p.304).

8 The missionary's report of Friday's description of his former religious practices, which included prostrating himself several times a day and praying to "Allah," seems to indicate that Friday had been a devout Muslim before being kidnapped in Africa (Harrison, 1893).

9 Also see Stewart (2001).

10 Also see Amoah and Oduyoye (1990). They offer a critique describing "the missionary's self-image of a benevolent paternal figure who knows what is best for African converts," and the continued appropriation of classical western Christologies by churches in Africa faithfully carrying on the legacy of western missions, including an understanding of Jesus as Lord—as a benevolent ruler (p.37).

11 My understanding of *sui generis* religion is influenced by McCutcheon (1997). He explains in the introduction: "Simply put, the discourse of sui generis religion deemphasizes difference, history, and sociopolitical context in favor of abstract essences and homogeneity"(p.3).

12 At the federal level, there are 1,138 rights and protections related to taxes, property, and other areas of political-economic life. See U.S. General Accounting Office, "Defense of Marriage Act: Update to Prior Report," 2004, www.gao.gov/new.items/d04353r.pdf (accessed September 25, 2011).

13 This emphasis could possibly resonate with the liberator Christ for African women that theologians Amoah and Ouyoye (1990) describe, who liberates from the burden of "the

ostracism of a society riddled with blood-taboos and theories of inauspiciousness arising out of women's blood" (p.43).

14 Womanist theologian JoAnne Marie Terrell stresses the need to understand Jesus' death as having saving significance because of his life that preceded it. She describes the death of her own mother at the hands of an abusive intimate partner as well as "countless other black women, who suffer abuse and die at the hands of patriarchal, violence-driven persons" as examples of lives that we must learn from. She asserts: "Jesus' own life and *sacramental* example of affirming the intrinsic worth of women enable humankind to see women's blood as sacred" (Terrell, 1998, p.143).

References

Addo, Ebenezer Obiri. *Kwame Nkrumah: A Case Study of Religion and Politics in Ghana.* Lanham, MD: University Press of America, 1999 [1997].

Amoah, Elizabeth and Mercy Amba Oduyoye. "The Christ for African Women". In Virginia Fabella and Mercy Amba Oduyoye, eds., *With Passion and Compassion: Third World Women Doing Theology.* Maryknoll, NY: Orbis Books, 1990.

Chapman, Louise Robinson. *Africa, O Africa: Twenty Years a Missionary on the Dark Continent.* Kansas City, MO: Beacon Hill Press, 1945.

Douglas, Kelly Brown. *The Black Christ.* Maryknoll, NY: Orbis Books, 1994.

——. *What's Faith Got to Do With It? Black Bodies/Christian Souls.* Maryknoll, NY: Orbis Books, 2005.

Earl, Riggins R. *Dark Symbols, Obscure Signs, God, Self, and Community in the Slave Mind.* Maryknoll, NY: Orbis Books, 1993.

——. "Loving Our Bodies as God's Luminously Dark Temples: The Quest for Black Restoration." In Anthony B. Pinn and Dwight N. Hopkins, eds., *Loving the Body: Black Religious Studies and the Erotic.* New York, NY: Palgrave Macmillan, 2004.

Fitzgerald, Timothy Fitzgerald. *Discourses on Civility and Barbarity: A Critical History of Religion and Related Categories.* New York, NY: Oxford University Press, 2010.

Harrison, Renee K. *Enslaved Women and the Arts of Resistance in Antebellum America.* New York, NY: Palgrave Macmillan, 2009.

Harrison, W.P., ed. *The Gospel Song among Slaves; A Short Account of Missionary Operations among the African Slaves of the Southern States.* Nashville, TN: Publishing House of the M.E. Church, South, Barbee and Smith, Agents, 1893.

Hinga, Teresa M. "Jesus Christ and the Liberation of Women in Africa." In Mercy Amba Oduyoye and Musimbi R.A. Kanyoro, eds., *The Will to Arise: Women, Tradition, and the Church in Africa.* Maryknoll, NY: Orbis, [1992]. Reprint, Eugene, OR: Wipf and Stock, 1995.

Hopkins, Dwight N. *Down, Up, and Over: Slave Religion and Black Theology.* Minneapolis, MN: Augsburg Fortress, 2000.

Jennings, Willie James. *The Christian Imagination: Theology and the Origins of Race.* New Haven, CT: Yale University Press, 2010.

Lincoln, Andrew T. *Truth on Trial: The Lawsuit Motif in the Fourth Gospel.* Peabody, MA: Hendrickson Publishers, 2000.

Martin, Joan M. *More than Chains and Toil: A Christian Work Ethics of Enslaved Women.* Louisville, KY: Westminster/John Knox, 2000.

McCutcheon, Russell T. *Manufacturing Religion: The Discourse on Sui Generis Religion and the Politics of Nostalgia.* New York, NY: Oxford University Press, 1997.

Moses, Wilson Jeremiah. *Alexander Crummell: A Study of Civilization and Discontent.* New York, NY: Oxford University Press, 1989.

Ng'weshemi, Andrea M. *Rediscovering the Human: The Quest for a Christo-Theological Anthropology in Africa.* New York, NY: Peter Lang, 2002.

Oduyoye, Mercy Amba. "Jesus Christ." In Susan Frank Parsons, ed., *The Cambridge Companion to Feminist Theology.* New York, NY: Cambridge University Press, 2002.

Raboteau, Albert J. *Slave Religion: The "Invisible Institution" in the Antebellum South.* New York, NY: Oxford University Press, 1978.

Shama, Arvind, ed. *God, Truth and Reality: Essays in Honour of John Hick.* New York, NY: St. Martin's Press, 1993.

Stewart, Dianne. "Christian Doctrines of Humanity and the African Experience of Evil and Suffering: Toward a Black Theological Anthropology." In Anthony B. Pinn and Benjamin Valentin, eds., *Ties that Bind: African American and Hispanic American/Latino Theology in Dialogue.* New York, NY: Continuum, 2001.

Tehranian, John. *Whitewashed: America's Invisible Middle Eastern Minority.* New York, NY: NYU Press, 2009.

Terrell, JoAnne Marie. *Power in the Blood? The Cross in the African American Experience.* Maryknoll, NY: Orbis Books, 1998.

Walker, Alice. *The Color Purple.* New York, NY: Harcourt Brace Jovanovich, 1982.

Yancy, George. *Black Bodies, White Gazes: The Continuing Significance of Race.* Lanham, MD: Rowman and Littlefield, 2008.

8

WHO BELONGS TO CHRIST?

Josiah U. Young III

Luke's gospel and Paul's 1 Corinthians do not address racism directly. Luke and Paul probably never imagined a Middle Passage or something as horrific. One can infer from them, however, that the *risen* Christ has opposed and opposes racist ideology and practices. If God has raised Him and if He is thus no longer a historical person, if His personhood is eschatological (as Acts 1:9–11 indicates), then He surely opposes the sins Luke and Paul never heard of. Yet, there are churches that have worshiped Him as their Lord but nonetheless harbor racism. Do their doctrines of justification and sanctification—both of which claim the counsel of the Holy Spirit—compel them to embrace white-supremacist ideologies? Why didn't they eschew racism, for God's sake?

The fact that Christian soteriology and racism have not been and are not mutually exclusive for many suggests to me that anti-racist Christologies depend on Christ's arrival ("Parousia") for substantiation. What else *but* the Parousia would prove compellingly that Christ opposes racism? One hopes that He would denounce white privilege and lift up those who have struggled against it upon His arrival. Until then, anti-racist Christologies are on tenuous ground. Jürgen Moltmann (1992) suggests as much to me in writing that

> faith … expects a future of Christ in the resurrection from the dead and in "the giving of life to our mortal bodies" (Rom. 8:11). This future is therefore a time which bears the impress, no longer of Christ's struggle but of his kingdom. This time is determined no longer by transience, but by a *tarrying and abiding in the felicitous moment.* No one participates in the messianic struggle of Christ against the powers of destruction and annihilation without a hope for such a *"fulfilled time"* in a victory of life of this kind. Anyone who lives in … contradiction to the laws and powers of "this world" hopes for a new world of

correspondences. The contradiction suffered is itself the negative mirror-image of the correspondence hoped for.

(p.200. Emphases added)

Without the *irrefutable* presence of the Christ in the midst of history, like a force field invulnerable to transience and corruption, every anti-racist Christology is a waning candle in the dark. As I see it, the reason for this is not just the fact that racism persists in some white North American churches and has the power of a pro-white history behind it. The paradoxical character of the Bible is also a problem. Since the Bible is the church's sacred text, one has to deal with its paradoxes until the Christ comes to clear things up. Nevertheless, His promise to return is the most important dimension of the gospel; and one must venture to say what His arrival would mean in relation to some of the most vexing problems of the day. Racism is one of them. In what follows I will discuss Luke 4:18–19 and 1 Corinthians 15 in the light of the problem and the promise of the Parousia.

Luke 4:18–19: to set at liberty those who are oppressed?

Luke's Christ says in 4:18–19,

> The Spirit of the Lord is on me,
> because he has anointed me
> to proclaim good news to the poor.
> He has sent me to proclaim freedom for the prisoners
> and recovery of sight for the blind,
> to set the oppressed free,
> to proclaim the year of the Lord's favor.

One knows by the time he or she reads this passage that Jesus of Nazareth has been the Christ—the "Son of the most High," true heir to David's throne—from the time when His mother conceived Him by the Spirit's power. He has triumphed, in addition, over the "devil" in the aftermath of His baptism and anointing with the Spirit of God. So, when the Christ, reading from Isaiah 61:10, declares that the "Spirit of the Lord is upon" Him and has anointed Him "to bring good news to the poor," none is surprised that He tells the synagogue assembly that the Isaiah prophecy is fulfilled in Him: Filled with the power of the Spirit, He will make the blind see and "let the oppressed go free." The rest of Luke narrates how the Christ relieves the suffering of the poor through healing them and feeding hundreds of them with next to nothing. Could He have done such things if the Lord's Spirit were not upon Him, if He were not the Son of God? Even when it seems that He had spoken a bit too boldly in the synagogue—for the Romans in collusion with the established Jewish priesthood put Him to death—He rises bodily from the dead. The Lord who has anointed Him vindicates Him. He is exactly who He said He was—God's champion of a pariah people. Is He also the Messiah for those who suffer until today from racism? Does

Luke's quoting of Isaiah 61 prefigure the release of those held captive by unnatural and early death? If His resurrection from the dead means that the liberation He proclaims is fulfilled in *Him*, and if this liberation extends eschatologically to those who are dead as He was, then there is hope. The countless victims of racial injustice, the casualties of the ruthless accumulation of New World wealth, would have in the risen Lord a true champion. Liberation wouldn't get any better than that. There is a problem though.

"The year of the Lord's favor," as found in Luke 4:18–19, alludes to Leviticus 25, which has to do with the Jubilee, the year in which the well-to-do Israelites were to release the indentured servants and slaves in their debt. But the non-Hebrew slaves from "the nations" had no Jubilee rights. According to Leviticus, YHWH permits the Hebrew people to pass those slaves (*aliens*) down to their "children as inherited property," for they are "slaves for life" (Leviticus 25:44–46). So much for proclaiming "liberty throughout the land to all [*sic*] its inhabitants" (Leviticus 25:8–10): The good news—*set the oppressed free, proclaim the year of the Lord's favor*—is not so good for some.

The Lucan parables that refer to slavery are similarly troubling. Luke 12:37–48, for instance, commends slaves for not sleeping on the job. These parables are not about setting people free or abolishing caste. These parables uphold the privileged caste. I recognize that one must place the gospel in its first-century context; but I'm unwilling to accept master–slave language of any sort. According to the parable, the household master (*kurios*) who finds his slaves "awake when he comes" would invite them to dinner and wait on *them*. What is more, if the household steward keeps the other slaves in good order—has given "them their allowance of food at the proper time"—the master would "put that one in charge of all his possessions." But if the steward stuffed himself with food, got drunk, and abused the lesser slaves, the master, having caught the unruly steward, would "cut him to pieces." Slaves complicit in such shenanigans, in addition, would "receive a severe beating." One wonders: *Would Luke's Jesus set all the oppressed free?* Neither the ancient Hebrew enslavement of the aliens nor the master–slave dialectic of the parables is helpful in pondering the question, "What would Jesus do about white privilege?"

On one level, then, Luke 4, when placed in its Jewish and Christian contexts, offers little support to those who claim that Jesus Christ's God—and His Spirit, and Jesus Himself—sides with those suffering from the effects of racism. Who can miss the affinity between the black North American slaves of yesterday and the ancient slaves who take center stage in the parable and Leviticus? And yet, the gospel and its literary twin, Acts, depict a very humane Messiah. This depiction is part of the hopefulness of the gospel. It is not a perfect hope—obviously; but hope connotes faith, as in trust, in the power of goodness to trump evil. Goodness has to with the Christ's healing of the sick, His partiality to the oppressed (however truncated in this case), and refusal to become like the evil He struggled against. His refusal to become wicked is integral to His crucifixion, His ostensible passivity in the face of those who mortified Him—His non-violent, but transformative, resistance to ignorance, corruption and injustice. For all that I find troubling about Luke, I also see hope in the gospel.

That hope brings to mind Marxist philosopher Ernst Bloch's (1986) notion of the "Not-Yet Conscious." *Hope*, he argues,

> is the *discovery and unmistakable notation of the "Not-yet-Conscious."* That is: a relatively still Unconscious disposed towards its other side, forwards rather than backwards. Towards the side of something new that is dawning up, that has never been conscious before, not, for example, something forgotten, something rememberable that has been, something that has sunk into the subconscious [*sic*] in repressed or archaic fashion.
>
> *(p.13)*

Bloch, in criticizing Freud, argues that we have thought of our consciousness as "only 'backward dawning'. ... People thought they had discovered that everything present is loaded with memory, with past in the cellar of the No-longer-Conscious." According to Bloch, though, everything that is present to our psyche does not stem from the past. An inkling of what we have yet to experience is also innate to us. We are not conscious of what is to come, but we are predisposed toward it. For Bloch, then, our species looks "forwards rather than backwards." The distant shore attracts us much more than the point of departure. What makes history is the journey toward the Promised Land, rather than the memory of Egypt land. The antithesis between the two is integral to Bloch's philosophy because he was profoundly influenced by his Jewish heritage. As Bloch (1986) sees it, Judaism and Christianity are largely responsible for the insight that we strive toward the unprecedented, the something *new*—the Not-Yet-Become. This "broken-off and broached material does not take place in the cellar of consciousness, but on its Front" (p.11).

That Judaism marked Bloch indelibly and that he has influenced Christian theologians such as Moltmann lend credibility to my sense that Bloch and Luke go together. In fact, Moltmann (1992) claims that "theologians began to rediscover their own biblical, i.e., Jewish and Christian, horizon of hope" because of Bloch (p.143). The evangelist Luke could not have known anything about "the peculiar institution," whose ramifications cripple many African-Americans until today. Still, given Bloch's perspective, I see nothing wrong in considering the upward path of the gospel as an example of "the Not-Yet-Conscious" in our species, which "belongs completely to the Not-Yet-Become, Not-Yet-Brought-Out, Manifested-Out in the World" (Bloch, 1986, p.11). From that point of view, one cannot separate the hope intrinsic to the gospel from what twentieth-century theologians have made of it.

Luke had no consciousness that Martin Luther King Jr.—whose paternal great grandfather was a slave—would, in his acceptance address to Dexter Avenue Memorial Baptist Church, tell Dexter's saints, "I have felt with Jesus that the spirit of the Lord is upon me, because he has anointed me to preach the gospel to the poor; to heal the brokenhearted, to preach deliverance to the captives, and to set at liberty them that are bruised" (Carson, 2007, p.167). The first-century context in which slavery was acceptable among Gentiles and Jews has passed away, as has the more ancient context responsible for the pro-slavery Priestly Law of Leviticus. Yet, the hope for deliverance has endured; and this hope is not beholden to first-century ethics but to the Not-Yet-Become. In a way that Luke could not have imagined, King exemplifies that the good news makes an *open* claim—namely that the Messiah's ascension from Judahite territory (Bethany) heralds God's coming to the nations. Would it make any sense to call this openness good news if God's kingdom were only for certain kinds of people? What purpose would that serve? Why would anyone hold that such divine bias is good? But as Orthodox theologian John Zizioulas (2008) points out, faith "does not draw its being from what it is now" (or, let me add, from what was then). Faith "is rooted ontologically in the future, the pledge and earnest of which is the resurrection of Christ" (p.64). If one posits "an infinite and qualitative distinction" between Luke as theologian (*past*) and Christ as the risen/ascended and coming Son of God (*future*), then it does not seem wise to value the pro-slavery, privilege-upholding ethics that contradict the *liberating* implications of His Lordship.

1 Corinthians 15: those who belong to Christ

One might say, the Not-Yet-Become is Paul's main concern in 1 Corinthians 15. For Paul, the risen Christ is "the firstfruits of those who have fallen asleep" (15:20). His resurrection *from* the dead, moreover, is as archetypical as Adam's sin-induced death, which Paul reckoned to be the reason for mortality. The risen Christ is, therefore, the prototype of an eschatological species liberated from sin and death. "For as in Adam all die, so in Christ all *will* be made alive" (emphasis added)—but in sequence:

> Christ the firstfruits, then at his coming those who belong to Christ. Then comes the end, when he hands over the kingdom to God the Father, after he has destroyed every ruler and every authority and power. For he must reign until he has put all his enemies under his feet. The last enemy to be destroyed is death. For "God has put all things in subjection under his feet." But when it says, "All things are put in subjection," it is plain that this does not include the one who put all things in subjection under him. When all things are subjected to him, then the Son himself will also be subjected to the one who put all things in subjection under him, so that God may be all in all.
>
> *(15:23–28)*

In his essay on 1 Corinthians as found in *The Oxford Bible Commentary*, John Barclay thinks it likely that the end, the point at which the Son hands His kingdom over to the Father, will occur "at that same moment" that those who belong to Christ are raised. Barclay (2001) points out, however, that some see the Son's transfer of His kingdom to the Father as "a further phase," "when God's kingdom is complete and all enemies of his rule are defeated" (p.1131).

Moltmann is among those for whom the transfer signifies a further phase—namely the eschaton *after* the millennial reign of Christ. Moltmann's pre-millenarian eschatology thus posits that those who belong to Christ will enjoy vindication in *history*, for the second round of the resurrection from the dead—the bridge as it were to the destruction of Death—is only for those who paid, to allude to Bonhoeffer, the cost of disciple-ship. For Moltmann, moreover, "The Thousand Years' reign of Christ, 'the kingdom of peace,' is … indispensable for every alternative form of life and action which will withstand the ravages of the world here and now. Without millenarian hope, the Christian ethic of resistance and the consistent discipleship of Christ lose their most powerful motivation" (p.201). From this perspective, the apocatastasis would come at the very end, when the Son hands His kingdom over to the Father (Moltmann, 1996, p.201). The "millenarian expectation" thus "mediates between world history here, and the end of the world and the new world there" (Moltmann, 1996, p.201). Given Moltmann's reading of Paul, I wonder. *Would those who truly believe in Christ and who were alive at His coming never die? Would those who did not believe prior to His coming pass away—"sleep" until the Great Transfer?* Whatever Paul (or Moltmann) has in mind, it's clear that the resurrection from the dead is, in part, for those who stood up for Christ when public devotion to Him put the believer in danger. To quote Moltmann (1996),

> the millenarian hope is a *hope for martyrs*. The praxis of this hope is resistance in the godless kingdoms of the world, and the refusal to conform to their idol worship and cults of power. It is not just the hope that must be called messianic and millenarian; it is the resistance and martyrdom itself that precedes the hope [i.e., resistance and martyrdom are also messianic and millenarian]. For in that resistance the relative, conditioned and often so ambivalent Here and Today is made the point in time of an eschatological, absolute and unconditioned decision.
>
> *(p.152)*

Of course, Paul, like Luke, was no revolutionary. His concern was the kingdom of God. He wished to maintain proper church discipline—to hold the ecclesia together, until the Christ's arrival. He tolerated a form of slavery, as is borne out by 1 Corinthians 7, and thus did not trouble the status quo. (Paul writes in 7:21, "Were you a slave when called? Do not be concerned about it.") He thought this age of sin and death was passing away. Why make waves over what had no future? Okay—but why would Paul's setting in life determine how we deal with institutions that perpetuate injustice today? Why should those of us who are discriminated against because our bodies are black keep quiet about racism or fail to trouble the institutions in which racism is alive and well? Because a *first-century theologian* accommodated the Roman Empire's mores? What is more important theologically—his parenesis which advises enslaved persons to be content with their status in the aeon which is passing away, or his idea of the coming reign of Christ?

If Paul has *current* apocalyptic significance, then the time in which we are living stands in stark contrast to what is to come. Life as we know it is, as Douglas Knight puts it, "part of a process and a history, enabled by the Holy Spirit which, because we must all participate in it, unfolds through time. Waiting for other people"—notably those who belong to Christ—"is what time is" (cited in Zizioulas, 2008, p.xix). If Christ were to return in the way Paul claims He will, and, moreover, if those who belong to Him will reign with Him, then that number should include the people who gave their lives in the struggle against white supremacy. It should also include those who were destroyed by it. (Remember Emmitt Till?) They should be up front with Him. I have already suggested that the very idea that the Parousia would uphold white privilege is an idea too bitter to swallow. *Why* should whites be so privileged? Has the playing field ever been so level that one can say truthfully that blacks, in particular, *deserve* the obstacles that have been placed in our way?

Bloch (2009) suggests that the "*Futurum* of hope was thought of as a property of God's being," a property that "distinguished him from all other gods." As a result, the anticipation of the Not-Yet-Become—the refusal to accept the present as final—is "the hope that is [God's] essence" (p.250). As Moltmann (1992) explains, "Bloch is concerned only with a functional criticism of religion" (p.151). He seeks to determine whether religion advances the quest for freedom or retards it. According to Moltmann (1992), then, Bloch seeks to gauge whether "belief in God along the lines of messianism" is hospitable to the future (p.151). Christology, it seems to me, ought to be hospitable to the future. Christology should argue "that belief in God has a liberating, stimulating and mobilizing effect on the real overcoming of real misery" (Moltmann, 1992, p.151). Movement toward God's future is passionate activity that mirrors (however dimly) what is hoped for. We are to fight for our interpretation of the arrival of the Messiah. For, as Douglas Knight argues in his Introduction to Zizioulas's *Lectures in Christian Dogmatics*, "God intends that we be free and his invitation to freedom is what the future is. If the future were fixed or necessary, it would not be *future*, but simply more of the present." What is more, "no future can be foisted on us. We can only be said to be beings with a future if we become, and remain, free" (Knight, cited in Zizioulas, 2008, p. xix). Free people (consider Dietrich Bonhoeffer, Martin Luther King, Jr., Engelbert Mveng) strive to be like the future they pray for daily, "for our identity will not be decided without our collaboration" (Knight, cited in Zizioulas, 2008, p.xix). The faith that justice and the love of God are coming in Spirit justifies the question, "What would Jesus do about the problem of racism?" Render it No-Longer-Conscious, I *hope*. Then, there would be no doubt about who belongs to Christ. In the meantime, we must decide what our hermeneutics are, do our theological work accordingly, and be, as James Baldwin (1979) puts it in one of his novels, *the song we sing*.[1] *Maranatha*.

Note

1 Baldwin (1979, p.46): "you can't sing *outside* the song. You've got to be the song you sing. You've got to make a confession."

References

Baldwin, James. *Just above My Head*. New York: Dial Press, 1979.
Barclay, John. "65. I Corinthians," in *The Oxford Bible Commentary*, edited by John Barton and John Muddiman. Oxford: Oxford University Press, 2001.
Bloch, Ernst. *Atheism in Christianity*. New York: Verso, 2009.

——The Principle of Hope, Volume One. Cambridge, MA: The MIT Press, 1986.

Carson, Clayborne. The Papers of Martin Luther King, Jr., Volume VI: Advocate of the Social Gospel, September 1948–March 1963. Berkeley: University of California Press, 2007.

Knight, Douglass. "Introduction," in John D. Zizioulas, Lectures in Christian Dogmatics, edited by Douglass H. Knight. New York: T & T Clark, 2008.

Moltmann, Jürgen. History and the Triune God: Contributions to Trinitarian Theology. New York: Crossroad, 1992.

——The Coming of God: Christian Eschatology. Minneapolis, MN: Fortress Press, 1996.

Zizioulas, John. Lectures in Christian Dogmatics, edited by Douglass H. Knight. New York: T & T Clark, 2008.

9

UPSTART MESSIAHS, RENEGADE SAMARITANS, AND TEMPLE EXORCISMS

What can Jesus' peasant resistance movement in first-century Palestine teach us about confronting "color-blind" whiteness today?

James W. Perkinson

"Are we not right in saying you are a Samaritan and have a demon?"

—John 8:49

The guiding question for this gathering of essays, "What would Jesus do?" is suggestive in the subjunctive, but begs a more concrete exploration in the indicative. What is Jesus doing about whiteness? Black theologian James Cone is a sharp-sighted critic here, pushing us past our mere imaginings to insist that the God of the oppressed is already active in the circumstance of exploitation (Cone, 1975, 126, 136). We discern what Jesus would do by asking what he *did* do, and then, in light of that, develop an eye to see what he is doing *now*. Cone insists that Jesus is black in contemporary North America because he was a Jew in first-century Palestine (Cone, 1975, 134). But of course, savvy about the recursive loops (think hip-hop sampling or break-dance ciphers or black church call/response) of any project of hermeneutics, our inchoate sense of what Jesus is doing now, already informs how we "read" what he was doing back in the day. The loop spirals and returns, crosses over, inverts, becomes itself again, but now different—a reverb, a rhythm, even a *logos* on a "dia-logue" mission. (Not just of confirmation, but of fractal novelty and freedom. The loop itself recurs in time and so is never really the same as the last time.) And this is why presuppositions are so important in the tradition, why the outcomes of parables about seeds, for instance, are decided so often by the soils in which they are sown.

In keeping with such a conviction, this reflection will first lay out a quick-sketch vision of the take on whiteness that informs my response to the question, and then get down to the business of profiling a provisional answer. The answer will actually unfold "antiphonally"—juxtaposing ancient text and contemporary conundrum, letting meaning strike in the tension between. Such a method is informed one more time by the black wisdom Cone intones, the sensibility of a "call/response" mode of knowing things. That first reflection on whiteness will establish the call. The response will coalesce in terms of a particular reading of the Good Samaritan mode of "parable-telling," in which Jesus throws up an explicit category of ethnicity to expose an inchoate text of purity/impurity that organizes first-century Palestinian space and governs social behavior. That reflection will lead to re-evaluating the centrality of Jesus' Temple exorcism as critical to his struggle to break open the hegemonic structure of perception and discourse that used the Torah to control and sanction political economy and debt. A large-scale public action becomes necessary to rupture the link between the situation of poverty/debt and the discourse of sin/impurity and begin to dislodge the stigma the latter had visited on an oppressed Jewish peasantry as well as to open up a space of questioning inside the presuppositions of the elite.

The final part of the chapter—responding to the response—will then characterize the way whiteness/color have functioned as modern analogues to purity/impurity to give ideological ramification to our own globalizing structures of development/under-development and wealth/poverty. Here the poly-rhythm will be scored by mapping the way a protest action at Chase Manhattan Bank, shutting it down for part of a day during the 2010 Social Forum gathering of activists in Detroit and galvanizing a continuing campaign to secure a moratorium on foreclosures, serves to expose the link between foreclosures and a default norm of whiteness, eager to "ethnically cleanse" the urban core as part of a long-term strategy to gentrify the city and return it to white control. The burden of such a two-step writing is to uncloak whiteness as a force of cultural habituation, styling itself politically as color-blind and economically as merely "individual" and "responsible," that insinuates itself continuously into the silences underneath our mediated public discourses, with ruthlessly disparate effects for peoples of color at home and abroad. Confronting its power today is as tricky and fraught, I will argue, as the struggle that Jesus engaged in first-century Palestine to "call out" the branding potency of impurity-perceptions and galvanize a social movement of resistance capable of restoring dignity to an impoverished peasantry while inverting the meaning of the stigma.

Presuppositions

Whiteness! What would Jesus do? Certainly whiteness exists today as a political demand and a moral quandary, no matter what one's religious conviction. It balloons before our partially blinkered eyes as a conundrum of the global system that is at once commanding and insipid. Existentially, it shows up by disappearing before the eyes of those who live its brand. It intrudes as a hidden transcript of the visual that rules without name. It is today a game of skin made into a topography of power, serving an economy of empire. With roots in Euro-Christian colonial take-over of cultures multi-hued and dancing, whiteness emerges only gradually in modern history, as an explicitly named social position, largely negative in citation: a deeply sighed, desperately clutched—"Whatever else I am, sure glad I am not that! Not black, or brown, or red-yellow-olive dark, with jungle vines and swamp mud, grabbing at my toes!"

Indeed, whatever else it asks, whiteness demands an accounting of the history under our feet (yes, "our," for I, too, am snarled in this peculiar tonality, this winding sheet of death, despite the fight I yet engage to step free). That accounting will not be easy, for the very idea of whiteness is itself elusive, an identity inhabited by people with light skin tones and European genetic lines, that only shows its face here and there, when its norms of behavior are violated or the resources it has locked behind gates and passwords, immigration authorities and corporate laws, are named "plunder" and questioned. Then it shows its teeth and rage. It is a fiction of superiority hiding a history of violence. But for one such as myself—in the tradition here held up to kindle vision and aspiration—that history is not original to this phantom called whiteness, but part of an older struggle. The blood on the ground is finally Abel's, of biblical fame. The one killed by Cain. The slaying that the Genesis account marks, primordial in figure, raw and ever-repeated in the 10,000 year procession of events we call "civilization," now coats the entire planet in red. White is the modern lie about this red, the desire to tread on bones without a crunch, a grasping for sky and light against the terror of ever-threatening night and comeuppance. While the blood on the soil cries out unrelentingly.

Abel has died screaming for a century of centuries—a hunter-gatherer/pastoral nomad/horticultural death rattle before the onslaught of expansionist agricultural "advance" that has rolled over the bodies and silenced their moans across the face of a planet. The truth underneath that silenced groan? A ceaseless *conquest*—clearing land, killing animal, uprooting plant, fencing forest, closing commons, chopping heads, raping according to gender, impressing labor, building machines, drilling for oil, fashioning ever-more outrageous liens of debt, conjuring rights in fictions of laws, screening lies and violence in the ruse called "money," a 10,000-year-old, planetary-wide promulgation of kleptocracy[1] and control, ever vaunting itself scribally (and now by way of CNN) as "achievement." Biblically, I would argue, Abel's cry animates the entirety of recorded history, until it is gathered into the archetypal city of end-times projection, summing up all urbanity everywhere. Babylon of the Book of Revelation is the emblem and substance of every turn to a metropolitan concentration of resources appropriated by force from elsewhere, inside whose walls and in whose goods is stored the blood of "all of those slain through the ages," until that cry of disappeared indigenous and crucified peasants and slaughtered slaves and mangled workers, like a Jericho trumpet, brings down the entire monstrosity (Rev. 18:1–24). Babylon is the secret truth of every city, the warning sign over civilization, arcing from the Genesis primordium of Cain-like farmers killing Abel-like nomads, to the final pull-back of the curtain of Oz, revealing the truth of the trek towards urbanized "urbanity"—culminating in Babel's infamous towers and lethal confusion— as "fall" (Gen. 4:1–17; 11:1–9; Rev. 18:2). White is merely the contemporary weave of that heavily weighted curtain of time, hiding all the blood. But its whiteness is not simply the dominance of a phenotype at a particular historical juncture.

White domination

In the words of W. E. B. Du Bois, writing in his famous *Souls* at the end of the beginning of industrialization in the United States, race descends on the "sons of night," for whose welfare and rights he struggles continuously, as a mysterious "Veil," see-through as gossamer, but chain-mail-strong in its powers of containment and incarceration (Du Bois, 1961, pp.15–17). Here we have a modernist text subtly signifying on ancient apocalyptic tradition (literally, a tradition of *apo-kalypsis* or "un-veiling"). In his particular case, the veiling issues from the eye of a girl of his early years, falling like a curtain of confusion on his simple expectation that exchanging greeting cards in his grade school classroom could only be a "merry good time." Her sudden refusal of his card—"peremptorily," communicated solely in a glance without a word—rings down a shroud and shatters a little boy's world. Her eye sees color onto his being, like an act of primal creation. On his side of the enveloping veil, the shadow-tone branding all the bodies, ranging from high yellow to deep ebony, will be a single, inescapable hue. In time, he will learn that his tawny skin, and all it harbors, is "black." On the other side of the divide, however—as seemingly innocuous as that girl's simple act of looking—a ghost of whitely innocence will haunt the shades from pink to cream, pearly-gray to red-and-embarrassed. To be white will bring no necessary struggle in its wake, no writhing under a magic blanket of shame. It will not even usually involve—as its absence in Du Bois' text cannily reflects—the qualifier "white," indicating a difference from the darkness just conjured, but merely a presumed transparency embodying an unassailable certainty, reigning (even in a grade school student) over the engulfing meaning. "To be white"—in the eye of one who assumes such a stance—is simply to *be*, without having color trouble one's ontology at all. It is also to be (in one's typical imagination of the situation) without victims.

So in quick sketch of a broad background, I offer the ideology of white racial supremacy as the quintessential modern "sleight of hand"—or more accurately, a trick of the eye created by a discourse of the tongue—hiding a ruthless history of genocidal practice. Under its influence in the Americas at large, Euro-heritage peoples disappeared 95 percent of the roughly 100 million First Nations peoples whose lands they stole over the course of a half millennium, and precipitated the early deaths of 30–50 million Africans who were killed in the process of enslaving the 12 million transported alive to the New World. In the U.S. alone, this same ideological hubris resulted in the invasion, annexation, and domination of half-a-continent's worth of *Mexicanos* from 1848 onward, and the importation of multiple regimes of Asian laboring forces (Chinese—in the wake of the opium wars, Filipinos—after massacring a million or so in "liberating" and "civilizing" their islands) to erect its infrastructure and harvest its crops. And in the process—in a typical conflation of race and gender—white male desire "read" the peoples it dominated as "female" races, subject to "penetration"[2] at will, even as it likewise (often enough) raped, worked, and sometimes burned (as "witches") white women into early graves. Over the course of its emergence globally as the normative category of human identity over recent centuries (through colonization and mass media), whiteness has re-created dark appearance as its paradigmatic opposite. In the process, white ways of thinking have transfigured a kaleiscopic range of African and Asian and Amerindian skin tones into a monolithic and damning meaning of darkness, swallowing entire peoples in its hungry economy and phobic gaze, while simultaneously consolidating itself as the (supposedly) supreme achievement of nature's grand design for our species. And what this veil of differentiation continues to hide today—by proclaiming it a merely regrettable mistake of the past that has since been overcome—is simply the ruthless perpetuation of this history of gore and exploitation.

The ten millennia-long progression of domination that we call "civilization"—made "natural" for most of its course by religious proclamation claiming divine legitimation for whoever managed to rule the mountain of plunder, and made scientific or at least sociological for most of its recent history as explicit white supremacy—today styles itself colorblind and user friendly. Domestically, this white dominance now reigns as a form of meritocracy. It continues to project historic blackness as a primal baseline for its relentless political economy of racialized otherness whose contemporary euphemisms— "criminal," "illegal," and "terrorist"—govern the burgeoning operations of our prison-industrial complex, our immigration bureaucracy, and our foreign policy, respectively. As neoliberalism in the global South, white-dominated corporate power works through a "fundamentalist" technocracy that differentially routes elite self-interest and popular aspiration into fated market outcomes of wealth and poverty by way of the "Invisible Hand" of World Trade Organization (WTO), World Bank, and International Monetary Fund collusion with finance capital and military force. In spite of its now celebrated multiculturalism and self-congratulatory inclusivity, how-ever, this corporate whitewash is "see through" if one attends to the broken bones and diseased or disappeared flesh. Historically, corporate accumulation has largely piled up inside "white-gated" communities and countries (and among their crony constituencies in the developing world). And most of the dead bodies and living bereaved have been of color.

In shorthand equation, then, whiteness today is not only a rough cipher for enti-tlement (a presumed right to "property," as legal scholar Cheryl Harris has argued), but is the color of Wall Street (Harris, 1993, p.1). At one deep level in the United States, it is the default assumption of merit that allows 1 percent of the population to own more assets than the bottom 90 percent together. If that 1 percent were majority black or Latino, there would be revolution in the streets. (Indeed, the contemporary emergence of China as a global force economically, militarily, and demographically con-stitutes the first world-historical challenge to the hegemony of de facto white supremacy in its 500-year career in modernity). Disrupting the power of whiteness, then, means clarifying the big bank as ground zero for pain on the planet, at once shrine and sepulcher whence white well-being and dark demise give rise to each other under the guise of worship and under-taking. Its unveiling—the exposure of this connection between cultural whiteness and big finance—is the minimum for any contemporary messianism worthy of the name.

What Jesus did do

When we seek perspective on such a broad-based rendition of white racial domination by way of ancient text and cultural distance, a revealing place to begin is with the embattled category "Samaritan" as it appears sporadically in the gospels of Luke and

John. As a term pointing towards a disparaged hybridity in first-century Palestine, "Samaritan-ness" anchors the operative discourses of stigma and shame mapping the social landscape of the time of Jesus. Historically, Samaria emerged as a mestizo polity, after the Assyrian conquest of northern Israel in 721 BCE, resulting from the co-mingling of Jewish *'am ha'aretz* ("people of the land") and certain other conquered peoples transplanted by the regime into the northern Palestinian hill-country from elsewhere. As a creole folk—neither Jew nor Gentile—Samaritans bore the opprobrium typical of peoples who don't fit the normative schemas of a social order. In the outback of Israel, at the margins of Roman imperial "civility," Samaritan-ness marked, for Jewish culture, an unassimilable miasma—an ethnic zone of compromised bloodlines and "bastardized" spiritual practices, whose very existence shouted uncleanness and danger. Of interest for our analysis here is the fact that, apart from one off-hand remark by Matthew, the term appears only in Luke and John, where in each case—though uniquely so within the particular perspective of each author—"Samaritan-ness" emerges in connection with confrontation with the authorities in the Temple in Jerusalem. In Luke, as we shall see, it first shows up as soon as Jesus sets his face to march *to* Jerusalem. In John, it marks an encounter with a woman and an entire village that stands in marked contrast to the surveillance and plotting that shadows Jesus as he flees *from* the Temple, immediately after his action there. The particular way that these gospels "work" the discourses and tropes of Samaritan-ness in connection with Jesus' own ethnic identity will prove provocative for the question on whiteness.

Tactical Samaritan-ness

In one place only does Jesus teach the term explicitly. Ironically, it becomes perhaps the best-known trope of the entire tradition. From the imperial pulpits of Christendom, historically, as well as in modernity subsequently, the Good Samaritan story has usually been offered as a cipher for nice neighborliness (Lk. 10:25–37). It is taught to children as exemplary and enters popular discourse as a metaphor for altruism. But read carefully in context, it explodes easy notions of morality. It is more realistically a "conscientizing" parable, as scholars today rehearse, thrown up like a grenade of offense in a system of rapacious domination. It proceeds from the inquiry of a lawyerly type, presumably sent from Jerusalem to "test" the upstart prophet from Galilee (somewhat like an emissary of J. Edgar Hoover of more recent notoriety, trying to get the goods on Martin King), hoping to provoke a "damning soundbite," useful for the disinformation campaigns and courtroom trials to come. He asks after eternal life, but is quickly queried in kind—in effect, "called out" by Jesus—to open up how he himself "reads," to disclose what he presupposes, where he comes *from*, in his questioning. He answers well, equating loving God with loving one's neighbor, and is commended in return with the simple admonition, "that's right, do it!" However, he is not really seeking theological clarity, but entrapment. So he asks again, and this time more pointedly, "and who is my neighbor?"

The invitation is to a game of Bible battleship—"I'll lob a text at you and you throw one back at me to see who is blown up first." Jesus refuses, in favor of a story followed by another counter-question. The story is the parable proper featuring a hero-Samaritan caring for a mugging victim, as we shall see in a moment, but the real hook of the exchange with the lawyer is a kind of Socratically flipped script, asking in seeming repetition of the lawyer's own question, "And which of these proved neighbor to the victim on the ground?" But it is a question with a difference. Where the lawyer began with his own self-assured certainty organized around his own pre-sumed identity—"Who is *my* neighbor?"—the question in kind inverts the structure of the asking. "Who is neighbor *to*?" presupposes the supine one on the ground as the new center of identity, whose condition as broken and in need puts everyone who sees *in* question, as now no longer assured of inclusion in the community of divine approval, but standing in need of proving themselves worthy of the Torah category of "neighbor" by *how they act towards* that suffering body. On Jesus' lips the question is not about the victim, but about oneself. In reality, the lawyer was actually asking, "Who is *not* my neighbor?" Who is *not* included in that category, to whom I need *not* bother responding? For the rabbi from Nazareth, "neighbor" is not a category that is anchored in oneself but in any person who appears on one's horizon in a condition of need. The shift is subtle, but seismic, a difference of world-orientation. And the battle of categories thus hinted, one with large stakes.

But it is the parable itself that is of special interest for our purposes here. Like any good pedagogue of popular renown, Jesus has launched his little vignette in careful resonance with his audience. Rabbinic stories of the time typically featured a cast of "usual suspects," known character types, elaborated in sequence to structure the story-line. Here the cast would have been, in descending order of social import in the hierarchy of the time, "Priest," "Levite," and "Jewish layperson." Jesus begins down that road. Though actual peasant expression may have been laconic, we can surmise at least a tacit belly response as he runs the expected sequence (something like, "Yes, Lord, break it down! We're with you! Teach!"). Until he hits the third character, and throws up a despised Samaritan as the archetype of faithful "Jewish" action in this story. The offense could hardly be more pointed. A heresy-espousing, false-Temple-attending, compromised-blood-line-carrying, ethnically abhorrent "miscreant"—whose gene-pool is worthy only of the dozens!?[3] Preposterous! Like some preacher today offering up a Guadalupe-loving fruit-picker from the barrio or Nation of Islam paper-seller on the ghetto streets as icon of a suburban Protestant Christian ethic. But even here, we need to slow the appreciation.

The code that determines the behavior is not explicit. Priest and Levite turn away … for no reason the text gives, but that everybody from that culture knows. The body may be bleeding or dead and contact will result in pollution. At stake—governing response and anchoring the bite of the gambit—is an inchoate set of categories. Pre-suppositions of purity/impurity structure perception, foster avoidance, explode with relevance once the action is culminated. This is a situation mapped definitively in a discourse that not only predicts action sufficiently to leverage the story but invites continual reflection on the extent of the send-up offered. The Samaritan is impurity incarnate in the culture of the time—a body marked by compromised ethnicity daring to join another body compromised by physical violation, in a shared abjection.

The story enjoins the risk of community-in-impurity—commonly embraced jeopardy!—as the very beginning of neighborliness. And one more time, in a long line of gospel inversions, throws down a mind-bend as necessary to heart-change and a better world. But we can go still further.

Mapping the space

The implicit markers of social position in the Good Samaritan parable—the operative "categories of consequence" that we have been considering—also map a sacral geography. Jesus, at this point in Luke, is on the road, marching toward a high-noon showdown with the powers that be in Jerusalem, having apparently decided, out of his encounter with another intrepid one (the Syro-Phoenician woman in the Tyre–Sidonian region according to the Markan chronology that Luke follows), that public confrontation of power is imperative. He, like the victim of the story he tells, is traversing dangerous terrain, subject to outlaw encounters and hold-ups. His home turf of Galilee is the reputed center of a "gangbanging" activity notorious throughout the nation, where the caves around the local "Sea" harbor renegade Jewish males—desperate after being foreclosed from their ancestral land domains, creating their own rogue toll system, and living on the run, sometimes celebrated as Robin Hood champions of the poor, sometimes feared as predators. He knows the risk of the outback environment. His story presumes a similar "street ethic." Mugging is not an equal-opportunity eventuality. As in most polities—contrary to what might otherwise be thought logical for thievery—it is not the rich who are most likely to get popped or jacked. They normally have the resources to wall-off such banditry, or secure their passage through dangerous terrain. It is usually the poor who are vulnerable to the most desperate forms of pillage. And thus we need to probe the geography of mugging that the story limns in its spare outline.

It has a correlate scene that it references only by way of implication as the narrative unfolds. But it is a spatial ordering of kleptocracy that Jesus will make explicit and definitive in the Jerusalem encounter towards which he has "set his face" (Lk. 9:52). The "priest" and "Levite" in his story reference a place of robbery, as well. And Jesus will name it such, when the time comes. Here it is merely requisite to recognize the hint that the narrative supplies—and the pedagogical tactic at work. For whom is the story being told? The lawyer?—in hopes that he will suddenly give up his positioning in power—a full-bellied lifestyle of elite pilferage, using credit to tangle up peasants in debt, courts to foreclose the land, managerial agents to switch the crop from (the staple) barley to grapes for export (re-hiring the displaced as tenants and pushing the younger sons into day labor and begging), while convening fat harvest parties to celebrate with cronies and enjoy repute as "scribes and elders"? Or for the peasants themselves?—stigmatized in the "common sense" of the day as "unclean sinners," an "accursed rabble," who do not know or keep the law, frequently in arrears on loans, unable to pay the Temple tithe (accruing to priestly wealth) alongside the Roman tax, preyed upon by the toll collectors and the money changers and the estate lawyers, whose leverage in cahoots with the priestly "aristocracy" they can hardly resist? For whom is the uplifted "Samaritan" an icon of inversion that is likely to provoke guffaws and real thinking? And what are the terms of offense whose trespass might give gladness for the crowd that forms the base of the movement Jesus leads?

Opening the stigma

In the Lukan narrative line, rhetorical combat has been relentless. From the beginning, the task for the Nazareth prophet has been one of unmasking the way that Torah has been made to serve wealth accumulation and using its covenant traditions to reconstitute peasant village communities in the outback of Galilee in an alternative political economy focused on "kingdom of God-like" practices of sabbath and Jubilee (Horsley, 2011, pp.131–53; Myers, 1988, pp.154, 169–86; 2001, pp.23, 46). In so doing he has merely entered the lists of a long line of prophetic brokers of Hebrew memory-touting models of living against the grain of empire and city alike (Horsley and Hanson, 1985, pp.135, 256–57). Jesus begins his public engagement by "initiatory involvement" in the most provocative social movement of his time (Pieris, 1987, pp.62–63). His will not be a lone-ranger verbal critique of the order of the day, but a strategy of fostering a contrast campaign of local social formation, opening zones of alternative discipline ("daily bread" sharing and "regular debt-forgiveness") rooted in folk wisdom and the "little tradition" of the marginalized. And he will shape this strategy out of his own discipline of schooling himself in Prophet John's "forerunner" organizing activity, concentrated on re-establishing the ancient vision of debt- and purity-code interaction articulated in the oldest parts of the tradition.

In the earliest memories of Israel, the land-gift of Canaan was comprehended by the "outlaw" (*hapiru* or "Hebrew") band of escaped slaves as primal indebtedness to YHWH, requiring, for its continuance, adherence to regular practices of land-, labor-, and debt-release (the Sabbath Day, the Sabbath Year, and the Jubilee Year) as well as allowance for gleaning rights and redistributive tithes for the poor (Myers, 1998, pp.73–78). In effect, these decided who was "pure" or "justified" ("righteous") in the eyes of the law. But by the first century, the equation had been reversed and purity now decided access (Borg, 1994, pp.51). Failing to adhere to the scribally adjudicated provisions of Torah, or pay the Temple tithe, meant "branding" as "sinner" and exclusion from the holy place until and unless purification had been secured through sacrifice (bought, of course, from Temple officials, who banked the proceeds in the Temple treasury and who also enjoyed rights to the animal parts so offered). In the rural outback of Israel, among the fields and peasant villages, a single bad crop year or other misfortune meant the necessity of turning to fat-cat landlords for credit, with one's ancestral holding put up as lien. Once inveigled into debt, small farmers rarely got out, as legal innovations like the "prosbul" enabled landowners to sidestep Jubilee requirements that land be returned (Trocme, 2011, p.29). And it is no surprise then that debt release and land restoration articulate the very core of Jesus' program (once we get back to the actual Greek underlying our English-translation emphasis on individual "forgiveness" and "heavenly" inheritance)[4]—even as debt extension and double taxation increasingly foreclose smallholders into tenant farming or day laboring and begging (and, often enough, early death).

Against such a background, Luke's version of the Great Sermon takes on pointed meaning (Lk. 6:17–26). Here we catch sight of the central pedagogical struggle. The Galilee Griot steps into the very middle of the nexus of exploitation, and inverts its terms. The primal Torah categories organizing perception and sanctioning relative positioning were strategic deployments of the priestly–scribal–elder[5] "triumvirate" of local power. The "righteous" were such because they were obviously being "blessed"—after all, their bellies and tables were full, their houses large, their holdings secure, their status impeccable. The struggling multitudes—the "crowds" or "people" against whose back-wardness and impiety the authorities continually rail—on the other hand, were clearly "cursed," just as clearly because they were Torah-violating "sinners."[6] These two sets of binaries ("righteous"/"sinner" and "blessed"/"cursed") functioned as the definitive markers of social concourse and political possibility—both enforcing and explaining the life-differences they organized—by mapping the landscape of purity and impurity in no uncertain terms. They were the "terminal" weapons of the elites.

And Jesus takes them up and throws them down in exact polemic challenge of their usual denotations in his famous field homily, which is laid out as a covenant-renewal ceremony for reconstitution of the peasant village-life that is the strategic core of his movement. In his declaration, it is the "poor" and "hungry" who are proclaimed blessed, the "rich" and "sated" who are publicly cursed (in a kind of "street theater" re-enactment of oath swearing common to the courts of the day). Those who grieve family members buried early are succored, those who laugh it up at their 100 shekel-a-plate dinners are damned. The stigmatized—and here is the issue writ large: those who labor under impossible codes of condemnation, policing their every action—are elevated as bearing the same honor as the "prophets of old," while their "reputable" counterparts are likened to the whispering sycophants so hated in the diatribes of a Jeremiah or Isaiah. This question of wrestling stigma off the backs of the "rabble"—of breaking up silence by cracking open shame—is the paramount game that the Jesus movement must engage. And it requires naming "victims" as already approved and loved—exactly in their pain and struggle—and, by implication, calling them also to agency and resistance beyond the stereotype! And likewise naming the stigma-creators to their face and excoriating their instigation! This is, in effect, "ritual exorcism" of public space, giving focused expression to deeply felt resentment[7] by way of reclaimed Torah codes, transforming the collective anger of the peasant crowds into potent excitement at the prospect of a different future. But public repartee in the hills of Galilee is hardly the place from which the most powerful popular resonance could be unleashed. Rather, we need to turn attention to the very event towards which Jesus so resolutely moved after the seeming failure of his Galilee campaign.

Exorcising the stronghold

Lukan attention to Samaritan particularity begins precisely at the moment that Jesus "sets his face" toward Jerusalem (Lk. 9:51ff). Indeed, his resolve causes offense to the nearby village of that hybrid folk whose hospitality he desires for a day, to prepare his trek south. Presumably they interpret his restlessness as more of the Jewish same—dis-ease with their ethnic difference and fear of taint—and refuse his request. Likely they desired more robust time together. The disciples react with bombast, itching to call down fire. Jesus, however, rebukes their reiteration of that most quintessential Jewish antipathy, begins his march of drama (think Gandhi strutting towards the sea) and, on the way, offers up his "Samaritan pedagogy" in the form of the parable already examined. Despite the miffed response of the village, he apparently remains impressed by the Samaritan propensity for hospitality (if John's gospel accurately details the memory, they had eagerly opened their doors to him; Jh. 4:40). The parable lifts up Samaritan care as archetypal and exemplary—even for Jews. But precisely concern to honor traditions of reciprocity and hospitality among the marginalized peasantry (and how much more so, then, among the even more despised "Samaritan half-breeds") requires the aim towards Jerusalem. There is the center not only of power, but of its ideological promulgation and ritual legitimation. The Temple is broadcast central for normative values and the discourses that underwrite them. So he hits "the road" (more like some pre-apocalyptic Cormac McCarthy protagonist than a merely fascinated Kerouac) in tragic-prophetic necessity, drawing near the city of demise and "forth-telling" its coming calamity. (The road, indeed! Not a De Certeau-ian "place,"[8] as we have seen, but the space of opportunistic seizure by those without the capital to claim ownership and hire security.) And he tells a parable of mugging, begging reflection on the reality of kleptocracy in a scene of imperial pillage.

The parabolic road winds, susceptible, between Jerusalem heights and Jericho's outpost on the border. As rehearsed, the Samaritan proves hero where the jacking is raw and wanton. But the antagonists in the mini-script hint a deeper question. In avoiding the violated body, priest and Levite enact the implicit codes of purity that also beg a geography. The archetypal space of propriety they reference is the Jerusalem Temple, where priests are paramount, Levites the resident acolytes, and purification and its opposite are produced for the entire nation by the daily liturgy. It is also the storehouse of all records of indebtedness (in the Temple treasury). Purity and its payoff are thus anchored in the site of the holy, but meet their uncertain boundary where the bloody body lies by the side of the road. Might there be an implicit connection between the "holy place" of legitimated accumulation and this outlaw space of renegade expropriation that the parable seeks to make thinkable?

Jesus himself labors under similar stereotypical predication related to the rural environs in which he has nurtured his movement. Setting out for the urban epicenter of things Jewish, he has had to repudiate the most obvious title shouted his way by an aroused peasantry, keen to follow. "Messiah"—in the media of the day—denoted any upstart rebel, galvanizing a countryside following, who was bold enough to begin inducting his followers into economic exchanges alternative to the tribute/tithe system enforced by Rome and authorized by comprador elites. Its meaning, in the courts of power, was roughly synonymous with "social bandit," as Horsley has demonstrated. And the Jesus movement, with its focus on Jubilee release and peasant reciprocity, is not merely suspect, but guilty. The upstart protagonist of the gospel story has ducked this more dangerous alias and sought temporary cover under the more enigmatic *bar 'enash* ("son of man" or "human one"). But once inside the city and in full prophetic mode at the head of his peasant horde, he enters the sacred precincts like an outlaw "David," sabotages the front-line machinery of exploitation (the money changing and pigeon selling), and convenes a day-long sit-down strike and teach-in (Lk. 19:45–46; Mk. 11:10, 15–19). He names the very place itself as "thug-central" ("den of thieves"). And, for the day, reinstates its primal role as refuge for the marginal (the lame and blind and loud street urchins, who immediately begin hawking his audacity; Lk. 19:46; Mt. 21:14–16).

And here, we might say, the Samaritan parable finds its deep hermeneutic. If empire, by any realistic account, is itself merely legalized piracy, then the raw "muggery" of the road (in the parable) is merely emblem of the entire situation. The "cave of robbers" epithet had most immediate reference, in the discourses of the day, to the renegade bands of displaced poor, holed up in the grottos and caverns lacing the hills of Galilee, or the bluffs above the Dead Sea, whose outlaw raids and "turf gang" tolls were notorious. But Jesus sideswipes the epithet to "send up" the Temple situation and "throw down" a central challenge to the system of stigma and plunder. His "mob" enacts an exorcism of place, exposing the religious–intellectual–economic alliance (priests, scribes, and elders) as a kind of Temple–synagogue–agribusiness syndicate, ramifying colonial relations by imposing debt-slavery on an increasingly displaced peasantry, forcing desperate choices and predatory action as the condition of survival "on the street" (or back-country road). The purity discourses—policing access to the holy place and leveraging tithes and sacrificial offerings "upward"—licensed the take and demonized the taken-from. If such a stigma was to be exploded, its shame broken, and its system revealed, verbal assault in the rural outback (as seen in the Sermon on the Plain) would scarcely suffice.

The need was, rather, to lead ostracized bodies into the very heart of maximal exclusion, name the game, open the pain for uncensored expression, proclaim a different regime of truth and value, give sharp voice to the shared anger, and face the likely arrest (or even, the swords or "nails") that might come in consequence. The reading so constructed suggests the Temple-action was the necessary apex of Jesus' prophetic pedagogy. In a sense, it was that towards which his entire ministry pointed as the inevitable place of a final polemic. It embodied, not just in his own individual persona but in the movement collectivity he orchestrated, a dramatic reversal of the organizing tropes of shame and exclusion exactly at the central symbolic site of the time—both shrine and bank—that concentrated the loot and pontificated the rationale. But was it successful in effecting the release it promised?

Such a question cannot be decided inside the text, but rests with any of us who still "read." For the record, followers huddled in fear in the near term, but quickly found their sea legs immediately after the days of terror, and just as quickly returned to the site of sharpest contention. In the Lukan take (in the Book of Acts), Galilean peasant rubes like Peter and John find voice—and trouble—right back in the Temple theater of things political, once convinced the messianic upsurge cannot be contained by grave-stones and lies. And the movement in short order embraces the alternative organization of goods[9] and codes and hunkers down for a long fight. Despite its continual buy-off and large-scale capitulation to imperial seduction and demand over the ensuing centuries—and, indeed, a millennial history of cooperation in genocide and slavery, witch-burning and colonial plunder—the question remains insistent and Sphinx-like. It is ours to answer.

Becoming the Samaritan

But first there is one last polemic worth contemplating among the gospel tactics of code-switching and dramatic confrontation. In John's gospel, Jesus' last Temple appearance is the scene of a rhetorical showdown that points up the stakes and import of his symbolic sit-in action. John, too, will center the question of thievery in this particular social geography. Chapter 10 unfolds a figurative discourse around shepherds and robbers whose implication is clear: it is not disparaged herders who constitute the real threat of pillage, but the leaders whose haunt is the holy place. Though cast in cryptic metaphor, this is John's version of the "cave of robbers" send-up that we find in the synoptics. But in John it issues directly from a Temple riposte whose anvil of contention is the supposed shame and implication of being Samaritan. Chapter 8 captures the polemic in a public debate between Jesus and leadership elites on the Temple grounds, just before his fate is sealed.

In the exchange outlined there, this stock stigma suddenly peeks briefly up from the basement of social relations and is just as quickly eclipsed in a deft deconstruction by a manic messiah. Like MCs in battle-mode, or street players engaging in a high-stakes game of "signifying,"[10] capping on respective mother-lines, Jesus and an elite officialdom bent on his arrest square off and spit their diss rhymes—though actually, the setting in the Temple is only one step removed from the courtroom, and the targeted pedigree in this case is the "father." Genealogy is the contention, relation to Abraham the question, demonic inspiration the charge, capital punishment the intention laid bare. At the climax of the contestation, Jesus is "served" with a charge straight from a "hidden transcript" of the elites: does he not harbor a Samaritan blood-line and thus suffer from "demon possession"? This is in response to his own allegation about them. He has denied the elites' claim of descent through Abraham by conceding the truth of their claim biologically, while simultaneously denying any implied spiritual kinship with that vaunted patriarch, in view of their intent to kill (him and others). They are, rather, "of their father, the devil" (Jh, 8: 44). Now, as they reciprocate the accusation, the shrewdness of the representation comes fully to the fore. In response to their cross-weaving of Samaritan genes and diabolical schemes of influence (Jh. 8:48)—"if you are Samaritan you must be harboring a demon"—Jesus is represented as refusing the spirit-side of the equation. He contends that he is not "possessed." But tellingly, he *refuses to refuse* the label Samaritan. The silence here is golden ... and provocative. In combating the way a category of ethnicity supposedly implies complicity with the underworld and its terrors, Jesus assents to *inclusion in the ethnic designation*. He will not repudiate being thought of as "Samaritan." What he won't do is accept the implied vilification. He breaks the equation. What in Luke's Good Samaritan parable he throws up as startling exemplar for Jewish behavior, here he allows to come home to himself. Not only does he lock down the Temple mount for a day, he occupies that space as a default "Samaritan"!

And in this category-crossing—pointing toward a scandalous social practice of trespassing ethnic boundaries and political meanings—there lurks a subtle Christological implication. Not only do the gospels give us, as Cone has so powerfully argued, a Jewish messiah whose bio-cultural particularity and ethno-political oppression in first-century Palestine imply that, theologically—in modern-day America—Jesus *must be black* (among other possible subaltern significances the messianic Spirit might be said to haunt, such as Latino, woman, gay, indigenous, etc.). But further, we can say, he is represented in the gospels as having been willing to be inscribed, as a Jew, into an even more stigmatized ethno-political category when occasion warranted—refusing the pejorative associations that Jews might be tempted to take up to leverage their own Jewish marginality as "at least, thank God, *not* 'Samaritan!'" Though already himself facing subjugation and stigmatization as a Jew, when crunch time comes, he does not flinch. If pushed, he will plunge even further into opprobrium in calling out the system. This is a Jewish Jesus *who is also willing to be identified as* Samaritan. And whatever such might mean for one who is already black, for whites, it represents heavy food for thought—especially and precisely for those whites tempted to think, "Cone's black Jesus is well and good for the black community, but has nothing to do with me as white." Cone himself has been clear from the beginning about his use of the category of blackness, that it might include even "black people in white skins," as he says in his first book (Cone, 1989, p.3). For him, it is a *theological*—not merely or simply biological—category of race. It stands as a cipher for—as well as material location of—oppression. And it implies that whites—no matter how fraught the enterprise—must dare to cross over "into" blackness at some real level of political alliance and shared jeopardy, if they are to claim true access to the God of this tradition. (Indeed, the contemporary analogy might be something on the order of whites faced with the demands of active solidarity with an African American Protestant leader risking arrest or worse in leading a White House sit-in against banking policy or the wars in Iraq or Afghanistan, who is him- or herself facing vilification as a terrorist sympathizer or covert Muslim.) Whatever marks out impurity and ostracism marks out the place of a necessary embrace and even "immersion."

What Jesus is doing: the Social Forum and Chase Bank

Fast-forward two millennia. So what is Jesus doing today? My own answer, as is already obvious, is once again beholden to Cone's vision. Writing in the late 1960s, he insisted that Christology of the day in the USA found deepest echo and most trenchant salience in the Black Power movement (Cone, 1989, p.1). And he offered it directly in the face of white equivocation. The central message of Jesus to America of the late twentieth century was to be found not in churches white or brown, but in the movement that refused to back down from confrontation. For Cone, it was the combination of Martin and Malcolm—as both those names were ciphers for continuous public action—that most cogently articulated the meaning of Jesus for the emergency of the hour (Cone, 1991, pp.273, 280, 290). Black Power—stepping beyond the integration–aspiration that might grudgingly grant provisional access into the institutions and rights of whiteness for some dark bodies—leaned deeply into an alternative vision and economy, given programmatic expression in Panther discipline and compassion, and popular foreshadowing in a new level of public pride in being black. Certainly the movement was compromised at the core—shot through with sexist hubris and homophobic rancor—but nonetheless, a gesture towards something more than reigning white power could countenance. For the first time[11] in the republic's gory history, an explicitly non-white possibility of being human was asserted, collectively and politically, in the public square and there, in the full glare of a livid national media, refused either to move or to stay silent. Closed fist and thunder-cloud 'fro remained uncowed and defiant. The movement—in both its Civil Rights and Black Power rites of public passage—had effectively cut loose the centuries-long knot of threat "noose-ing" black heads in a silencing memory of terror and shame. "Black" stepped out into the streets shrewdly proud, publicly beautiful, and named "the great white ugly" out loud and to its face. And though forced to pay harsh prices ever since, that genie has never been returned to the bottle!

Today a new movement is afoot—or really a movement of movements. From my own modest perch inside the poster-child of de-industrialization and core city blight, I offer testament to a glimpse of an entire planet refusing the siren-song of white comfort and propriety. I write from Detroit, Michigan—whose hardcore inner-city streets and hardscrabble populace have been my place of abode and schoolhouse of initiation and training for a quarter century now. In June of 2010, the prototypical black metropolis of the country stepped forward into a preview of the future by hosting the United States Social Forum. The event was a regional version of the World Social Forum, begun in 2001 in Porto Alegre, Brazil as successor initiative to the large-scale street protests attending gatherings of world leaders (such as the WTO or OAS [Organization of American States]) ever since the (in)famous "Battle in Seattle" in 1999 began raising sharp issue with the neoliberal agenda championed by those elite policy-making bodies. (The latter "alter-globalization battle" had itself emerged from the resistance gauntlet thrown down by the Zapatista Movement in challenge to the priorities of the North American Free Trade Association in 1994.) After the Seattle crowd (as large as 100,000, according to some estimates) effectively closed out WTO deliberations that year, subsequent mass demonstrations had drawn down increasingly heavy-handed police response, and grass-roots coalitions of activists decided in 2001 to develop their own counter-forum to reimagine the world from the ground up. Attracting on average 100,000 people per event from a vast array of oppositional engagements, the forums have enfleshed a vision of Martin King's Beloved Community beyond anything he could have imagined—everything from labor union and Gay Pride organizers to feminist raconteurs and anti-racism ranters, from deep-ecology renegades and anarcho-primitivist animists to war resisters and neo-Marxist theorists, alter-globalization activists and Third World farmers making common cause with street-theater performance artists and spoken-word poets, alternative media inventors using hip-hop rhymes and punk sensibilities to promote community-gardening pioneers and disability-rights champions, alongside religious leaders singing down Jubilee and sunshine and sending up *suras* and chants—and all of it led by indigenous rights leaders and peoples of color of every hue (Perkinson, 2011, pp.11–12).

The Detroit Forum was only the second U.S. regional gathering of its kind (Atlanta in 2007 pioneered the first) and drew 20,000 to the hot streets of Motown for the June throw-down of workshops and performances, skills-trading and networking, send-up celebrations and cool-off story-telling in bars and bistros after each day of hard-pursued exchange. The choice to locate the Forum in this epicenter of the industrial revolution was both cautionary and encouraging. Detroit has been undergoing outsourcing of plants and jobs and people since the 1950s and stands as a stark emblem of the destructive outcome of neoliberal policy priorities (Boggs et al., 2011, pp.105–11). It also stands as an icon of a hopeful future of re-localizing and human-scale organizing, in having incubated, over recent years, all manner of close-to-the-ground experiments in community urban farming, do-it-yourself (DIY) media construction and broadcast technologies, and street-art embellishing blight with beauty using the detritus and refuse of the city as its palette and canvas. The Forum is by constitution a space for incubation of vision and stimulation of dialogue and not of policy generation or action, but is also accompanied by a tandem set of meetings (People's Movement Assemblies) designed to craft policy calls and hatch various forms of intervention or campaigns for change. And here is the rub for this writing.

One such action that I participated in (planning for months prior to the actual Forum and now continuing afterward) initiated a rally during the Forum of some 800 people, conjoining faith and labor leaders in particular, marching from a downtown church to the door of Chase Manhattan Bank, calling for a two-year moratorium on foreclosures in Detroit (as well as demanding that Chase use its capitalization influence over R.J. Reynolds Tobacco Co. to leverage a negotiating meeting with the Farm Labor Organizing Committee, seeking to challenge the slave-labor practices of North Carolina growers importing undocumented workers from Mexico every year to work the fields under heavy duress and impossible conditions). Obviously, the so-called "sub-prime crisis" has been far from an equal-opportunity debacle, targeting, as it did, highly disproportionate numbers of blacks and Latinos,[12] and leveraging the largest transfer of wealth in the history of the country from the lower levels of society to the top tier (not exclusively a re-arrangement out of communities of color and into those identified as white, but not inconsequentially effecting that kind of transfer either). In Detroit, in particular, the foreclosure process has been working hand in glove with numerous allied initiatives of gentrification, rendering housing cheap for young "cultural creatives" bearing university pedigrees and white visages, closing down public schools in favor of privatized charters, mobilizing foundation dollars in service of plans for a "right-sized" city, cleansed of homelessness and poverty and street crime, gated in propriety, secured in "eye-in-the-sky" technology, and clubbing in postmodern venues of minstrelsy (hip-hop and techno flavors in the parties and galleries). In resisting such, a number of us (lighter and darker hued) prepared to do civil disobedience if Chase refused to meet, and committed to a national campaign of disinvestment from Chase, should the negotiations that our action sought to open prove fruitless.

The action was heady at the moment—a face-off with the preeminent power of our time, orchestrating ongoing pillage of public assets into private control by way of financial manipulation around the globe. Grabbing arms in a tight circle at the bank's door, eye-to-eye with the dark-blue-suited core of Detroit's finest, who cordoned off egress, it was easy to imagine a twenty-first-century Jesus taking the next step— crashing the entry, leaping desks, throwing down computers, convening a kneeling prayer circle for an hour in the lobby with that 800-fold following. Of course, well-trained police would try to keep such a scene out on the steps and the result would undoubtedly be blood in the streets and bodies in the jail (but then that is the result anyway, by the more covert means already tracked above). ... But the bank opted, rather, to stall and to offer promise of meeting later in the summer. The crowd had little recourse but to assent to the bank's small show of good "faith"—certain that it was mere tactic but needing nonetheless to honor the public ritual in kind and allow for negotiation by winding up the action short of initiating a sit-in. The corporate media proved itself faithful accomplice in keeping the action "private"—not a single minute of exposure on prime time, or any other time, local or national.

Today, more than a year later, we are in full swing of a national campaign calling for a massive response to bail *out of* Chase, since negotiations have gone nowhere and there is no large-scale fest on the horizon comparable to the Social Forum celebration to gather a crowd and perhaps gain broad attention. And so it all feels likely to be about as effective an attempt to interrupt imperial business-as-usual as the gesture of a renegade band in a small shrine in out-of-the-way Palestine in the first century. As was (and is) the case with the gospel of Mark, in particular, the ending here is a non-resolution, an open space of longing and pain, begging further response. ... Opting for a willingness to engage in civil disobedience did little, in the moment, to change the juggernaut of evictions, but it certainly served as a small test for clarification of one's own existence. How far would one be willing to go to interrupt "white" business as usual?

(In)Conclusion

The issue that the moratorium campaign invokes remains compelling. Who will dare refuse the silence so ruthlessly maintained by policy and authority around the mechanisms of domination of our time—and do so with their bodies on the line, alongside of the bodies already being rendered homeless and disappeared? The question of the chapter here is not merely or primarily one of "reading a text," but of engaging a situation. Discerning where "Jesus" is at work on the contemporary scene is no more obvious than it was under Roman rule. It does not come with a clear label, but in outlaw form against the reigning order of oppression and killing. Catching its significance requires *active* discernment of a spirit inside a movement *already* in motion, with no guarantees that the discernment is correct. It takes a savvy "sussing out" of the way labels manage structures in the current context and requires courageous intervention in public actions probing the operative "Powers" for weakness and exposure. I take for granted that "Jesus" is already on the front lines, under many guises, teaching, story-telling, cursing and blessing, acting outrageously … and is already surrounded, or being led(!) by intrepid ones who have broken through the shame and fear—offering their bodies and spirits in enthusiastic resolve to get in the way, name, refuse, dance, party, and practice otherwise! (not least in the last year, for example, in certain sectors of the so-called "Arab Spring"). I see already in motion a postmodern version of that Palestinian enterprise, re-creating a "multitude"[13] in disciplines of gift-exchange and do-it-yourself innovation, taking risks, bellowing and laughing, putting bodies on the line in ways small and not-so-small. The "text" of their offering is no more perfect than the gospels' witness is infallible. And their movement of "another world happening"[14] has no more of a monopolistic grasp of right behavior or univocal claim to truth than did the movement that issued from the Galilee–Jerusalem initiative of first-century peasants rallied around their upstart prophet. The burden remains for all of us to stammer and grope, choose and work and die, inside the upwelling possibilities of our day.

What does appear clearly peculiar to our time is the hegemonic thrall of a light/dark binary of meaning, reigning like a global pall of sanction and blindness over the ongoing dance of wealth and death. Under its mists and mystification, a world has lately been divided—roughly, according to color. The question it implies for faith, however, is old and patent. How to interrupt the silence? How to break the code attending the pallor—"outing" the norms of propriety, challenging the presumption of entitlement, opening up the domestication of emotion, breaking down the restriction of boundaries, refusing the seduction of distraction, and halting the flow of accumulation? The response it demands is not doctrinaire confession, but a continuing improvisation. The major gauntlet I wish to throw down for those of us who look like me is simply this—that improvisation is already in motion! Will we plunge in like those flocking to John in the Judean desert of an earlier empire, go down into the turmoil, come up experimental, reconstitute a local commons, and join in the multi-hued and multi-faceted efforts to shatter the stigma? Or hold back in suspicion and stake our hope in a fantasy of purity (inside a lifestyle, a national border, a doctrine, an economic ideology)? "Whiteness" today is largely the cautionary approach to world suffering—afraid to risk its stockpile of stolen goods or fictive status as meritorious—when faced with all the bodies by the side of the road (supine and angry in ghettos and prisons, refugee and immigrant across borders, desperate and strapped down in "Third Worlds," etc.). It prefers to cross to the other side of the road and await a second coming. But there is no "second." There is only a first one—which began long before Jesus twinkled in Mary's eye and continues far outside any monolithic creed of belief. *That* "Presence" has never ceased happening—led now, as then, largely by visionaries of color[15]—in movements large and small, all around us. It is up to us to step up … and in.

Notes

1 See Jared Diamond's description of religion once it begins serving larger-scale social orders (Diamond, 1997, p.269).

2 See the work of Jon Michael Spencer in discussing what might be called "the racial politics of penetration" (Spencer, 1991, p.1; 1995, pp.166, 171; Perkinson, 2010, pp.197, 206).

3 "Playing the dozens" references African American practices of "signifying," initiating a ritual exchange of insults "capping on" or putting down the mother-line of an opponent's genealogy.

4 See Myers's discussion, emphasizing that while the Greek words for "sin" (*hamartia*) and "debt" (*opheileema*) are different, in the Aramaic of Jesus they are one and the same word. Even more tellingly, in New Testament Greek, the same verb (*aphiemi*) renders both "forgiveness" of sin and "release" of debt (Myers, 2001, p.24).

5 In Mark's gospel, this threesome only begins to be invoked (as the institutional coalition that will conspire to secure his demise) once Jesus sets his course for the capital city and begins to prepare his inner circle for what will happen after his Temple action (Mk. 8:31).

6 See the clear association of "crowds" and "accursed" in Jh. 7:49.

7 See Horsley's discussion of the "oppositional emotion" and popular resentment, resulting from suffered indignities, that provided the infrastructure for Jesus' ritual actions in restoring the covenant relations among the peasantry (Horsley, 2011, pp.160, 176).

8 The reference is to the way in which Michel de Certeau has differentiated "place" and "space." Place is the provenance of strategies of domination; in its operation, dominating forms of power constellate, secure, and attempt to valorize a particular location. On the other hand, the tactics of resistance are more opportunistic; subordinate powers seize spaces in momentary takeovers that usually must be quickly abandoned (de Certeau, 1984, pp.xiv, xix, 35–39).

9 As Acts makes clear, the early church took Sabbath–Jubilee seriously as a practical ethic of living, pooling assets and making lands into a kind of communally shared "commons" (Acts 2:43–47, 4:32–37).

10 See the work of Henry Louis Gates, Jr. in his 1988 book *The Signifying Monkey* for a dense unpacking of African American traditions of using nimble rhetoric to escape or displace the epistemic violence of oppression (Gates, 1988, pp.45, 54, 75, 79–80).

11 Certainly many other modes of living have struggled for air in our national polity— beginning with pre-contact social orders of native communities that never ceased to struggle for their right to be, separate from the defining constraints of European legal codes or "doctrine of discovery" usurpations of sovereignty (Newcomb, 2008, pp.xxiii, 129–30). Indeed, "tri-cultural isolate" communities of maroons, natives, and disaffected whites, like the Seminole "Indians" of South Florida fame, quickly emerged (and were just as quickly submerged), in our national history, as prophetic foreshadowings of the kind of cross-cultural alliances now becoming requisite simply for survival's sake, as a species (Loewen, 1995, pp.107–8, 126–27, 151). These clearly gave public embodiment to an alternative reality and fought the dominant social order as evil and unjust, but did not have the technology of mass media to name or counter the domination in a way that confronted the entire white community with a compelling image of something it could not control. Arguably, the Black Freedom Movement successfully invoked and significantly challenged a broadly shared white terror whose recriminatory reactions have not ceased up to the present.

12 See, for instance, the analysis of Tim Wise in his book *Colorblind: The Rise of Post-Racial Politics and the Retreat from Racial Equity* (Wise, 2010, pp.97–101).

13 To invoke the category constructed by Michael Hardt and Antonio Negri in their recent writings on empire (Hardt and Negri, 2009, pp.x–xi, 39–55).

14 The watchword of the 2010 United States Social Forum was "Another world is possible, another US is necessary, another Detroit is happening!"

15 Though the occasional John Brown does appear.

References

Boggs, Grace Lee, Glover, Danny, and Kurashige, Scott. 2011. *The Next American Revolution: Sustainable Activism for the Twenty First Century*. Berkeley: University of California Press.

Borg, Marcus. 1994. *Meeting Jesus Again for the First Time: The Historical Jesus and the Heart of the Contemporary Faith*. San Francisco: HarperSanFrancisco.

Cone, James. 1991. *Martin and Malcolm and America: A Dream or A Nightmare*. Maryknoll: Orbis Books.

——. 1989 [1969]. *Black Theology and Black Power*. New York: Seabury Press, 1969; 20th anniversary reprint, San Francisco: Harper & Row.

——. 1975. *God of the Oppressed*. New York: Seabury Press.

de Certeau, Michel. 1984. *The Practice of Everyday Life*. Trans. S. F. Rendall. Berkeley: University of California Press.

Diamond, Jared. 1997. *Guns, Germs, and Steel: The Fates of Human Societies*. New York: W. W. Norton.

Du Bois, W. E. B. 1961. *The Souls of Black Folk*. New York: Fawcett Publications, Inc.

Gates, Henry Louis, Jr. 1988. *The Signifying Monkey: A Theory of Afro-American Literary Criticism*. New York: Oxford University Press.

Hardt, Michael and Negri, Peter. 2009. *Commonwealth*. Cambridge, MA: The Belknap Press of Harvard University Press.

Harris, Cheryl. 1993. "Whiteness as Property." *Harvard Law Review*. Vol. 108, No. 6.

Horsley, Richard A. 2011. *Jesus and the Powers: Conflict, Covenant, and the Hope of the Poor*. Minneapolis, MN: Fortress Press.

Horsley, Richard A. and Hanson, John S. 1985. *Bandits, Prophets, and Messiahs: Popular Movements at the Time of Jesus*. San Francisco: Harper & Row.

Loewen, James W. 1995, 2007. *Lies My Teacher Told Me: Everything Your American History Textbook Got Wrong*. New York: Touchstone.

Myers, Ched. 2001. *The Biblical Vision of Sabbath Economics*. Washington, DC: Church of the Savior.

——. 1988. *Binding the Strong Man: A Political Reading of Mark's Story of Jesus*. Maryknoll, NY: Orbis Books.

Newcomb, Steven T. 2008. *Pagans in the Promised Land: Decoding the Doctrine of Christian Discovery*. Golden, CO: Fulcrum Publishing.

Perkinson, James W. 2011. "The 2010 US Social Forum as Sign of Martin King's Beloved Community: Ecumenism in the Hour of Planetary Crisis." *The Ecumenist*. Vol. 48, No. 2, Spring 2011, 8–15.

——. 2010. "Queering White Male Fear in the Mirror of Hip-Hop Erotics." In *The Embrace of Eros: Bodies, Desires, and Sexuality in Christianity*. Ed. M. D. Kamitsuka, Minneapolis, MN: Fortress Press, 197–213.

Pieris, Aloysius. 1987. "Speaking of the Son of God in Non-Church Cultures, e.g., in Asia," *An Asian Theology of Liberation*. Maryknoll, NY: Orbis Books.

Spencer, Jon Michael. 1995. *The Rhythms of Black Folk: Race, Religion and Pan-Africanism*. Trenton, NJ: Africa World Press, Inc.

——. 1991. "Introduction," *The Emergency of Black and the Emergence of Rap* (A special issue of *Black Sacred Music: A Journal of Theomusicology*). Ed. Jon Michael Spencer, Durham, NC: Duke University Press, 1–11.

Trocme, Andre. 2011. *Jesus and the Nonviolent Revolution*. Ed. C. E. Moore. New York: Plough Publishing House.

Wise, Tim. 2010. *Colorblind: The Rise of Post-Racial Politics and the Retreat from Racial Equity*. San Francisco: City Lights Books, 64–97.

10

JESUS, WHITENESS, AND THE DISINHERITED

William David Hart

> Jesus is the answer for the world today
> Above him there's no other
> Jesus is the way.
> > (A children's song)

> Traditionally, Christ-Myth theorists have argued that one finds a purely mythic conception of Jesus in the epistles and that the life of Jesus the historical teacher and healer as we read it in the gospels is a later historicization. This may indeed be so, but it is important to recognize the obvious: *The gospel story of Jesus is itself apparently mythic from first to last.*
> > (Price, 2000, p.260)

Introduction

In *White Like Me* (2008), Tim Wise, the wise provocateur on matters of white privilege, recalls the first time he raised the question of Jesus' whiteness before an audience of white Christians. In response to his provocation, the students at this Catholic college were quick to insist that Jesus' "race" was irrelevant, while vigorously resisting the invitation to imagine him as black. Their resistance gave the lie to their claim that Jesus' race is irrelevant. Their failure of imagination, indeed, their outright resistance to imagining a black Jesus, reveals just how deeply racial ideology[1] has affected the Christian imagination (Wise, 2008, pp.54–56). In this chapter, I take Howard Thurman's classic text, *Jesus and the Disinherited*, as pretext and context for thinking about Jesus and whiteness. I regard whiteness as a covering term for (a) the ideology of race, (b) the practices of racism, and (c) the residual structures of white supremacy. Without pretending to possess Charlie Parker's skills (and allowing for differences in media),

I attempt to "riff" on Thurman's account of Jesus in the way that Parker improvises on the popular song "Cherokee"—and to answer the question, "What would Jesus do (about whiteness)?"

Jesus and Blackamericans

If we construe the Jesus of popular piety, however well informed by elite opinion, as the "little tradition," then the "great tradition" regarding Jesus has three broad streams of interpretation: Christology, the quest for the historical Jesus, and "Jesus myth theory"—that is, agnosticism regarding the actual existence of a historical Jesus. Though dependent on these traditions, this chapter is not an act of scholarship within any of them. My account is an essay in cultural hermeneutics. I regard Jesus as a discursive object, a site of ideological contestation, and a form of cultural capital in a struggle of position among social groups.[2] The ongoing conflict around the residual (and/or reconstructed) phenomenon of racial ideology, structured by white supremacy, is an example of that struggle. In light of this conflict, what kind of signifier is Jesus? As a historical matter, I am skeptical of the relevance of Jesus' praxis to the problem of whiteness. Apart from Christology or an equally strong non-historical (mythological) interpretation, Jesus' praxis is largely irrelevant. To claim otherwise, it seems, would be anachronistic. Though shadowed by the "Christological capture" of the historical Jesus, I wonder whether Thurman (1976) provides an alternative. Consider the following remark:

> The significance of the religion of Jesus to people who stand with their backs against the wall has always seemed to me to be crucial. It is one emphasis which has been lacking—except where it has been a part of a very unfortunate cor-ruption of the missionary impulse, which is, in a sense, the very heart of the Christian religion. My interest in the problem has been and continues to be both personal and professional. This is the question which individuals and groups who live in our land always under the threat of profound social and psychological displacement face: Why is it that Christianity seems impotent to deal radically, and therefore effectively, with the issues of discrimination and injustice on the basis of race, religion and national origin? Is this impotency due to a betrayal of the genius of the religion, or is it due to a basic weakness in the religion itself?
>
> (p. 7)

Thurman presents the issues about as starkly as possible. Insofar as Christianity is an artifact of Greco-Roman, European, and Western culture, is its hostility to racial, religious, and national others inevitable or accidental? According to William Apel, "Thurman made an important distinction between the religion *of* Jesus and the religion *about* Jesus. He felt he could speak without the unnecessary burden of defending the doctrines and practices of historic Christianity" (Mitchell, 1990, p.70). This is a liberal Protestant view and suggests that Thurman has the same desire that motivates the quest for the historical Jesus: to get behind the accrued doctrines and practices of historic Christianity, the religion *about* Jesus, and access the religion *of* Jesus.[3] This is no easy task. Some critics claim that it is an impossible task. They insist that the Jesus we can know is a thorough artifact of Christology, the Jesus of faith, a wholly mythological figure (see Price, 2000). Thurman appears to disagree. Several decades of scholarship (seems to) vindicate his view.[4] Though not a historian, he casts his lot with the historical approach to the life and meaning of Jesus.

Thurman establishes parallels between the life of Jesus and the experiences of Blackamericans. As a Jew, Jesus was shaped by his ethnicity, as were Blackamericans; furthermore, he was poor and a member of a despised minority group dominated by a great imperial power. To use Thurman's preferred metaphor, their "backs were against the wall." Jews and Blackamericans were disciplined and punished. Thurman (1976) remarks that "This is the position of the disinherited in every age. What must be the attitude toward the rulers, the controllers of political, social, and economic life? This is the question of the Negro in American life" (p.23). It's a threshold question, an answer to which lies at the beginning of any act of accommodation or resistance. Under such circumstances, accommodation or resistance and the subtle shades between is an either-or choice; or, in the language of William James, a "forced option." Both Jews and Blackamericans were existentially involved in the choice they had to make: it was a "live choice," bearing down on them as collective and individual subjects. And this choice was "momentous": a matter of life and death.

Though I am drawing out explicitly what is only implicit in Thurman's account, he does note another parallel between the circumstances of Palestinian Jews during Jesus' lifetime and the condition of Blackamericans, that is, a cultural challenge to their very distinctiveness as a "nation," ethnos, or people of "common" natality. First-century Jews struggled to maintain their distinctiveness within the all-pervasiveness of the Roman Empire's Hellenistic culture and the pressure to assimilate. Blackamericans struggled to create and maintain a sense of peoplehood against an American identity that was historically predicated on their exclusion and/or subordinate inclusion. To be American was to be free and white; over time, the formulation "free and white" became redundant. Thus Blackamericans struggled against the exclusionary *and* assimilating power of what W.E.B. DuBois (1990) describes as "white Americanism" (p.9). Thurman uses the complexities of Jesus' social world to signify on the Blackamerican condition. Specifically, he examines the competing responses of various Jewish groups—Sadducees, Pharisees, Zealots, and the Jesus Movement—to the challenge that was Rome. He draws a sharp distinction between resistance and nonresistance, while allowing for shades of difference within those categories. In Thurman's schema, Herod and the Sadducees are assimilationists. Where Herod assimilates completely, mimicking Roman ways in minute detail, capitulating in every respect to the Empire and its demands, the Sadducees, despite their true love of Israel (but they loved security even more), are mitigated assimilationists (Thurman, 1976, 23–24). In contrast, the Pharisees are passive resisters; their resistance takes the form of a terrible contempt of all things Roman. Strong anti-assimilationists, they seek to isolate themselves from Roman influence while cultivating the purity of their traditions. The Pharisees' form of resistance (contempt of Roman authority, and efforts to keep their traditions pure) is just shy of active resistance; indeed, Thurman argues, it may be regarded "as an appositive dimension of resistance." Though Thurman has all forms of nonresistance in mind when referring to this apposition or "near resistance," it seems especially apropos of the Pharisees and their contempt. "Obviously such an attitude is a powder keg. One nameless incident may cause to burst into flame the whole gamut of smoldering passion, leaving nothing in its wake but charred corpses, mute reminders of the tragedy of life. Jesus saw this and understood it clearly" (Thurman, 1976, p.25).

The Zealots fully embraced this tragic dimension of life. They crossed the dividing line between nonresistance and resistance by arming themselves for bloody struggle against the Empire. The fact that fanaticism tinged their rebellion, Thurman argues, is not a vote against it. Though he acknowledges the point obliquely, he might have added explicitly that on some accounts Jesus was touched by fanaticism too, by the same persecution-induced certainty that characterized the Zealots. But Jesus chose a different form of resistance. On Thurman's interpretation, Jesus cultivated an intense inwardness (the "Kingdom of Heaven is in us") that was the optimum response for an oppressed people. Aware that his interpretation is counterintuitive, Thurman (1976) attempts to preempt critics by acknowledging that Jesus' response to Roman authority *appears* to be an act of capitulation if not betrayal: "a kind of groveling and stark cowardice," self-deception, whistling in the dark. In opposition to that reading, he places a lot of weight on Jesus' "inwardness":

> He recognized with authentic realism that anyone who permits another to determine the quality of his inner life gives into the hands of the other the keys to his destiny. If a man knows precisely what he can do to you or what epithet he can hurl against you in order to make you lose your temper, your equilibrium, then he can always keep you under subjection. It is a man's reaction to things that determines their ability to exercise power over him.
>
> *(p.28)*

I have difficulty seeing how Jesus' inwardness is different, more transformative and revolutionary than, say, a Stoic—"you can kill my body but not my soul"—kind of inwardness. According to Thurman (1976), Jesus' inwardness funds "the work of redemption for all cast-down people in every generation and in every age." This reference to "redemption," he argues, apart from any theological or meta-physical interpretation, is literal. I take this to mean that he uses redemption in its original (pre-theological) "political sense" as liberation from slavery, debt, and other human-all-too-human forms of oppression (pp.28–29).

In light of his reflections on the complexities of Jesus' Jewish history, Thurman (1976) remarks: "The striking similarity between the social position of Jesus in Palestine and that of the vast majority of American Negroes is obvious to anyone who tarries long over the facts. We are dealing here with conditions that produce essentially the same psychology. There is meant no further comparison" (p.34). In both cases, an oppressive denial of citizenship, where both inclusion and exclusion are abusive, produces a problem of creative survival. The Jesus Movement in first-century Palestine was one response. The Blackamerican freedom movement, under different circumstances, is another response.

The Jewish/black dyad

Howard Thurman published *Jesus and the Disinherited* in 1949 on the cusp of the Supreme Court's 1954 *Brown* v. *Board of Education* decision that ushered in one of the most spectacular periods in the long civil rights movement. Though it is clearly a precursor of black liberation theology that emerged in the late 1960s, Vincent Harding argues in the preface that Thurman's text should not be reduced to that theological development. In any case, Thurman's interpretation of Jesus seems compelling. But what compels some repels others: Jesus is a fiercely contested signifier. Consider the following: "At noon on Saturday, May 6, 1939," ten years before Thurman published his text, "a group of Protestant theologians, pastors and churchgoers" in Nazi Germany celebrated the inaugural meeting of the Institute for the Study and Eradication of Jewish Influence on German Church Life. In *The Aryan Jesus*, Susannah Heshel (2008) remarks:

> Rejecting Jesus's Jewishness and defining him as Aryan was about not only redefining Christianity, but racializing Europe: reassuring Europeans that they were white. Images of Jesus were crucial to racism in establishing the primary criterion of whiteness: Christ himself. It is not the Caucasian male who was the model of the authentic white man, but rather an idealized "White Man," namely Christ. For the European male to define himself as a "white man" he had to fantasize himself as Christ, a Christ who had to be imaged not as a Jew but as Aryan. Deleuze writes, "If the face is in fact Christ ... then the first deviances, the first divergence-types, are racial: yellow man, black man, men in the second or third category ... They must be Christianized, in other words, facialized. European racism as the white man claims has never operated by exclusion, or by the designation of someone as Other. ... Racism operates by the determination of degrees of deviance in relation to the White-Man face. ..." Yet by converting to Christianity, blacks did not become white, any more than Jews became Aryan.
>
> *(p.28)*

At the heart of Christianity, Heshel discerns a supersessionist desire to appropriate and displace the Jewish history, texts, and imaginary on which it depends. From Marcion in the second century through the contemporary period, persistent efforts to "dejudaize" Christianity are evident. In the very act of affirming Jesus as messiah, traditional Jewish interpretations are displaced. In constructing Christian texts as New, Jewish texts are rendered Old; thus "fulfilled," their centrality and authority are superseded. Heshel (2008) remarks that "Within the Christian theological economy, the conflict [between Jewish origins and Christian supersessionism] reached a crisis with the emergence of modern racism and the dangers and desires of miscegenation that were racism's central trope" (pp.26–27). Lest we succumb to the "tired argument that racism is about biology," Heshel underscores the racist perception that body and spirit are indissoluble, that the former endangers the latter, and that, as sites of moral degeneracy, the two are isomorphic. Modern racist discourse constructs a mirroring relationship between body and spirit that channels the "body-soul dilemma at the heart of Christian metaphysics" and Western philosophy. Racist discourse (with its dominant black–white polarity) reinscribes the classical Christian distinction between Judaic carnality and Christian spirituality (Heshel, 2008, pp.23–24).

Within the thought world defined by the "white problem," whiteness replicates spirit, blackness replicates carnality. On this reading, there is no simple way of insulating Jesus—as historical figure or as Christ, an object of faith—from the apparatus of whiteness. The ideology of race, the practices of racism, and the structures of white supremacy, that is, the apparatus of whiteness, are predicated (in a double sense) on a Jewish–black dyad: *Jesus is simultaneously ethnically deracinated and racialized*; he becomes an Aryan, the prototypical white man, and *Jews are associated racially* with black people.

Jesus and the "elevator effect"

In the brilliant first chapter of *Black Bodies, White Gazes*, George Yancy (2008) describes the following scenario:

> Well dressed, I enter an elevator where a white woman waits to reach her floor. She "sees" my Black body, though not the same one I see reflected back to me from the mirror on any number of occasions. Buying into the myth that one's dress says something about the person, one might think that the markers of my dress (suit and tie) should ease her tension. What is it that makes the markers of my dress inoperative? She sees a Black male body "saturated with meaning, as they [Black bodies] have been relentlessly subject to [negative] characterization by newspapers, newscasters, popular film, television programming, public officials, policy pundits and other agents of representation." Her body language signifies, "Look, *the* Black!" On this score, though short of a performative locution, her body language functions as an insult.
>
> *(p. 4)*

In this section, I intend to read Jesus in relation to the phenomenological, existential, and psychological dynamics of the "elevator effect." I do so in further pursuit of the relevance, if any, of Jesus to the problem of whiteness. Now some might view this as a stretch, an anachronism, or, even worse, as blasphemous. On this pious view, Jesus is not subject to our categories. Obviously, I do not share this view and will not try to convince those who do. And while my analysis is a stretch, it is an appropriate kind of stretching and is hardly anachronistic, since bigotry characterized Jesus' social world every bit as much as ours. Obviously, my analysis has nothing to do with the actual presence or absence of elevator technology in first-century Palestine. Rather,

I shall be discussing the dynamics revealed by Yancy's account. Indeed, considering Jesus' social world and Jewish notions of purity and sacred space, we might translate the elevator effect as the "temple" or "purity effect."

According to the Jesus scholar Bruce Chilton (2000), "Purity was Jesus' fundamental commitment, the lens through which he viewed the world" (p.90). To use the phrase made famous by the anthropologist Mary Douglas, he saw things in terms of "purity and danger."[5] This purity–pollution economy was literally embodied in Jew and non-Jew. Romans (with their Hellenistic culture) and their Jewish collaborators such as Herod Antipas were particular vectors of impurity and danger. Jesus' view of who was pure and who was impure—that is, dangerous—was deeply ethnocentric. Like all of us with respect to some people and certain matters, Jesus was a bigot. Consider Chilton's (2000) account of Jesus' encounter with the Samaritan woman at the well. Jesus shared the widely held Galilean bias against Samaritans. "To the Jews (that is, the Judeans) the Samaritans were apostasy and defeat incarnate, a perfect example of what the people of God should not become: hopelessly mixed up with the Gentiles that the Assyrians and later conquerors settled in their land" (p.67). These mixed-up remnants of the "ten lost tribes" of Israel were objects of contempt. Again, Jesus shared that contempt. Now Jesus' bigotry should not surprise us. After all he was human-all-too-human: limited, imperfect, and fallible like everyone else. And when he encounters the Samaritan woman he cannot imagine her as being anything other than what his prejudice said she could be: a woman of ill repute, an adulterer if not a prostitute. If the white woman on Yancy's elevator could not see through the terministic screen of blackness to his specificity as *this particular black male* and not *the predatory black male of stereotype* that haunts the white imagination, then the ethnicity ("saturated with meaning") of the woman at the well obscured Jesus' view also. Let's forget for the moment that Jesus acted against his bigotry and consider the probable nature of his initial perception of the Samaritan woman.

One can imagine all the important elements of the "elevator effect" playing out in this encounter. Indeed, Chilton provides his own phenomenology of the encounter: hesitant, Jesus is surprised as he hears himself asking the woman for a drink of water; he registers her surprise at his request. Chilton describes the quality of her surprise as bemusement. The wonder of it all: a Jew asking a Samaritan for help, his very willingness to address her at all. Chilton (2000) imagines Jesus as curt in manner. Without a greeting or preamble of any kind, he issues a demand: "'Give me to drink'" (p.67). Taking both his ethnic and gender superiority for granted (a God-given right), he makes this demand in a cultural context where he had imbibed the wisdom of rabbis who taught that, as menstruants from birth, Samaritan women were eternally impure; that Samaritans of all genders were idolaters because they worshiped in a temple on Mount Gerizim and not in the one true temple in Jerusalem. Chilton establishes an interesting parallel between the impurity that Jews ascribed to Samaritans as *marginal outsiders* and Jesus' status as a *marginal insider*. Jesus was a *mamzer*: "an Israelite of suspect paternity." This category included the children of incest and anyone born of a "prohibited sexual union" (Chilton, 2000, pp.12–13). Such children were scandalous not because they were "illegitimate" (Jews were generally tolerant of premarital sex) but because their mothers were suspected of having sex with the wrong person. As a *mamzer*, Jesus was a "marginal" Jew, "second class," an outcast within Jewish society. "The doubts about the parentage of a Galilean accused of being a *mamzer*," Chilton adds, "paled in comparison to the suspicion with which Jews regarded Samaritans" (pp.67–68).

In a conjectural account of Jesus' (likely) reaction to the Samaritan woman, I turn to Frantz Fanon's *Black Skin, White Mask* (2008), where he captures the fearful reactions of a small (white) boy to the presence of a black man: "'Look, a Negro! *Maman*, a Negro!'" (p.93). In the following passage, Fanon (2008) elaborates on the phenomenology of the boy's perception:

> The Negro is an animal, the Negro is bad, the Negro is wicked, the Negro is ugly; look, a Negro; the Negro is trembling, the Negro is trembling because he is cold, the small boy is trembling because he is afraid of the Negro, the Negro is trembling with cold, the cold that chills his bones, the lovely little boy is trembling because he thinks the Negro is trembling with rage, the little boy runs to his mother's arms: "*Maman*, the Negro is going to eat me."
>
> *(p.93)*

Now imagine Samaritans in the role of the Negro and Jesus as the white boy. Visualize Jesus' hyper-vigilant body language as he reflexively attempts to keep himself "pure" in the presence of a Samaritan woman:

> The Samaritan is an animal, the Samaritan is bad, the Samaritan is mean, the Samaritan is ugly; look, a Samaritan woman, it's hot, the woman is faint because she is hot, Jesus is trembling because he fears that she is hot with an adulterer's if not a prostitute's iniquity and that she will contaminate him; fanning the heat, she seeks to quench her thirst, the hand of Jesus is trembling because he thinks that this impure, dangerous Samaritan woman is soliciting him or gesturing in contempt (and because he is unaware of his repressed sexual desire). Abba, he says to himself, will this woman, one of those "menstruants from the cradle," defile me?

The Samaritan woman recognizes an insult when she sees one. She can see Jesus visually "scaling" her body, constructing her as an adulterer: impure, unworthy, *the Samaritan woman of Jewish stereotype* and not as *this particular Samaritan woman* drawing water from a well. Of course, as a matter of fact, she might have conformed to this stereotype. But Jesus could have only assumed this to be true; he could not have known. The biblical text, however, with its hagiographic style, portrays Jesus as having supernatural foreknowledge of the woman's life, of already knowing that she was a serial adulterer. And yet, Jesus overcomes his bigotry sufficiently to solicit water from her and to extend the promise of the kingdom of God to all the children of Israel, even the despised Samaritans. But, as Chilton remarks, this victory over ethnocentrism is not complete. Jesus' sly if not rude comments about the woman's marital status "you have lived with five husbands, and the current man is not your husband" is an ethnocentric residue. She is doing what he expects *people like her* to do. "His deep conviction," Chilton (2000) adds, "that God was in the process of purifying and pouring out his Spirit on all of Israel, even Samaritans, did not completely wash away the cultural bias of his Galilean upbringing" (p.69). Jesus was not the first holy man to say unholy things, nor will he be the last. (Thoroughly androcentric, religious traditions, great and small, say comparatively little about holy women. But I do not think that gender materially affects the previous remark.)

Now let us compare explicitly Yancy's first-person account of his encounter with a white woman on an elevator and the Samaritan woman's encounter with Jesus at the well. Yancy (2008) claims that "Blackness functions as a stipulatory axiom from which conclusions can be drawn" (p.3). I think that this is clearly true, and he provides examples to support his claim. It seems equally clear to me that, for Jews of Jesus' time, "Samaritan" functioned the same way. Only a kind of pious prejudice prevents us from seeing what is obvious in the text, even though it was written by authors determined to present Jesus in a positive light.

Unlike the white woman on the elevator, Jesus *does* reorient his bodily performance toward the other, even if he cannot, on Chilton's account, completely reorient his cognitions or his verbal performance. Whether he comes out better, according to Yancy's criteria, is not clear, since Yancy (2008) calls for both cognitive and bodily reorientation (p.5). Unlike the white woman on the elevator, Jesus performs (on the somatic level) an act of bigotry-overcoming by accepting a drink of water from the Samaritan woman, thus cutting against ethnocentric prohibitions on Jewish–Samaritan interaction. Even though he retains bigoted ideas about Samaritans—women in particular, whether literally menstruating and adulterous or not—he violates a powerful taboo and pushes past deeply ingrained notions of purity and ethnocentric notions of superiority. This partially counts in favor of those who wish to argue that Jesus' praxis, as an example that can be appropriated and reconfigured, provides resources in the struggle against whiteness. This may be true, but I do not see his act as particularly remarkable. It merits praise, but we shouldn't be excessive in doing so. After all, if we hold Jesus to the same standards that Yancy holds the white woman on the elevator, where any account she gives of her bodily comportment becomes evidence of racism, then my account is far too generous. Closer scrutiny of Jesus' bodily comportment in the presence of the Samaritan woman might reveal all the ticks, tell-tale signs, and affects[6] that Yancy discerns in the white woman's response to his presence (p.5). On Yancy's criteria, the claim that the Samaritan woman, as I construct her, has "simply misread" Jesus' intentions does not hold. Her "privileged take on things" is no different than Yancy's take on his elevator encounter with the white woman (Yancy, 2008, p.6). Furthermore, if we compare Jesus' engagement with the Samaritan woman to contemporary antiracist white people, who have worked hard on both their racist cognitions and their bodily comportment toward black people, then they are ethically more advanced than him (relative to their historical circumstances and to his) and appear to be better than him.

Homi Bhabha (2004) interprets the encounter between the black man and the white boy as an artifact of colonialism (p.117). I want to extend Bhabha's account of colonialism and stereotyping to Jesus and the Samaritan woman. The stereotype—in one case, of a predatory, cannibalistic black man and in the other, of an adulterous, menstruating Samaritan woman[7]—does not lie in creating a false image that becomes the scapegoat for discriminatory acts. Bhabha (2004) argues that things are more ambivalent (and I would add ambiguous), with projections and introjections, "metaphoric and metonymic strategies, displacement, over-determination, guilt, [and] aggressivity" that both mask and split official and phantasmagoric knowledges in the very act of constructing the subject positions of racist discourse (p.117). Though this interpretation has much to recommend it (and though some of it is applicable to Jesus' encounter with the Samaritan woman), my appropriation of Bhabha's analysis does not quite work in regard to Jewish–Samaritan conflict, since they did not have a colonizer–colonized relationship. Nevertheless, the analogy does shed some light.

Jews and Samaritans were subordinate groups within the Roman Empire. They had an antagonistic relationship to the Roman imperium and to each other. In a real sense, the relations between Samaritans and Jews were undermined by the imperial practices of the Assyrian Empire in the eighth century B.C.E. According to historians, the Samaritans of Jesus' time were the remnants of the ancient Northern Kingdom of Israel, in whose territory the victorious Assyrians settled many non-Israelis who intermarried, interbred, and engaged in extensive cultural exchange with the remnants of the indigenous population. Israelis in the Southern Kingdom (Judea) regarded this "mixed" population with contempt. They saw them as impure and the vectors of religious error. After several centuries, during which Judeans themselves were subjugated by a series of imperial powers—Babylonia, Persia, Macedonia, the Seleucids, and Rome—the residents of the old Southern Kingdom, the Judeans (Jews), still regarded the Samaritans, remnants of the old Northern Kingdom, as beneath them. Rather than responding with compassion to the descendants of those victimized by Assyrian imperialism and making common cause with them against the Romans, Jews expressed contempt. The feeling was mutual. Samaritans were contemptuous of Jews. Both found reasons to despise the other, despite their common subjection to Rome. From this case, we might analogize to the antagonism between Blackamericans and Latinos (regardless of "racial" designation, immigration and/or citizenship status) as they compete and (sometime cooperate) for recognition and "free space" within the American imperium.

As was true with Samaritans, Jews, and Rome, there is a triangular relationship among Blackamericans, Latinos and the American Empire.[8] While there are obviously contextual differences between the two sets of triangular relations that qualify any claim I might make, in both cases mutual antagonism makes cooperative resistance difficult. Without denying the differences, it is still possible to consider a "structural" similarity, namely, the Jewish view that Samaritans were impure and the view held by many Blackamericans that Latinos, especially Mexicans, are "illegal aliens" or that their citizenship is otherwise suspect.[9] Claudia Sandoval (2009) describes the consequences as follows:

> The negative discourse on immigration in the mass media has shaped the interactions that Blacks and Latinos have with each other, particularly in

inner-city communities where many member[s] of both groups live. The mechanism through which racial power works has various implications in this debate: One, it strategically aligns African Americans with white Americans by recognizing them as American citizens. Two, African Americans have the advantage of *racial naturalization*—a form of belonging that is still exclusionary in nature, but is useful for putting into effect the first implication—while Latinos are continually *racially alienated* regardless of actual citizenship status. Combining these two implications can potentially have a strong impact on Black and Latino relations, leading to the reinforcement of the white power structure already in place.

Beyond platitudes, it is not clear what Jesus' ethic has to offer for problems such as Blackamerican-and-Latino conflict, which are partially funded by the ideology of race, the practices of racism, and the residual structures of white supremacy. This is especially true when we recall that Jesus struggled with a "Samaritan Problem"—his equivalent of the "Negro Problem" of white Americans and, as Claudia Sandoval might put it, the "Latino–Alien Problem" of Blackamericans. To reiterate, Jesus developed his disposition toward Samaritans within a context of imperial domination, mutual antagonism, ethnocentrism, and bigotry (much like the Blackamerican–Latino relationship). While there are reasons to admire Jesus, we should not exaggerate his virtues. In his encounter with the Samaritan woman, Jesus reminds us of the white American (racial) liberal who partially and with great ambivalence overcomes her bigotry. Lest I be misunderstood, it is not my intention to diminish the moral achievement of white liberals. Moral progress is difficult, slow, and fragile; reversals and backsliding are common. So I tend to evaluate white racial liberals highly, despite my own ambivalence toward them. Though their response to whiteness is hardly utopian, I see it as an important ethical–political achievement—and, quite possibly, as the best we can get, most of the time. (This judgment is a measure of my "mitigated realism.") Among Blackamericans, white racial liberals have long elicited an ambivalent, eyebrow-raising, and sarcastic response. Though frustrating in its partiality and ambiguous in results, I think that white liberals strike a genuine blow for racial justice. An ambivalent response to their ambivalence is appropriate. This same ambivalence toward Jesus is appropriate, especially when we consider appropriating his praxis—analytically rather than dogmatically—in the contemporary struggle against whiteness.

Given their despised status among Jews, the very notion of a "Good Samaritan" (like the "good black") is an oxymoron. The term encodes the presumption that Samaritans (like promiscuous black females and predatory black males) are, ordinarily, bad people. We should not forget these facts when attempting to draw ethical–political lessons regarding whiteness from the story of the Good Samaritan or from other examples in Jesus' storied life. Indeed, in the ongoing struggle against the ideology of race, the practices of racism, and the residual structures of white supremacy, (some) white liberals are a better resource than anything that the life of Jesus might offer.

Conclusion

Howard Thurman paints an arresting picture of Jesus as patron of the disinherited. This portrait seems to have some merit as long as we remember that the scope of Jesus' patronage was narrow and ethnocentric. In *The Incredible Shrinking Son of Man*, Robert Price (2003), the influential Jesus scholar, remarks: "We have arrived at the conclusion that the gospel tradition seems completely unreliable. That is, most of the sayings and stories alike seem to be historically spurious. If any of them should chance to be genuine, we can no longer tell" (p.349). If Price is right, then Jesus is virtually a fictional character, an artifact of the many ways that we have imagined him. Our knowledge of him is even less reliable than the knowledge we acquire from an autobiography, with its highly fictive narratives. Indeed, on the fictional–factual continuum, our knowledge of Jesus is closer to novelistic than to biographical. Apart from various Eros-driven interpretations (desiring faith and faithful desire), and insofar as there is evidence at all, there is nothing special about Jesus' praxis that speaks to the issue of whiteness. So: "What would Jesus do (about whiteness)?" If, as the competing, antag- onistic, and even diametrically opposed interpretive traditions suggest, Jesus is a creature of our desires, then he would act and speak ambiguously. Among other incarnations, he would appear as a patron of Thurman's disinherited *and* as a prototypical Aryan—that is, as a patron of those who dispossess, disinherit, and push others against the wall. The lyrics of the children's song that introduced this chapter notwithstanding, Jesus is not the answer to whiteness. He is a contested signifier, a site of struggle *for and against* the ideology of race, the practices of racism, and the residual structures of white supremacy.

Notes

1 For an influential analysis of race as an ideology see Barbara Fields (1990).
2 My use of "ideology" and "discourse" in the same breath may cause some eyebrows to rise. However, on this matter, I find that Edward Said's creative eclecticism better accounts for the evidence (like particles and waves in physics) than do either/or approaches.
3 In his magisterial study of Jesus, John Dominic Crossan remarks: "This book is about the historical Jesus and not about the history of earliest Christianity." See John Dominic Crossan (1992), p.422.
4 This consensus view is the foundation for Bruce Chilton, *Rabbi Jesus: An Intimate Biography* (2000). I rely heavily on this "biography" in my analysis.
5 See Mary Douglas, *Purity and Danger: An Analysis of the Concepts of Pollution and Taboo* (1988). In this classic text, Douglas analyses several concepts of pollution, including those in Leviticus. Undoubtedly, the "Rabbi Jesus" whom Chilton describes was fully aware of the Levitical codes regarding pollution and taboo.
6 One probable exception to Yancy's account is the fear of sexual assault. While the woman on the elevator may have had such a fear, no matter how unjustified, Jesus is unlikely to have had a comparable fear.
7 The latter case is my interpolation. The logic of his analysis, I am arguing, applies to his example and mine.
8 Some object to the claim that the United States is an empire.
9 This is not to suggest that Blackamerican–Latino conflict is a "black problem." Whether American-born or immigrants, and often irrespective of their racial designation, Latinos share a racist formation that places blacks of all nationalities at the bottom of the racial hierarchy.

References

Bhabha, Homi. 2004. *The Location of Culture*. New York: Routledge Classics.

Chilton, Bruce. 2000. *Rabbi Jesus: An Intimate Biography*. New York: Image Books.

Crossan, John Dominic. 1992. *The Historical Jesus: The Life of a Mediterranean Jewish Peasant*. San Francisco: HarperSanFrancisco.

Douglas, Mary. 1988. *Purity and Danger: An Analysis of the Concepts of Pollution and Taboo*. London: Routledge.

Du Bois, W.E.B. 1990. *The Souls of Black Folk*. New York: Vintage Books, 1990.

Fanon, Frantz. 2008 (1967). *Black Skin, White Masks*. New York: Grove Press.

Fields, Barbara. 1990. "Slavery, Race and Ideology in the United States of America," *New Left Review*, CLXXXI (May/June), 95–118.

Heshel, Susannah. 2008. *The Aryan Jesus: Christian Theologians and the Bible in Nazi Germany*. Princeton, NJ: Princeton University Press.

Mitchell, Mozella G. (ed.), 1990. *The Human Search: Howard Thurman and the Quest for Freedom, Proceedings of the Second Annual Thurman Convocation*. New York: Peter Lang.

Price, Robert M. 2000. *Deconstructing Jesus*. Amherst, NY: Prometheus Books.

——. 2003. *The Incredible Shrinking Son of Man: How Reliable is the Gospel Tradition?* New York: Prometheus Books.

Sandoval, Claudia. 2009. "Allies or Aliens? Black-Latino Relations and Perceptions of Political Membership in the U.S." Unpublished manuscript, University of Chicago. http://chicago. academia.edu/ClaudiaSandoval/Papers/756264/Allies_or_Aliens_Black-Latino_Relations_ and_Perceptions_of_Political_Membership_in_the_US.

Thurman, Howard. 1976. *Jesus and the Disinherited*. Boston: Beacon Press.

Wise, Tim. 2008. *White Like Me: Reflections on Race from a Privileged Son*. Berkeley, CA: Soft Skull Press.

Yancy, George. 2008. *Black Bodies, White Gazes: The Continuing Significance of Race*. Lanham, MD: Rowman & Littlefield.

11

LOOKING LIKE ME?

Jesus images, Christology, and the limitations of theological blackness

Anthony B. Pinn

The history of white supremacy and the struggle against the ramifications of that history have in part been worked out through the nature and meaning of Jesus' presence on earth. And this Christological emphasis has involved a physical and spiritual aesthetics as well as a system of ethics ("What would Jesus do?"). Mindful of this, I argue that efforts to challenge whiteness as normative through the dual aesthetics presented in the story of Jesus' "look" and through efforts to mimic Jesus' system of ethics fall short. This is because both are based on biblical mythology and cultural considerations that can be manipulated and made to support multiple stories of whiteness. In a word, the symbolic importance and visual representation of Jesus' "look," life and ministry can be used to support either a critique-of-whiteness discourse or an embrace of it. Furthermore, both discourses of whiteness (and corresponding discourses of blackness) are too limiting in that both present truncated ways to identify one's humanity. In either case, one's humanity is recognized only to the extent that it can be defined by this one marker of life meaning. More to the point, both fail to wrestle with the fundamental nature of moral evil—a denial of the right to occupy time and space physically and discursively in complex and transformative ways. Instead of attempting to counter the damage done by whiteness discourse through claiming Jesus' blackness—either as a symbolic *more* or ethical mandate—it is, as I argue in this chapter, more useful to recognize the limits of Christology as a model for human self-understanding, and begin one's ethics with this recognition.

What the "look" of Jesus means

There are ways in which visual images of Jesus the Christ promote a particular social cohesiveness and a sense of collective identity at the cultural–political level (Morgan, 2005, pp.247–55).[1] The aesthetics of divinity as represented by Jesus the Christ (the "God/man") also legitimize a moral and ethical posture toward the world, or a particular sense of the public sphere and proper involvement in it. The visual image communicates—when transfixed and rendered a trope of relationship—civil religion as tied to a particular "look" (Morgan, 2005, pp.248–49). "The significance and power of popular religious imagery," writes David Morgan, "resides precisely in its contribution to the social construction of reality, whether in the everyday domain of visual and epistemological recipes that guide people through the day or the liminal passages of crisis and transformation that dramatically shape their lives" (p.17). The image becomes natural, and confirms communal aesthetics in support of a particular ethics of life (Morgan, 2005, p.18). Morgan (2005) writes, and this is key: "the devout seek in his depictions an image of what they wish the world to be" (p.123). And white Americans were not alone in working through a vast array of issues and concerns vis-à-vis the imagining of Jesus.

Black folks and a Jesus who understands "us"

Christology and images of Jesus in particular were meant by African Americans as positive and creative effort to craft themselves in light of their understanding of the Christian faith. Early discussions and depictions of Jesus Christ within the African American imagination did not necessarily fix on the physical presentation of Christ as similar to that of enslaved Africans. Instead, much more emphasis was given to a shared image based on ethics and epistemology, meant to short-circuit white supremacy and advance African American self-understanding.

Beginning with the spirituals, enslaved Africans measured the terror and absurdity of the world over against the cultural world inhabited by Jesus and by his response to that world. In certain respects, Jesus Christ served as religious symbol and ethical trope over against the dehumanization of enslaved existence. If enslavement represents a form of social death, as Orlando Patterson (1985) argues, Jesus Christ provided a reconstituted self (physically and socially significant) through the details of his life and resurrection. Time and historical context, in this instance, give way to the pain shared by the righteous and the empathy of God toward those faced with existential angst and embodied pain. Jesus and enslaved Africans share knowledge:

> Don't ever feel discouraged
> For Jesus is your friend
> And if you lack of knowledge
> He'll ne'er refuse to lend.[2]

The idea that enslaved Africans are ontologically and existentially adrift, detangled from the workings of cultural worlds that once sustained them, is matched by a counter force of familiarity with a cosmic presence having significant power and capacity:

> Ride on King Jesus!
> No man can hinder him

Ride on King Jesus!
No man can hinder him.

And,

I was young when I begun
No man can hinder him
But now my race is almost run
No man can hinder him.[3]

Compassion and power in a historically targeted pattern are highlighted within the context of the spirituals, as the enslaved and their descendants work through the trauma and joys of life. Little attention in this early Christology is given to the biological reality of Jesus the Christ; instead, enslaved Africans emphasized his relationship to suffering humanity and the consequential demand for justice. In general, the color of Jesus was of less importance, a lesser marker of the value of black (enslaved) bodies than was a shared relationship to God. Both Jesus and enslaved Africans marked out the reality (in differing ways of course) of the *imago Dei*. Jesus was their kin, not necessarily in look, but clearly in knowledge and the context of misery. As the song proclaims, "nobody knows de trouble I've had nobody knows but Jesus."[4] The Jesus Event presents a moral compass and an ethical posture toward the world that serves the enslaved, helping them to recognize the manner in which Jesus Christ presents both the form and content of transformed existence:

Children Jesus died to set me free
Nailed to that cross on Calvary.[5]

By making this epistemological and ontological link, it was possible to expose as white supremacy the rhetoric covered by theological assertions that made exclusive claims of white Americans to Jesus. Some, however, would go further and seek to replace literally a white Jesus with a black Jesus.

When Jesus becomes black

Salvation history holds the marks of "ethnological development" (Pinn, 2002, pp.132, 133). Assuming the reality of the groupings presented in Genesis, minister James Theodore Holly argues:

> the converted Ethiopian eunuch, as well as Simon the Cyrenian, who carried Christ's cross, and the Canaanitish woman whose faith our Lord declared to have been greater than any He had found in Israel, all go to show how the descendants of Ham continued to mingle in the designs of Almighty God down to the development of the Gospel dispensation. Hence, it may appear that the Semitic race has given us the written thought of God's Divine Plan; the Japhetic race has openly proclaimed this thought in the printed and

preached WORD; but both alike await the forthcoming ministry of the Hamitic race to reduce to practical ACTION that spoken word, that written thought.

(Pinn, 2002, p.139)

Put differently, blackness *is* the mark of Jesus' salvific work in the world. Within this more robust Christology is the unapologetic embrace not only of Jesus Christ as sympathetic to the plight of God's "dark" children, but of Jesus Christ as embodying blackness.

While implied in the Doctrine of God offered by figures such as Holly (Pinn, 2002) and Henry McNeal Turner (1971), it is with the mid-twentieth century that the physical representation of Jesus Christ as black gains its most significant ground. Deep within the civil rights movement was a vision of renewed life based on the demise of white supremacy and the rise of humanity recognized beyond the superficial markers of racial and ethnic difference. And for Christians seeking to articulate this new vision, the re-thinking of Christ imagery was a necessity. Yet, whereas Turner softens his polemical proclamation of God as black by offering a preference for the color of God more deeply associated with the colors of the natural world—if whites will also release God from their image—some within the civil rights era and post-civil rights black consciousness ideology reclaimed the blackness of Christ as epistemological, ontological, and political reality. The notion of "black is beautiful" was brought to bear on the aesthetics of political life, as well as being a hermeneutic by which to strip away whiteness (and all its implications) from the metaphysical underpinning of black Christian life. Gone were the blonde hair and blue eyes. In their place, an afro, brown skin and brown eyes: one was more likely to see the children of Christ in the troubled terrain of inner-city communities than in carefully crafted suburban communities. Not all preaching and physical church structures (e.g., stained-glass windows) embraced this move, but those doing so marked out a new theological platform, one that attempted to wrestle with the embodied and psychological consequences of negative color symbolism.

The challenge to both physical and epistemological whiteness is given its strongest theological articulation in the work of late twentieth-century black and womanist theologies. Whereas figures such as minister Albert Cleage argued for the physical blackness of Jesus Christ (i.e., a black revolutionary whose recorded perspectives and opinions nurture the late twentieth-century black Christian nationalist impulse), black and womanist theologies have been less concerned with physical blackness as the primary (if not sole) marker of importance. "Although Jesus' ethnicity and dark-skinned complexion are certainly important aspects of Christ's blackness," writes theologian Kelly Brown Douglas (1994), "to call Christ Black points to more than simply ancestry or biological characteristics" (p.1). To the contrary, a sense of God as being ontologically black (Cone, 1986, ch. 4) suggests an image of Christ as connected to the liberative impulse of African American communities and embodied within their very struggle for social transformation. "What does Jesus Christ mean for the oppressed blacks of the land?" asks James Cone (1986, p.111). And the answer: Jesus must be disassociated from images of a white Jesus meant to safeguard white supremacy. Instead, Jesus is "the Oppressed One" who struggles on behalf of African Americans to bring about liberative existence. In other words, "in a society that defines blackness as evil and whiteness as good, the theological significance of Jesus is found in the possibility of human liberation through blackness. Jesus is the black Christ!" (Cone, 1986, p.121).

Theologian J. Deotis Roberts (see, for example, Roberts, 2005) notes the manner in which Jesus Christ must be free from reified and limiting notions of incarnation, and instead must be recognized as bearing in his actions and commitments the full range of humanity. Cone, however, understood late twentieth-century blackness (in association with black power) as the paradigmatic status of Christ. For Cone, Christ is black, but this involves not so much a biological statement as much as it is an epistemological and ethical statement—meaning that Jesus Christ is known visually through the placement of black bodies in time and space, and is present wherever effort is made to fight racism and challenge white supremacy's basic logic. This involves a redefining of blackness over against whiteness, whereby the former becomes the basic hermeneutic of life's meaning. This, for Cone and those who follow his lead, has something to do with a metaphysically sanctioned alteration of power marked out through an ontological shift privileging the once-despised. Even negative reaction against this "new" depiction of Jesus Christ points to the problematic assumptions of whiteness guiding thought and action in the United States. "The same white theologians," writes Cone (1975), "who laughingly dismiss Albert Cleage's 'Black Messiah' say almost nothing about the European (white) images of Christ plastered all over American homes and churches. I perhaps would respect the integrity of their objections to the Black Christ on scholarly grounds, if they applied the same vigorous logic to Christ's whiteness, especially in contexts where his blackness is not advocated" (p.134).

Visual representation of Jesus as black, based on a set of socio-political, economic and cultural markers, damages the theological undergirding of white supremacy while also, at its best, allow for attention to the challenges of gender found in any attempt to "depict" Christ. For theologian Jacquelyn Grant (1989), the reality of Jesus is experiential in nature – based on the ability of Jesus to dwell where suffering women are and respond to their plight with liberative possibilities. In a word, "black women's affirmation of Jesus as God meant that White people were not God" (Grant, 1989, p.213). Through the insightful and sharp critique of womanist theologians, blackness was freed from the assumption of masculinity. Or, as Brown Douglas (1994) remarks, "the Black Christ explicitly disavows White oppression of Black people. The problem is that it does not go beyond that. It does not portray the complexity of Black oppression. Specifically, it does not address the fact that Black people oppress each other, and that racism is not the only barrier to Black freedom" (pp.85–86). The image of Jesus for many womanist scholars revolves around ethics—what did/would Jesus do—as opposed to the look of the historical Jesus. Hence, Jesus is a paradigmatic representation of embodied activity in the world. This does not rule out the possibility of depicting Jesus Christ as visually and culturally black (male or female), but it does deny the ability of any one transfiguration of Christ to serve as normative. Jesus

Christ as the embodied and visual presence of liberative ethics is given priority (Brown Douglas, 1994, pp.108–9).

The dilemma of Christology

Christology has been a mainstay of African American Christian thought; in fact, it has been the central theological category used to frame the nature and meaning of human engagement with/in the world. However, this has come at a cost. In what remains of this chapter, I address briefly several of the problems associated with this reliance on Jesus imagery and Christology: (1) the normalizing of human suffering vis-à-vis a mythology of external redemptive mechanisms; (2) a persistent shadow presence of whiteness as the framework for African American self-realization; (3) a problematic fixing of power as resolvable by means of an ethics of gift.

Normalization of suffering

African Americans have at times posited the African American community as a transfiguration of Christ—the "one" whose suffering and pain will redeem the nation (Moses, 1982, pp.x–xi). The most notable marker of this perspective is the persistent notion of redemptive suffering whereby African Americans understand the resolution of moral evil to take place through suffering: "no cross, no crown." What this model prevents is creative engagement with the world that does not presuppose suffering, and does not use a relationship to suffering as the measure of both pain and progress. Instead, suffering becomes already and always. Furthermore, such a move positions African Americans as scapegoats, or the means by which transformation takes place. Their bodies become the necessary substitute for (socio-political and cultural) "sin." They are "pulled apart" and "consumed" for the sake of others. Embedded in this positioning of African Americans is the assumption that redemption comes by means of an external mechanism—an exchange by which particular bodies accept stigma in order to open space for large-scale social transformation. Or, drawing on René Girard (1977), one might understand that this depiction of blackness as constitutive of Christ entails a type of sacrifice concerned with the production of harmony. There is something of this meaning in theologian Delores Williams' (1995) understanding of the surrogacy role played by African American women over the course of US history; but rather than seeking to reject this role as she hopes to do, theologically many African American Christians have embraced it as a means of communal and social restoration. Sacrifice centers the transfiguration (Girard, 1977; Williams, 1995). In other words, "we inherit the tradition of Christian morality which makes self-renunciation the condition for salvation. To know oneself was paradoxically the way to self-renunciation" (Martin et al., 1988, p.22). Yet, this move simply re-enforces another stigma—the African American (collective) Christ figure as stigmatized figure whose suffering is redemptive (Goffman, 1963). A social stigma becomes theologically contrived and ethically enacted, and both undergird a meta-language (and conceptual paradigm) of race as already and always meaningful difference. It gives the stigma cosmic importance through the teleology of human suffering. It matters little whether this positioning of the stigmatized group is recognized or embraced by all. While not a strict correlation, the perspective offered by Erving Goffman (1963) is applicable to the situation of individual African Americans as well as the collective African American community understood in terms of this transfiguration of Christ. The demands of the larger society—as presented in/through a discourse of whiteness as normative—can be denied without significant impact as those claiming the stigma of the blackened Christ are "insulated by [their] alienation, protected by identity beliefs of [their] own, [they feel that they are] full-fledged normal ... [they bear] a stigma but [do] not seem to be impressed or repentant about doing so"(Goffman, 1963, p.6). In fact, the stigma becomes the marker of their importance, their contribution to the advancement of the moral and ethical nature of life. The stigma—blackness over against whiteness—becomes a sign of excellence, or deep meaning, in that categorical racism[6] is addressed through the transfiguration of a few vis-à-vis an altered Christ image and Christ-like postures toward the world (e.g., redemptive suffering). This proposition bears significant difficulties in that suffering easily becomes the standard of black life—the inescapable measure of black existence.

Shadow presence of whiteness

African American Christology challenges the status of whiteness as conceptual paradigm, but it does so in a way that maintains the embedded integrity of the racialized structuring of information and meaning. Whether in white or black, African American Christology continues to posit the significance of race formation as having "real" importance and meaning. (I wanted to separate the category of race from the felt damage of racism.) And, to the extent that this is the case, "black" Jesus imagery re-enforces whiteness, in that blackness remains a response to, or consequence of, whiteness. It is dependent on the "space" made available through the matrix of whiteness. A correction of whiteness through blackness continues the discourse of whiteness, and maintains a sense of race-based self-awareness as normative. That is to say, in either case, presentation of the African American continues to entail stigma (Goffman, 1963, p.73).

Some fifteen years ago, Victor Anderson provided a compelling explication and critique of this meta-symbol of whiteness lurking behind racial discourse. He gave particular attention to the ontological blackness that black and womanist theologies have used to describe both God and Christ. Through this projection of blackness as anti-whiteness, African American presentations and understandings of the self are truncated. One should be mindful of what Ann Branaman (1997) says regarding Erving Goffman's theory of the self, in that such a restrained understanding forces a defining of the self "in congruence with the statutes, roles, and relationships they are accorded by the social order" (p.xlvii). Rejection of whiteness as having theological and ontological importance depends on the perpetual target of whiteness. While the blackening of Christ might symbolically and ethically render African Americans Christ-like, the necessity of whiteness for this development renders whiteness god-like

(Anderson, 1995, pp.91–92). Put another way, "because black life is fundamentally determined by black suffering and resistance to whiteness ... , black existence is without the possibility of transcendence from the blackness that whiteness created ... existentially, the new black being remains bound by whiteness" (Anderson, 1995, pp.92, 93).

Problematic fixing of power

African Americans attempted to use theological categories to visually alter their status over and against the ramifications of whiteness as normative. This assumes that recasting of the black body vis-à-vis applied Christology effectively alters power and its impact, as if this new articulation of the blackness "on" black bodies places African American Christians outside the "social fiction" of whiteness (Sullivan, 2001, p.2). Even this Christ-like black body is a symbol of the social system, and therefore power continues to define and shape it. To the extent that Christology anchors theological anthropology and ethics, it seeks to address issues of domination and control by means of a passive act of surrogacy—marking out transformation as a process of moralized suffering. Transfigurations of Christ, then, seek to generate new schematics of life. Connected to this idea, however, is a flawed assumption: power is "held" by embodied bodies, and that power can be secured through actions that counter the dominant social motif. Instead, I find compelling Michel Foucault's (1995) understanding of power as working in and through bodies, but not held by particular individuals or groups. So understood, the presentation of a messianic figure—even with "black"—maintains an illusion, a misunderstanding of power and its function that serves to re-enforce the workings of power to control discourse and thereby life's meaning.

The basic meaning of the Christ Event suggests that it is possible to view and work on problems of power (e.g., whiteness and limitation on life) from outside the structures of oppression. Christology also seems to suggest that power can be arranged and controlled through particular ethical acts. However, it is more likely that power is not so easily understood, does not relate to particular truths, and is present in and through this reconfiguration of Christ and Christology. In this regard, "human subjects and historical events are not firm and discrete (id)entities but are fragmented and changing sites across which the flows of power move" (McHoul and Grace, 1993, p.41). This may involve a different "mapping" of the body through a Christological repositioning of *imago Dei*, but even this mapping bears the marks of a racial discourse that still controls the nature and meaning of African Americans and their bodies. This theological turn is an "improvement" of the status and meaning of blackness, but even this involves reflection against whiteness. This altered Christology is still the "blackness that whiteness created" because it amounts to "racial apologetics" writ theologically.[7]

As I have argued elsewhere, fighting racism as a form of power relations does not entail fighting particular individuals or groups. Power is a series of relationships found in everything and through everything—making and informing bodies. Hence, an attack on white supremacy as expressed in relationship to particular groups doesn't end the problem when one considers the fluidity of power relationships and the

knowledge connected to them, as well as the manner in which these same power relationships flow from the "oppressed." Struggle, then, takes on connotations and possibilities
less robust and "meaningful" than those posited by liberation theologies. Black theology
and womanist theology seek to detangle black bodies from the power dynamics of
oppression, but perhaps, if Foucault is correct, such thinking is to misunderstand the
nature of power and knowledge, and to assume that the body has a pre-historical reality,
and that power does not flow through and by means of black bodies as well (Pinn, 2009).
Christology actually renders bodies docile—in line with the discourse of control and
relationship generating the status quo—rather than encouraging the formation of
embodied bodies that seek to expose the dynamics of power and control.

The transfiguration of Christ within the context of African American struggle
against white supremacy assumes a linear sense of progress, a certainty of transition in
that action (the activities of Christ manifest in the workings of African Americans
who are Christ-like) generates particular outcomes. This transfiguration of Christ
suggests that power is held and can be redirected based on the strength of moral and
ethical positioning. Christology as an effort to rethink theological anthropology so as
to counter the effects of whiteness and a discourse of domination involves reconstitution of black bodies at the level of discourse, the level of cultural construction.
Theology may map the body, but not in a way that isn't compromised by an always
present and already operative arrangement of power relationships—despite what is
theologically said about race as a mode of authority (Carrette, 2000, pp.112–13).

Theological anthropology presupposed by the blackness of Christ (over against
whiteness) involves a static sense of identity or meaning that limits African Americans,
and downplays the significance of how bodies occupy time and space. Christology
actually looks beyond the body—sees the body, but is only able to claim it as a
matter of discourse—shifting signs and symbols articulated. The challenge to visual
images of whiteness through an alternate Christology—or a blackening of transfigurations of Jesus Christ—may entail an effort on the part of some African Americans
to constitute African Americans as subjects, but the end-product is a theologized
body, a discursive body—with little impact on the embodied body that remains
restricted by social arrangements and political mechanisms of control. Material bodies
are born, live, grow old and die.

However, Christology is not concerned with the articulation of a relationship to
this embodied body, but rather seeks to stem the tide and focus on the culturally/
theologically constructed body—the one that gives itself and in the process seeks to
abandon our materiality, or our "finitude ... our inescapable physical locatedness in
time and space, in history and culture. ... " This materiality, which includes race and
gender, cannot be escaped through Christology; it simply determines who African
Americans are as the blackened Christ and who the blackened Christ is in light of
whiteness (Bordo, 1998, pp.89, 91).[8]

Notes

1 For information on the function and meaning of Jesus in North America, readers should also
see Stephen Prothero, *American Jesus: How the Son of God Became a National Icon* (2003).

2 "There Is a Balm in Gilead," www.negrospirituals.com/news-song/there_is_a_balm_in_gilead.htm. Viewed on March 21, 2011.
3 "Ride on King Jesus," www.negrospirituals.com/news-song/ride_on_king_jesus.htm. Viewed on March 21, 2011.
4 "Nobody Knows De Trouble I've Had," www.negrospirituals.com/news-song/nobody_knows_de_trouble_i.htm. Viewed on March 21, 2011.
5 "Buked and Scorned." www.negrospirituals.com/news-song/buked_and_scorned.htm. Viewed on March 21, 2011.
6 Here I am adopting Victor Anderson's sense of this as "a species logic in which every individual member of a species shares essential traits that identify the member within the species." See Anderson (1995, p.51).
7 This phrasing is drawn from Anderson (1995, pp.61, 78).
8 The ideas in this final section of the chapter draw on and extend thoughts found in Pinn (2009).

References

Anderson, Victor. *Beyond Ontological Blackness* (New York: Continuum, 1995).
Bordo, Susan "'Material Girl': The Effacements of Postmodern Culture," in Donn Welton (Ed.) *Body and Flesh: A Philosophical Reader* (Malden, MA: Blackwell Publishers, Inc., 1998).
Branaman, Ann. "Goffman's Social Theory," in Charles Lemert and Ann Branaman (Eds.) *The Goffman Reader* (Malden, MA: Blackwell Publishers, 1997).
Brown Douglas, Kelly. *The Black Christ* (Maryknoll, NY: Orbis Books, 1994).
Carrette, Jeremy R. *Foucault and Religion: Spiritual Corporality and Political Spirituality* (New York: Routledge, 2000).
Cone, James H. *A Black Theology of Liberation*, 20th Anniversary Edition (Maryknoll, NY: Orbis Books, 1986).
Cone, James H. *God of the Oppressed* (New York: Harper & Row, Publishers, 1975).
Foucault, Michel. *Discipline and Punish: The Birth of the Prison* (New York: Vintage, 1995).
Girard, René. *Violence and the Sacred*, translated by Patrick Gregory (Baltimore: Johns Hopkins University Press, 1977).
Goffman, Erving. *Stigma: Notes on the Management of Spoiled Identity* (New York: Simon & Schuster, 1963).
Grant, Jacquelyn. *White Women's Christ and Black Women's Jesus: Feminist Christology and Womanist Response* (Atlanta: Scholars Press, 1989).
Lemert, Charles and Ann Branaman, editors. *The Goffman Reader* (Malden, MA: Blackwell Publishers, 1997).
Martin, Luther H., Huck Gutman, Patrick H. Hutton, editors. *Technologies of the Self: A Seminar with Michel Foucault* (Amherst: University of Massachusetts Press, 1988).
McHoul, Alec, and Wendy Grace. *A Foucault Primer: Discourse, Power and the Subject* (New York: New York University Press, 1993).
Morgan, David. *The Sacred Gaze: Religious Visual Culture in Theory and Practice* (Berkeley: University of California Press, 2005).
Moses, Wilson Jeremiah. *Black Messiahs and Uncle Toms: Social and Literary Manipulations of a Religious Myth* (University Park: Pennsylvania State University Press, 1982).
Patterson, Orlando. *Slavery and Social Death: A Comparative Study* (Cambridge, MA: Harvard University Press, 1985).
Pinn, Anthony B. *Embodiment and the New Shape of Black Theological Thought* (New York: New York University Press, 2009).
Pinn, Anthony B. *Moral Evil and Redemptive Suffering: A History of Theodicy in African-American Religious Thought* (Gainesville: University Press of Florida, 2002).
Prothero, Stephen. *American Jesus: How the Son of God Became a National Icon* (New York: Farrar, Straus and Giroux, 2003).
Roberts, J. Deotis. *A Black Political Theology* (Louisville, KY: Westminster/John Knox, 2005).

Sullivan, Nikki. *Tattooed Bodies: Subjectivity, Textuality, Ethics, and Pleasure* (Westport, CT: Praeger, 2001).

Turner, Henry McNeal. "God is Black," in Edwin S. Redkey (Ed.) *Respect Black: The Writings and Speeches of Henry McNeal Turner* (New York: Arno, 1971, pp.176–77).

Welton, Donn, editor. *Body and Flesh: A Philosophical Reader* (Malden, MA: Blackwell Publishers, Inc., 1998).

Williams, Delores. *Sisters in the Wilderness: The Challenge of Womanist God-Talk* (Maryknoll, NY: Orbis Books, 1995).

12

THE (BLACK) JESUS OF DETROIT

Reflections on black power and the (white) American Christ

M. Shawn Copeland

In the early morning hours of July 23, 1967, a routine police vice-squad raid on an after-hours drinking club in a predominantly black neighborhood in Detroit, Michigan, escalated into one of the most furious racial rebellions in modern times. Five days later 43 persons were dead, more than 450 injured, more than 7,200 arrested, and more than 2,000 buildings destroyed. A little-known, yet highly symbolic, incident during those days involved a statue of the Sacred Heart of Jesus on the grounds of the major seminary of the Roman Catholic Archdiocese. At the intersection of West Chicago Boulevard and Linwood Avenue, two blocks west of the site of the rebellion, stands a statue of the Sacred Heart of Jesus, which looked out on a then increasingly black neighborhood, even as the seminary faculty and students remained predominantly white. On the second day of the disturbance, an African American housepainter reportedly applied black paint to the hands, feet, and face of the statue of the Sacred Heart of Jesus. At least twice, the color was removed, but black paint prevailed and, over the past four decades, the seminary has kept it fresh. In an interview during a 40th anniversary commemoration of the rebellion, the Assistant Dean of Sacred Heart Seminary's Institute for Ministry, John Lajiness, said, "the City really has no other positive visible symbol like it. [The painted statue] speaks less of violence and more of the internal struggle for identity and the human tension which, intentionally or not, bled into making this statue an icon" (Gallio, 2007).

The painting of the statue of the Sacred Heart of Jesus occurred in the thick of the black cultural nationalist movement. While the Newark-based poet and dramatist LeRoi Jones (later known as Imamu Amiri Baraka) is credited as the inspiration and developer of the Black Arts Movement, Detroit poets, dramatists, publishers, aestheticians, and social theorists made substantive contributions to the formulation of a black aesthetic and articulation of a sharp analysis of the urban condition. Although a "blue collar" town, Detroit boasted of a constellation of theorists with sound, seasoned, and pragmatic experience in the labor and black civil rights movements as well as in the arts. One need think only of social activists James and Grace Lee Boggs, attorney Ken Cockrel, publishers and poets Dudley Randall of Broadside Press (*Negro Digest/Black World*) and Naomi Long Madgett of Lotus Press, and the Reverend Albert B. Cleage (later known as Jaramogi Abebe Agyeman), who in 1953 founded the Shrine of the Black Madonna (formally known as the Central Congregational Church) and advocated a Black Christian nationalism (Collins and Crawford, 2006; Georgakas and Surkin, 1998). To borrow a well-known phrase from the Reverend Dr. Martin Luther King, Jr.: Perhaps, the housepainter had been tracked down by the *zeitgeist*— the spirit of the time! The ebonizing of the statue occurred approximately one year prior to the publication of Cleage's (1969) *The Black Messiah*, roughly two years ahead of the appearance of a "picture of a kinky-haired, broad-nosed Black Christ ... on the cover of *Ebony* magazine" (Douglas, 1994, pp.9, 119) as well as the publication of James Cone's (1969) *Black Theology and Black Power*, seven months after Vincent Harding (1967) wrote "Black Power and the American Christ," and a few weeks before the appearance of *Black Power: The Politics of Liberation in America* by Stokely Carmichael and Charles V. Hamilton (1967).

Whether or not Lajiness grasped the full import of his remark, he put his finger on a central concern of African Americans during the 1960s and 1970s—the meaning of Jesus Christ (and Christianity) to black cultural nationalism and to social (i.e., political, economic, and technological) struggle in urban America. As icon, the painted statue both commanded and transformed a "sacred precinct and [a] profane space" (Mondzain, 2005, p.118). The housepainter's iconic rendering of the Sacred Heart of Jesus protested the social, cultural, and spiritual aloofness of the Christian churches from the deteriorating social conditions of too many black and poor Detroiters of all racial–cultural backgrounds, and claimed Jesus indisputably as a co-sufferer in a suffering and oppressed urban situation. This iconic black Jesus resolved (although only temporarily) black people's fitful struggle with the blond-haired, blue-eyed, pink-and-white Jesus; concretely anticipated theology's turn to the black human subject and black identity; and signified a new economy capable not only of deconstructing whiteness, but of embracing blackness. Indeed, this iconic representation revealed the sacred heart of Jesus broken open in angry compassion at the urban rebellion's attempt to uncover and disentangle the American "cultural myth from [American] cultural reality" (Babb, 1998, p.175).

This chapter contributes to the volume's critical interrogation of Jesus and whiteness, first, by attending to the spirituals made and sung by enslaved Africans and their ebonization and reconfiguration of the (white) Jesus of slaveholding Christianity and second, by revisiting historian and activist Vincent Harding's "Black Power and the American Christ," which appeared at the crest of the black power movement and well before the advent of whiteness studies. Here, Harding offers a sketch of the major features of American colonialism, i.e., the structure of racial privilege, the introduction of a system of preferential patronage rooted in assimilation and existential self-denial, and the institution of mechanisms of control and suppression.[1] What is at stake in this reflection is black identification with the historical Jesus and the impact of a black messiah on the sacramental and social economy.

Reconfiguring Jesus Christ in slavery

From the seventeenth through the nineteenth centuries, slavery was all but synonymous with economy, with "a [black] person with a price" (Johnson, 1999, p.2). This terrible synchronicity violated the Christian sacramental economy manifest in history and inseparable from the human flesh of the Word (Mondzain, 2005, p.32), the flesh of Jesus Christ. Not even the sacrament of baptism could redeem black flesh from the damnation and predation of slavery; rather, baptism served to tame, to temper, to discipline the slave for ease of subjugation and profitability of service or sale. Hence, the slave would come to perceive grace only as emancipation or freedom or escape, but more likely as the release of death. In this "soul murdering" (Painter, 1995, p. 127) economy, black lived life was a situation of hermeneutical vigilance.

In making, crafting, and singing spirituals, the slaves formulated and expressed their interpretation of that economy. Although the Southern slaveholding class was accustomed to the singing of slaves, hearing it as so much "noise" (Cruz, 1999, p.45),[2] wide awareness of these moans, chants, and songs coincides with the Civil War. These sorrow songs emerged and were nurtured within the single sphere in which historians and cultural anthropologists agree that the slaves were able to exercise some measure of autonomy—the religious sphere.[3] The spirituals are saturated with biblical characters, images, places, themes; the language is vivid, poetic, even decorative, yet poignant, self-critical, and singularly free of all references to vengeance. Through the spirituals, the slaves discerned, distinguished, and registered coded disgust with those "phony, insincere Christians ... who practice selfishness and brutality ... who go to church on Sunday morning and come home and beat their slaves on Sunday afternoon" (Lovell, 1972, p.192). Thus, the spirituals protest such heretical perversion, differentiate authentic and inauthentic Christian practice, and resist any *kerygma* that would debase black humanity. Writing of the cognitive and emotional power of the spirituals, Frederick Douglass (1845) mused:

> I have sometimes thought, that the mere hearing of these songs would do more to impress truly spiritual-minded men and women with the soul crushing and death-dealing character of slavery, than the reading of whole volumes of its mere physical cruelties. They speak to the heart and to the soul of the thoughtful. ... Every tone was a testimony against slavery, and a prayer to God for deliverance from chains.
>
> *(pp.28–29)*

Even as the spirituals critique slavery's degradation, these songs point toward the precarious spiritual condition of the slaveholders and their blatant disregard and dismissal of the sacramental economy in the ruthless pursuit of profits.

With great subtlety and indirection, the crafters of the spirituals made visible the brutal suffering and oppression of slavery. At the same time, the slaves derived a critical metaphysics that reconfigured being human and human being: Righteousness, that is, authenticity as enfleshed in the person and praxis of Jesus Christ, rather than whiteness, functions as normative. Thus, Jesus formed the center, text, and subtext of the spirituals. What the slaves recognized, perhaps immediately, was Jesus' wide and open heart, acute sensitivity, and deep compassion for those in situations of material and spiritual want, physical suffering, and social and religious oppression: "Did you ever see the like before, King Jesus preaching to the poor/ My Lord's done just what he said, Healed the sick and rais'd the dead." Perhaps what the slaves recognized in the biblical stories about Jesus, in his parables of "welcome and warning" (Wright, 1996, pp.243, 280), in his ability to confuse and upend dominative power was a way navigating suffering and pain, evil and affliction with dignity. They realized that Jesus could be met in vision through prayer: "Ef you want to see Jesus, Go in de Wilderness" or "King Jesus is a-listenin' all day long, To hear some sinner pray." And like the poor, needy, outcast, and rejected of the New Testament, the slaves in faith expected his response. Indeed, the very name of Jesus held pharmacopeic power. Like sacred medicine, the name of Jesus delighted, instructed, and healed: "I love Jesus for his name's so sweet;" "Fix me, Jesus, fix me;" "I know the Lord has laid his hands on me."

The slaves assumed a familiar and intimate relationship with Jesus. He was their "rock in a weary lan'," their "shelter in a storm." He is addressed as a cherished friend who never will abandon them on the path through the hardships of a hard life.

> I want Jesus to walk with me;
> I want Jesus to walk with me;
> All along my pilgrim journey,
> Lord, I want Jesus to walk with me.
> In my trials, Lord walk with me;
> In my trials, Lord walk with me;
> When my heart is almost breaking,
> Lord, I want Jesus to walk with me.
> When I'm in trouble, Lord walk with me;
> When I'm in trouble, Lord walk with me;
> When my head is bowed in sorrow,
> Lord, I want Jesus to walk with me.

Jesus is a comfort in time of trouble or pain and in the most intimate moments of joy or anguish, the maker of the spiritual cries: "Give me Jesus, Give me Jesus, You may have all this world, Give me Jesus."

The predominant theme of the Christianity of the slaves was freedom. Their yearning and struggle for freedom did not fragment into diametric oppositions; rather, freedom for the slaves was holistic. The freedom for which the enslaved peoples longed, struggled, fought, and died was, at once, social and cultural, psychic and spiritual, metaphysical and ontological, this-worldly and other-worldly (Mitchell, 1975, p.120; Wilmore, 1998, p.217). For the slaves understood Jesus Christ as the Bringer of freedom, as their Savior. Yet, as Howard Thurman (1975) has observed, "It was dangerous to let the slave understand that the life and teachings of Jesus meant freedom for the captive and release for those held in economic, social, and political bondage" (p.16). To understand the fearless and dangerous Jesus was to break the spell cast by the prevailing dominative consciousness—to break with slave mentality. To understand the fearless and dangerous Jesus was to release the Word of God from the grip of the slaveholders and set it working free in the midst of those yearning to be free. Thus, the makers of the spirituals sang:

> Woke Up This Morning with my mind, And it was stayed,
> Stayed on Jesus.
> Can't hate your neighbor in you mind, If you keep it stayed,
> Stayed on Jesus.
> Makes you love everybody with your mind, When you keep it stayed,
> Stayed on Jesus.
> The Devil can't catch you in your mind, If you keep it stayed,
> Stayed on Jesus.
> Jesus is the captain in you mind, When you keep it stayed,
> Stayed on Jesus

During the civil rights movement of the 1950s, when this spiritual was sung, the word "freedom" was substituted for the name of Jesus. Still, this substitution was in keeping with the intentionality and the spirit of the slaves' grasp of the meaning and message of Jesus. Jesus was an answer to prayers for freedom; he was "God's Black Slave who had come to put an end to human bondage" (Cone, 1972, p.49).

It is no surprise that the spirituals accorded painstaking attention to the suffering, crucifixion, and death of Jesus. The enslaved folk knew what it meant to suffer, and in Jesus' suffering and death they recognized their own experience. Narratives about enslavement report an especially vicious form of brutality in which an enslaved man or woman would be "staked." The slave would be forced to lie face down on the ground with arms and legs extended and tied to stakes, then the person would be flogged. Another form of this punishment required that the slave's "hands ... be tied together with a rope, which was then thrown over the limb of a tree or over a beam." Then the slave would be "pulled up till [his or her] toes only just reached the ground, feet tied together, and a rail or fence thrust between the legs with a weight on it to keep the body at full stretch" (Blassingame, 1977, p.220). This form of punishment was not uncommon. We do not know whether it gave rise to the following lament, but in it the slaves poured out a tender anguish for the brutalized Jesus. Their love transcended the limitations of time and space; they stood with Jesus as he stood with them in their sufferings.

> They nail my Jesus down,
> They put him on the crown of thorns
> O see my Jesus hangin' high!
> He look so pale an' bleed so free:
> O don't you think it was a shame,
> He hung three hours in dreadful pain?

The resurrection of Jesus signified that death would not be the last word, that slavery would not be the last word. The God who vindicated Jesus would vindicate the slaves and that triumph would be, at once, eschatological and historical, other-worldly and this-worldly.

To paraphrase Walter Benjamin, the spirituals are shot through with chips of messianic time. The spirituals testify to a deep longing for concrete salvation in history, for the realization of the hopes and dreams of a long-oppressed people, for a new age in which the power of the slaveholders is vanquished, sinners are punished, and the righteous are rewarded. Freedom will mean the end of the auction block and the driver's lash, a mother's repressed anger and a father's tears. Freedom will mean reunion, not only with the beloved dead, who may now be honored fully, but also with those who have escaped chattel slavery. Jesus was God's inbreaking and transformation of their concrete historical condition. To these women and men Jesus was "a god of compassion and suffering, a promulgator of freedom and peace and opportunity, a son of an omnipotent Father" (Lovell, 1972, p.189) who would bring about their historic liberation.

The Jesus Christ reconfigured by the slaves was a "black" Christ, not in his racial pigmentation, but in his prophetic praxis that focused compassionately on the most abject in his society, that proclaimed and performed the presence of the reign of God, and that called for the renewal of Israel, despite the thick opacity of oppressive Roman rule (Horsley, 2002, pp.79–104). This Jesus Christ was black because he took upon himself the suffering and affliction, the hope and cause of freedom (i.e., the condition of racial oppression). Thus, God-made-flesh in Jesus Christ *is* black because God is one with, for, and on the side of oppressed black people. Jesus Christ is the Oppressed One, who signifies in word and deed the nearness of God and God's reign and reveals liberation as God's essential activity.

Black power and the (white) American Christ

By joining the New Testament notion of agapic love to Gandhian principles and techniques of nonviolent resistance, the Reverend Dr. Martin Luther King, Jr., demonstrated that Christianity could be an effective non-violent weapon in the struggle of black men and women for civil rights. But, in the summer of 1966, committed yet wearied and increasingly militant members of the Student Non-violent Coordinating Committee (SNCC or "Snick") called for black power.[4] Their demand underscored the barricades of segregation, reframed the issue of integration, and splintered the precarious harmony and fragile compromises that King's leadership had forged between blacks and whites. Black pastors and clergy had marched, enduring police brutality and racist assault, had supported the nonviolent movement of direct action, and had achieved passage of the Civil Rights Act (1964) and the Voting Rights Act (1965). Still, this progress benefited only a small percentage of the black middle class; it failed to effect change for the vast majority of black people trapped in poverty, squalid urban housing, unemployment, disease, inadequate and indifferent social services, blatant discrimination, and police brutality. As the decay, unrest, and frustration within the nation's inner cities became visible, many who had adhered to

King's strategies began to doubt. His wisdom and the "weakness of the moderate centrism of the Black Church" were challenged further not only by the preaching of Muslim Minister Malcolm X, but by protracted police and FBI probes of the Black Panther Party (Wilmore and Cone, 1979, p.69). The celebrations of the landmark legislation began to "seem gratuitous to ghetto-dwellers who did not have the price of dinner at a desegregated restaurant" (Wilmore and Cone, 1979, p.16).[5] Urban uprisings in New York in 1964, and in Watts in 1965, contested such celebration, and more was to come: In the summer of 1967, rebellions broke out in several northern New Jersey cities, including Newark and Jersey City, Phoenix, Washington, D.C., New Haven, and Detroit. "This was the 'long hot summer,' during which terrible riots, looting, and burning devastated the black sections of so many of America's cities" (Harris, 1998, p.ix). But, as Stokely Carmichael and Charles Hamilton (1967) noted in their examination of black power, the urban problems of the 1960s were not much different than those of 1920 (p.155). And as James and Grace Lee Boggs (1974) wrote, "the American Dream [had become a living] nightmare" (p.257).

King held that segregation formed a double contradiction of the country's democratic principles and its religious heritage. Segregation betrayed the country's best and most noble ideals of liberty and justice; however, King (1986, "The Current Crisis") maintained that the religious contradiction of segregation was the worst. "If we are to remain true to the gospel of Jesus Christ," he argued, "we cannot rest until segregation and discrimination are banished from every area of American life" (p.89). King (1986, *Stride Toward Freedom*) once remarked, "any religion which professes to be concerned about the souls of men [sic] and is not concerned about the social and economic conditions that scar the soul is a spiritually moribund religion only waiting for the day to be buried" (p.91). He held that the Christian church had a social mission rooted in its prophetic task and fidelity to the preaching of Jesus Christ. The "projection of a social gospel" was the only "true witness of a Christian life" in a segregated and oppressive America (1986, "The *Playboy* Interview", p.345). In a 1963 sermon at Atlanta's Ebenezer Church, King criticized the black church's excessive preoccupation with the other-worldly:

> There is something wrong with any church that limits the gospel to talkin' about heaven over yonder. There is something wrong with any minister … who becomes so otherworldly in his [sic] orientation that he [sic] forgets about what is happening now … forgets [about] the here. Here where men [sic] are trampled over by the iron feet of oppression. Here where thousands of God's children are caught in an air-tight cage [of poverty]. Here where thousands of men and women are depressed and in agony because of their earthly fight … where the darkness of life surrounds so many of God's children.
>
> *(Cone, 1991, pp.147–48)*

"A minister," King stated, "cannot preach the glories of heaven while ignoring social conditions in his [sic] own community that cause men [sic] an earthly hell" (Cone, 1991, pp.147–48)

Functionally, King's Christ was a black Christ, whose prophetic praxis was committed to the banishment of segregation and discrimination. But to "the seekers of black power ... the angry children of Malcolm X" (Harding, 1979, p.38), the Christ of the civil rights was not black at all. Rather, this Christ was far too meek and mild; he was the ineffectual, effete, compliant (white) American Christ. These young and not so young people responded to this American Christ with disaffection, disgust, and anger. This was the Christ whom the privileged and powerful of (white) American society made complicit in structures of domination in order to define and circumscribe, to alienate and segregate, to oppress and suppress the (black and poor) subaltern class. The insistence of James Cone that black people needed a savior who looked like them was an argument grounded on far more than simple psychological or existential or social or, even, aesthetic redress. Cone was making a genuinely soteriological and, hence, theological argument.

> [T]he blackness of Jesus brings out the soteriological meaning of his Jewishness for our contemporary situation when Jesus' person is understood in the context of the cross and resurrection. ... The cross of Jesus is God invading the human situation as the Elected One who takes Israel's place as the Suffering Servant and thus reveals the divine willingness to suffer in order that humanity might be fully liberated. ... [Jesus'] presence with the poor (read: blacks) today is not docetic; but like yesterday, today also he takes the pain of the poor upon himself and bears it for them. ... It is in the light of the cross and the resurrection of Jesus in relation to his Jewishness that black theology asserts that "Jesus is black."
>
> *(Cone, 1975, p.124)*

White racist supremacy needed and transmuted Christ into a "crossless puppet, running away from suffering with his flaxen locks flapping in the wind" (Harding, 1979, p.41). Black power sought to hold that Christ accountable for the suffering and pain of black people.

In "Black Power and the American Christ," Vincent Harding sketched out in lyrical, penetrating, and uncompromising prose a dialogue between the advocates of black power and the adherents of the American Christ. Harding's method was contrast, his purpose to make visible the "strong and causative link between black power and American Christianity" (p.36). Or, put differently: Harding wanted to show how the ideological manipulation of representations of Jesus Christ in American Christian preaching, teaching, and art served and advanced "racial hierarchy, racial exclusion, and racial vulnerability and availability" (Morrison, 1992, p.11) and, thus, served and advanced whiteness. Originally published in January 1967 in the *Christian Century*, a progressive mainline Protestant bi-weekly magazine, and well before the emergence of Whiteness Studies, Harding's article comprises seven sections, including, brief introductory remarks.

Harding uses the introductory remarks in order to locate the audience—"social-action-oriented Christians," black and white, "true believers," who are caught in nostalgia. Their stories and reminiscences are drenched in their certainty of the rightness of the civil rights cause and its commitment to integration; yet, Harding worries that these reminiscences all too easily might prevent the older generation of activists from recognizing and engaging new and creative possibilities, particularly the possibilities of black power (Harding, 1979, p.35). Borrowing W. E. B. Du Bois' trope of "the veil," Harding distinguishes the nostalgia of "then" from the frustration of "now." Like Du Bois, Harding assumes an interpretive standpoint that suggests that he grasps what is at stake on both sides of the veil, that is, the tension between those who combine "the terrible privileges of blackness and Christian commitment" and those who advocate black power and deprecate the (white) American Christ (p.36). In fact, Harding insists that fidelity to the radical hope of achieving our humanity as expressed in King's notion of the "beloved community" (King, 1986, "The Current Crisis," p. 87) required that black power be examined, because Christ *is* also the Lord of Black Power (Harding, 1979, p.36).

Harding draws out the multivalent and shifting meanings of the veil: The veil is black power in the judgment of the movement elders, thus it separates the younger generation of activists from the older. The veil also may be a wall, not so much for separation but for writing—on both sides; but can one side see the other, and who is writing? Finally, Harding likens the veil to the large sheet that appears to the apostle Peter during a trance as recounted in the New Testament Book of Acts. A large sheet is lowered from the heavens and is filled with all kinds of "four-footed creatures and reptiles and birds of the air. Then [Peter] heard a voice saying 'Get up, Peter; kill and eat.'" Peter protests that the animals are unclean and he has not eaten unclean food; but the voice dismisses his protest: "What God has made clean, you must not call profane." At the same time, Cornelius, a centurion of the Italian Cohort, has had a vision directing him to seek out Peter and has sent trusted men to find him. Peter's preaching to the group Cornelius has assembled wins converts to faith in Jesus Christ; he stays several days and eats with them. The Jerusalem church criticizes the apostle's decision to stay, preach, and share the table with uncircumcised Gentiles. But Peter's commitment to obeying his vision proves to be of greater worth than any momentary discomfort and signals the freedom of the believer (Acts 10:1–11:44).

In alluding to this key moment in the New Testament, Harding insinuates that the established elders of the civil rights movement (the Jerusalem church) ought not to view black power as unclean. In fact, the brutal, dehumanizing, vicious, and racist actions of the followers of the (white) American Christ have provoked the very response about which these elders now grumble and before which whites tremble. Harding outlines the initial move of white colonial power: the collusion of white missionaries and profiteers, the stench and misery of slave ships bearing the name of Jesus,[6] the rape of black female bodies, the murderous jettisoning of human cargo. The demand for black power evokes an axial moment not for whites alone but, and far more importantly, for blacks. Black power scours and cleanses: a scythe clearing a thickly covered path or purifying minds and hearts choked with brush. Once the path is cleared, the mind and heart purified, then self-definition is necessary and the emergence of a new people possible.

The title of the second section, "Glad to Be Black," predates James Brown's famed celebration of blackness in song, "Say It Loud, I'm Black and Proud!" No longer,

Harding writes, will young black people pander to the (white) American Christ, whose skin pigmentation mocks their blackness and commands an imitation of white life. Black power repudiated the "American culture-religion," (Harding, 1979, p.37) which had so disparaged and dismissed blackness—the blackness of skin and hair and facial features, the blackness of rhythm, the blackness of Africa. Here, Harding recalls the well-known African adage: "Before the white man came, we had the land and they had the Bible. Now we have the Bible and they have the land."[7] The white American Christ has been used to deny black people authentic homelands, whether on the African continent or in the broken and congested ghettos of their exile. Furthermore, the followers of the American Christ enacted another exodus—fleeing the deteriorating congested urban core where the weak and powerless, those whom Howard Thurman (1949) called the "disinherited,"[8] were trapped and warehoused. The advocates of black power had the pulse of this suffering community and sniffed out the hypocrisy of the statement, "we all love the same Christ" (Harding, 1979, p.38). To this mewling, Harding places these words in the mouths of the advocates of black power in the third section, "Sensitized by Apprehension:"

> To hell with you and your Christ! If you cannot live where we live, if your children cannot grow where we grow, if you cannot suffer what we suffer, if you cannot learn what we learn, we have no use for you or your cringing Christ.
>
> *(Harding, 1979, p.38)*

Through attentive observation, incisive probing, and critical reflection, the advocates of black power apprehended "the core problem within the ghetto ... the vicious circle created by the lack of decent housing, decent jobs, and adequate education" (Carmichael and Hamilton, 1967, p.155). Forced by urban renewal and highway clearance programs into deteriorating and crowded slums, blacks were cut off from the lifelines of the very country that their ancestors' hard, unpaid labor helped to create. Isolated by suburban zoning laws, relegated to substandard schools, and segregated in churches, *de jure* and *de facto*, black children, women, and men were (and in large part, remain) separated from whites. As psychologist Kenneth Clark (1965) famously concluded, "The dark ghettos are social, political, educational and—above all—economic colonies. Their inhabitants are subject peoples, victims of the greed, cruelty, insensitivity, guilt, and fear of their masters" (p.11).

The advocates of black power called for an embrace of that separation: "Let us use the separateness that the white Christians have imposed upon us. ... The American Christ is a Christ of separation and selfishness and relentless competition for an empty hole. We want no part of him" (Harding, 1979, p.38). Like Marcus Garvey before him, Albert Cleage embraced separateness. He addressed the angry young advocates of black power directly, preaching that the movement for black liberation *was* the (true and only) Christian Church in the twentieth century. Moreover, in the sanctuary of the Shrine of the Black Madonna, a black aesthetic answered Countee Cullen's (2000) poignant line, "Wishing he I served were black ... " (p.450). Cleage (1972) conjured Jesus as a black messiah, a "revolutionary black religious leader fighting for the liberation of Israel" (p.3).[9] By founding the Shrine of the Black Madonna of the Pan African Orthodox Christian Church, Cleage generated (almost *ex nihilo*) a potent space "committed to transforming the spiritual emptiness, economic powerlessness and social disorganization" experienced as "plagues" on the black community.[10]

"Groveling No More," Harding's fourth section, exposes the "limp," "half-hearted" pledges by whites "to correct old wrongs. [Our] hand may be extended grudgingly and patronizingly, but anyone who rejects that hand rejects his [*sic*] own best interests" (Harding, 1979, p.39). The advocates of black power refuse to grovel; moreover, they have schooled themselves in America's global use of power; in particular, the shadow of the anti-colonial national liberation struggle in Vietnam falls across this and the fifth section. Black power recognizes that the limp and bloodied Mississippi hand is the same hand that oppresses nonwhite people around the globe. The white Christ of Cicero, Illinois, is the same Christ that leads bombing runs, blesses soldiers on their way to invade Latin America or Asia, and sanctions a "blasphemous" peace redolent of the *pax Romana* (Harding, 1979 p.39).[11] To white colonial power, "the black power advocates sanely shout: 'Go to hell, you whited sepulchers, hypocrites. All you want is to cripple our will and prolong our agony, and you use your white Christ to do it.' To the black people they say, 'Don't grovel, don't scrape'" (Harding, 1979, p.40).

"The force of black power," James Perkinson (2004) recognized, "was not merely negative. ... Among other things, it constituted a popular rejoinder to the autonomies and antinomies of modernity" (p.83). The advocates of black power sought to coax forward in black people a new self-consciousness, self-understanding, and self-definition as "energetic, determined, intelligent, beautiful and peace-loving ... vibrant and valiant;" (Carmichael and Hamilton, 1967, pp.38, 39) a new consciousness of the antiquity and sophistication of African culture and history; and a new consciousness of community, rather than competition for individualistically based acceptance by whites. Further, black power called for serious interrogation of the old values and institutions of society; thoughtful search for and experimentation with new and different forms for organizing and structuring the social order in an effort to solve political and economic problems in a thoroughgoing way; and broadening the base of political participation so that more people from different class backgrounds and interests are included in policy decision-making (Carmichael and Hamilton, 1967, p.39). The advocates of black power sought to create "a new society where human misery and poverty are repugnant" (p.41) and "viable coalitions [are forged] between blacks and whites who accept each other as co-equal partners and who identify their goals as politically and economically similar" (p.84).

The lengthiest section of Harding's article, "Christian Blasphemers," is followed by the briefest and final, "Chance for Redemption." Authentic life and love are what is at stake. On the one hand, the advocates of black power charge that what white power offers black children, women, and men is survival, not authentic or abundant life and tolerance, not authentic love. Thus, what white power offers can be nothing but contingent upon self-denial and, hence, nothing but ersatz life and love. To the angry children of Malcolm X, white power declares:

You must love your enemies—if they're white and American and represent law and order. You must love them for your rotting houses and for your warped education. You must love them for your nonexistent jobs. Above all, you must love them for their riot guns, their billy clubs, their hatred and their white, white skin.

(Harding, 1979, p.40)

The advocates of black power meet this "vicious" exhortation to perverted self-denial with a cry of rage: "Give us no pink, two-faced Jesus who counsels love for you and flaming death for the children of Vietnam. Give us no blood-sucking savior who condemns brick-throwing rioters and praises dive-bombing killers. That Christ stinks. We want no black men to follow in *his* steps" (Harding, 1979, pp.40–41).

In his own voice, Harding warns (white and black) Christians who are eager to protect the white American Christ from what some perceive as blasphemy: "We [Christians] are the ones who take [Christ's] name in vain. We are the ones who follow the phony American Christ and in our every act declare our betrayal of the resurrected Lord" (p.41). The enduring power and truth of Harding's analysis is evident in the following quote:

It is we Christians who made the universal Christ into an American mascot, a puppet blessing every mad American act, from the extermination of the original possessors of this land to the massacre of the Vietnamese on their own soil. ... If judgment stands sure it is not primarily upon SNCC that it will fall, but upon those who have kidnapped the compassionate Jesus—the Jesus who shared all he had, even his life, with the poor—and made him into a profit-oriented, individualistic, pietistic cat who belongs to his own narrowly defined kind and begrudges the poor their humiliating subsistence budgets. These Christians are the ones who have taken away our Lord and buried him in a place unknown.

(Harding, 1979, p.41)

White power has distorted Jesus Christ in the American image, thus, black power represents the nation's only chance for redemption and liberation. In the hands of theologians like James Cone and Gayraud Wilmore, the meaning of such redemption and liberation necessarily and willingly includes those children, women, and men of all races who have been marginalized and made powerless by white hegemony. White supremacy posits liberation in the fulfillment of the market-made desire, while authentic liberation urges us to "become conscious of the fact that the humanizing struggle for life, hope, and true freedom in the world shows that God created all of us for freedom in God's self" (Wilmore, 2004, p.134).

Taking up this fragile chance for life and love calls for *metanoia*, for conversion of life. King recognized the concrete and social impact of sin in society. In one sermon, he exegeted our collective human enmeshment in sin and evil in light of the parable of the prodigal son. Like the prodigal, humankind has "strayed to the far countries of secularism, materialism, [sexual immorality], and racial injustice. [Our] journey has brought a moral and spiritual famine in Western civilization. *But it is not too late to return home"* (King, 1963, p.112).

To turn home is to turn to a God-Man startling strange, the black messiah, the black Jesus. He calls us to conversion of heart and mind—to transformation and change; to embrace the responsibility of resistance and creativity in order to honor and respect the human other, to enjoy human and humane life. Social (i.e., political, economic, technological) conditions in contemporary America beg for radical change. Most significantly, those who would follow the black Jesus must be alert to our vulnerable black, Latino, and poor white youth, who are lured by the glitter of violence and evil. We followers of the black Jesus must speak and act; already our silence and avoidance have sown a bitter crop. Moreover, we not only must counsel young people, but live rightly in the midst of vapid market values that swamp our ordinary daily choices. We not only must denounce violence and brutality, but develop strategies that expose the corrosive impact of the gestures, dress, and rhetoric of gang-life, which surround and tempt our youth. We must live a peace which does not merely suppress aggression, but which creatively and actively befriends others and ourselves. We must live the peace of the black Christ. Indeed Harding invites us to become "a gift of light," a "source of hope" for all living "daily under the threat of white America's arrogant and bloody power" (p.42).

Early on in "Black Power and the American Christ," Harding considers whether, God "is writing on the wall, saying that we Christians, black and white must choose between death with the American Christ and life with the Suffering Servant of God" (p.36). Those of us who would live with the Suffering Servant of God must be prepared to uncover and disrupt white hegemony, to enter into concrete solidarity with a suffering world and embrace the little ones as comrades and equals, to cast our lot with the black Jesus who challenges and changes the sacramental imagination and economy.

A concluding postscript

Perhaps the Detroit housepainter had been tracked down by the *zeitgeist*—the spirit of the time! Perhaps the housepainter was tired of being sick and tired, tired of praying to a white Christ. Perhaps he sought a witness—a witness to the changes in the city, a witness to the rebellion. Perhaps the housepainter wanted to shake up a Christianity that had given itself over to the principalities and powers of the age. Perhaps he wanted to signify the distance Christianity had traveled from the broken and abused body at its heart to seats of corporate power. It is probable that we shall never know. But, the painted black Jesus of Detroit disturbed more than the aesthetics of race; the ebonized statue problematized the iconic hegemony of the white American Christ. Albert Cleage (1972) was correct when he wrote, "You can take anything and paint it Black, but that does not make it Black if it is still serving white interests and if it still comes out of the white experience. ... A thing is not Black because it is painted Black" (p.14). Black theology repudiated a merely painted Christ: "Christ's blackness is both literal and symbolic. His blackness is literal in the sense that he truly becomes One with the oppressed blacks, taking their suffering as his suffering and revealing that he is found in the history of [black] struggle" (Cone, 1975, p.125). The black Jesus of Detroit subverted white hegemonic economic interests and kept alive the vibrant memory of the struggle of black and poor Detroiters of all racial–cultural backgrounds and claimed Jesus indisputably as a co-sufferer in a deindustrialized, crumbling city.

Notes

1 For prescient analyses of whiteness, see Du Bois (1920/1999, pp.17–29) and Baldwin (2010, pp.72–79).
2 See Epstein (1977).
3 The literature on the religion of the slaves has grown quite large since the 1970s; two pioneering, classic texts come from historian Albert J. Raboteau (1978/2004) and historian of religions Charles H. Long (1986).
4 The phrase "black power" may have originated with Adam Clayton Powell, who, in an address at Howard University on May 29, 1966, declared, "Human rights are God given ... to demand these God-given rights is to seek black power, the power to build black institutions." Quoted in Barbaus (1968, p.189); see also Nathan Wright Jr. (1967, pp.3, 13).
5 Nothing captured the raw urgency, apocalyptic hope and daring of the times more than the dramatic entrance of James Forman into Riverside Church on May 4, 1969. To a stunned congregation, Forman read the "Black Manifesto," which demanded that the white Christian churches and Jewish synagogues pay $500,000,000 reparations to the country's 30,000,000 black citizens.
6 According to the Trans-Atlantic Slave Trade Database, more than three hundred merchant slave ships bore some variant of the name of Jesus. This "christening" of slave ships mocks the Pauline letter to believers at Philippi: "at the name of Jesus, every knee should bend, in heaven and on earth and under the earth" (Philippians 2:10).
7 This adage is well-known to the indigenous peoples of the Americas.
8 In his foreword to the Beacon Press 1996 edition, Vincent Harding writes: "A postmodern and postindustrial American postscript: Although Thurman's message of the 1940s was focused on the needs of the Black representatives of the disinherited in the United States, by the last half of the final decade of the twentieth century it is clear that his message is now replete with significance for many other people as well. Latinos, Native Americans, Southeast Asians, and many women and gay and lesbian people are only the most obvious additions to Thurman's community of the wall" (p.7).
9 Cleage (1969, pp.35–47 and 1972, p.3).
10 A brief history of the Shrine of the Black Madonna is available online at www.shrine bookstore.com/church.aspx. In addition to the first Detroit site, the Pan African Orthodox Christian Church reports branches in Atlanta, Houston, and Calhoun Falls, South Carolina.
11 In 1966, Dr. King and the Southern Christina Leadership Conference planned several marches against segregation in Northern cities. Cicero, Illinois, a suburb of Chicago, was noteworthy for its racial hatred. After several aborted attempts, King decided against a march. However, the Reverend Jesse Jackson organized approximately 250 marchers to go to Cicero, where they were met by 3,000 law enforcement officers and an angry white mob (see www.pbs.org/wgbh/amex/eyesontheprize/story/12_chicago.html).

References

Babb, Valerie. *Whiteness Visible: The Meaning of Whiteness in American Literature and Culture* (New York and London: New York University Press, 1998).

Baldwin, James. "The White Problem," pp.72–79, in *The Cross of Redemption: Uncollected Writings* (New York: Pantheon Books, 2010).

Barbaus, Floyd B. *The Black Power Revolt* (Boston: Beacon Press, 1968).

Blassingame, John, ed. *Slave Testimony: Two Centuries of Letters, Speeches, Interviews, and Autobiographies* (Baton Rouge: Louisiana State University Press, 1977).

Lee Boggs, James and Lee Boggs, Grace. *Revolution and Evolution in the Twentieth Century* (New York and London: Monthly Review Press, 1974).

Carmichael, Stokely and Hamilton, Charles V. *Black Power: The Politics of Liberation in America* (New York: Vintage Books, 1967).

Clark, Kenneth B. *Dark Ghetto* (New York: Harper & Row, 1965).

Cleage, Albert B. *The Black Messiah* (New York: Sheed and Ward, 1969).

——. *Black Christian Nationalism: New Directions for the Black Church* (New York: William Morrow & Company, Inc., 1972).

Collins, Lisa Gail and Crawford, Margo Natalie eds. *New Thoughts on the Black Arts Movement* (New Brunswick, NJ: Rutgers University Press, 2006).

Cone, James H. *Black Theology and Black Power* (New York: Seabury Press, 1969).

——. *Spirituals and the Blues* (1972; Maryknoll, NY: Orbis Books, 1991).

——. *God of the Oppressed* (1975; Maryknoll, NY: Orbis Books, 1997).

——. *Martin and Malcolm and America: A Dream or a Nightmare* (Maryknoll, NY: Orbis Books, 1991).

Cruz, Jon. *Culture on the Margins: The Black Spiritual and the Rise of American Cultural Interpretation* (Princeton: Princeton University Press, 1999).

Cullen, Countee. "Heritage," p.450, in Rochelle Smith and Sharon L. Jones, eds., *The Prentice Hall Anthology of African American Literature* (Upper Saddle River, NJ: Prentice-Hall, Inc., 2000).

Douglas, Kelly Brown. *The Black Christ* (Maryknoll, NY: Orbis Books, 1994).

Douglass, Frederick. *Narrative of the Life of Frederick Douglass an American Slave* (1845; New York: Random House, Modern Library College Edition, 1984).

Du Bois, W. E. B. "The Souls of White Folk," pp.17–29, in *Darkwater: Voices from within the Veil* (1920; Mineola, NY: Dover Publications, Inc., 1999).

Epstein, Dena. *Sinful Tunes and Spirituals: Black Folk Music to the Civil War* (Urbana: University of Illinois Press, 1977).

Gallio, Daniel. "A Gathering of Hope," *Mosaic* (Fall 2007), www.aodonline.org/SHMS/Publications+5827 (accessed 22 April 2010).

Georgakas, Dan and Surkin, Marvin. *Detroit: I Do Mind Dying: A Study in Urban Revolution*, updated ed. (1975; Cambridge, MA: South End Press, 1998).

Horsley, Richard. *Jesus and Empire: The Kingdom of God and the New World Disorder* (Minneapolis: Fortress Press, 2002), pp.79–104.

Harding, Vincent. "Black Power and the American Christ," pp.35–42, in *Black Theology: A Documentary History, 1966–1979*, ed. Gayraud S. Wilmore and James H. Cone (1967; Maryknoll, NY: Orbis Books, 1979).

Harris, Fred R. "Preface to the 1988 Edition," *The Kerner Report: The 1968 Report of the National Advisory Commission on Civil Disorders* (1968; New York: Pantheon Books, 1988).

Johnson, Walter. *Soul by Soul: Life Inside the Antebellum Slave Market* (Cambridge, MA and London: Harvard University Press, 1999).

King, M.L. "What Is Man?" in *Strength to Love* (1963; New York: Harper & Row, 1968).

——. "The Current Crisis in Race Relations," in *A Testament of Hope: The Essential Writings of Martin Luther King, Jr.*, ed. James Melven Washington (New York: Harper & Row, 1986).

——. *Stride Toward Freedom*, in *A Testament of Hope: The Essential Writings of Martin Luther King, Jr.*, ed. James Melven Washington (New York: Harper & Row, 1986).

——. "The *Playboy* Interview" in *A Testament of Hope: The Essential Writings of Martin Luther King, Jr.*, ed. James Melven Washington (New York: Harper & Row, 1986).

Long, Charles H. *Significations: Signs, Symbols, and Images in the Interpretation of Religion* (Philadelphia: Fortress Press, 1986).

Lovell, John Jr. *Black Song: The Forge and the Flame* (New York: Macmillan, 1972).

Mitchell, Henry, Cp. *Black Belief* (San Francisco: Harper & Row, 1975).

Mondzain, Marie-José. *Image, Icon, Economy: The Byzantine Origins of the Contemporary Imaginary*, transl. by Rico Franses (Stanford, CA: Stanford University Press, 2005).

Morrison, Toni. *Playing in the Dark: Whiteness and the Literary Imagination* (Cambridge, MA and London: Harvard University Press, 1992).

Painter, Nell Irvin. "Soul Murder and Slavery: Toward a Fully Loaded Cost Accounting," 127, in *U.S. History as Women's History: New Feminist Essays*, eds., Linda Kerber, Alice Kessler-Harris, and Kathryn Kish Sklar (Chapel Hill and London: The University of North Carolina Press, 1995).

Perkinson, James W. *White Theology: Outing Supremacy in Modernity* (New York: Palgrave Macmillan, 2004).

Raboteau, Albert J. *Slave Religion: The "Invisible" Institution in the Antebellum South* (1978; Oxford: Oxford University Press, 2004).

Thurman, Howard. *Deep River and The Negro Spiritual Speaks of Life and Death* (Indiana: Friends United Press, 1975).

——. *Jesus and the Disinherited* (1949; Boston: Beacon Press, 1996).

Wilmore, Gayraud S. *Black Religion and Black Radicalism* (Maryknoll, NY: Orbis Press, 1998).

——. *Pragmatic Spirituality: The Christian Faith Through an Africentric Lens* (New York and London: New York University Press, 2004).

Wilmore, Gayraud S. and Cone, James H. (Eds.) *Black Theology: A Documentary History, 1966-1979* (Maryknoll, NY: Orbis Books, 1979).

Wright, N. T. *Christian Origins and the Question of God: Jesus and the Victory of God*, vol. 2 (Minneapolis: Fortress Press, 1996).

Wright, Nathan Jr. *Black Power and Urban Unrest* (1967).

13

THE MIMESIS OF SALVATION AND DISSIMILITUDE IN THE SCANDALOUS GOSPEL OF JESUS

Victor Anderson

Introduction

This chapter is a critical discussion of the relationship of Christian supersessionism, which is the idea that Christ's saving works supersedes all prior covenants, promises, and dealings with biblical Israel, as Christ is the fulfillment or recapitulation of God's soteriological aim to reconcile creation and all people to God. This aim is mediated not only in the person and work of Christ (Christology) but especially in the gospel that Jesus preached. I argue that the gospel of Jesus is a scandalous gospel that carries within itself its own history of supersessions, which mimetically join Christology and whiteness; for the gospel of Jesus is good news for some and bad news for others. This is its scandal, and everything matters for those who fall on the side of its bad news—whether Jews or gentiles, Pharisees or Sadducees, the synagogue or church, Christian or Muslim, European or savage, or white and black.

I never paid much attention to whether Jesus was white, black, brown, or yellow. His color was simply a matter of indifference to me growing up. I have stored away in my shed two sacred heart images of Jesus and the blessed Mother. They hung on walls over the beds in my bedroom. I knew that they were there to protect me. In the dining room hung a three-dimensional rendering of Leonardo Da Vinci's *Last Supper*. Images such as these hung everywhere throughout my home and were usually accompanied by pictures of Dr. Martin Luther King, Jr. and President John F. Kennedy. There was Jesus seated between his disciples or holding in his arms a white or black lamb. Sometimes, he is sitting on the edge of a hill over-looking the plains of Galilee or looking toward Jerusalem. Not only were these icons sprawled throughout my home, but one could easily find them in the homes of neighbors. They circulated throughout the black community through church and funeral home fans, family bibles, children bibles, and in Sunday school lessons. I recall with affection these images. In those days, they did not spark in me a critical concern about the apparent whiteness of Jesus. Yet, they operated as iconography, but not an iconography of whiteness.

I now see that the whiteness of Jesus is a mimetic effect within a history of the mimesis of salvation and dissimilitude (alterity). They represent Jesus as soft, gentle, and loving. Some picture him sitting on a rock with children gathered around him. Each child is depicted differently by a racial or ethnic group and skin color. The divine lesson of this iconography is not difficult to grasp. No matter what your race or ethnicity, Jesus' love *supersedes* all differences because Jesus loves everybody. It took many life experiences of sorrow and grief, senseless deaths and racial and ethnic violence, to wrest from my naïve childhood consciousness both my appreciation for the color-blind Jesus and the idea that Jesus really loves every one. What I discovered was that behind this mimesis of representations of "white Jesus" lay histories of mimetic desire, rivalry, violence, and scandal in the gospel of Jesus. This is the critical relation between Christology and whiteness.

Christology is Christian discourse surrounding the person and work of Jesus the Christ. God's soteriological aim to reconcile not only all to God, but all to all, is mediated in and through the person and work of Jesus as the bearer of good news. For some, Christ's person and work perform a "recapitulation" of the promises, covenants, and dealings with biblical Israel as God's elect among the nations. Within this mimesis of recapitulation, "there is no longer Jew or Greek, there is no longer slave or free, there is no longer male or female; for all of you are one in Christ Jesus" (Galatians, 3:28). However, it appears that such a biblical universalism, as articulated by Paul, is more the work of Paul and his followers than an articulation of the scandalous gospel of Jesus, which announces a repetition of "otherness" or dissimilitude.

However, Paul's mimesis of salvation levels all racial/ethnic distinctions within salvation history, for he preaches that "there is no distinction between Jew and Gentile; the same Lord is Lord of all and richly blesses all who call on him, for everyone who calls on the name of the Lord will be saved" (Romans, 10:12–13). Does this universalism represent a *supersession* of the all over the particular, of the kingdom of God over all nations, including Rome and Judea? Through his death, resurrection, and ascension, Jesus Christ ascends to the right hand of the throne of God as lord and savior of all. However, does this universal election of all in Christ simultaneously signify a prior supersession of the election of biblical Israel over the nations? Is Paul's biblical universalism of the "all" in Christ without dissimilitude? Does it entail a mimesis of salvation and dissimilitude with a price in which salvation is available to those who call on the name of Christ but for others what? This chapter explores this mimesis of salvation and dissimilitude (otherness) as the mimetic effect of the scandalous gospel of Jesus.

On the mimesis of supersession

Supersession is one of the most contested doctrines in Christology. In proclaiming and inaugurating the Kingdom of God, does this gospel of the kingdom simultaneously supersede all previous covenants, dealings, and the election of biblical Israel?

Does the new covenant replace, fulfill, or recapitulate God's promises to the Jews in the election of all in Christ? As a theological idea, supersession has special significance for Christian anti-Semitism and modern racism. My first contact with it was as a Bible College student at Chicago Bible College and Moody Bible Institute, where I was immersed in dispensationalism. Here, salvation history is parsed into stages in which the mighty works of God are ordered through dispensations of grace and covenants. God's covenants are made within distinct dispensations. And although God is faithful in keeping God's promises, God's promises transfer to others when the covenant is breached. For instance, God's covenant with Adam is superseded by God's covenant with Noah. Then God's covenant with Noah is superseded by God's covenant with Abraham. This is called the Abraham covenant. Abraham's covenant with God is then superseded by the Mosaic covenant at Sinai. And the Davidic covenant is superseded by the Messianic. The Messianic covenant is fulfilled in Jesus' ushering in the New Covenant. Each covenant is progressively superseded until all are finally consummated in the second coming of Christ and eternal bliss.

Sometimes covenantal supersession has been understood in light of what some theologians call "Replacement Theology." However, Michael Vlach says that "replacement theology" does not appear to be well received by some. Several have noted that they would rather be known as "fulfillment theologians" or some other title that is more positive. For some, replacement theology suggests that "the Church, Abraham's spiritual seed, had replaced national Israel in that it had transcended and fulfilled the terms of the covenant given to Israel, which covenant Israel had lost because of disobedience" (Vlach, personal communication). Others understand covenantal supersession in that "God chose the Jewish people after the fall of Adam in order to prepare the world for the coming of Jesus Christ, the Savior. After Christ came, however, the special role of the Jewish people came to an end and its place was taken by the Church, the new Israel" (Vlach, 2011). Still others take this mimesis of supersession to mean: "The New Testament affirms that Israel would no longer be the people of God and would be replaced by a people that would accept the Messiah and his message of the Kingdom of God" (Vlach 2011). Common to these views of covenantal supersession is that God makes covenants and that human breaching of these covenants means a reversal and transference of God's promises to others.

J. Cameron Carter (2008) argues that at the root of modern racism and anti-Semitism is the Gnostic heresy of supersession. He writes:

> At the genealogical taproot of modern racial reasoning is the process by which Christ was abstracted from Jesus, and thus from his Jewish body, thereby severing Christianity from its Jewish roots. Jewish flesh in this moment underwent a religious conversion: it was converted into racial flesh, positioned within a hierarchy of racial–anthropological essences, and lodged within a now racialized chain of being. In making Christ non-Jewish in this moment, he was made a figure of the Occident. He became white, even if Jesus as a historical figure remained Jewish or a racial figure of the Orient.

(p. 6–7)

For Carter, this whitening of Jesus was the mimetic effect of a prior supersession, namely, a Christological supersession of the divinity of Christ over the humanity of Jesus of Nazareth, the Jew.

According to Carter (2008), this supersession of spirit over the flesh was the work of Gnostic Christianity, with a complex metaphysics and anthropology that severed "Christianity from its Jewish roots. In decoupling Christianity from YHWH, the Abrahamic God, the Gnostics were able to re-imagine Christian identity in protoracial terms, terms that supported the supremacy of the pneumatics (or Gnostics) over the species of humankind" (p.23). Drawing on Elaine Pagels, Carter explains Gnostic supersessionism:

> The Gnostic seized on the Pauline doctrine of election in order to rewrite it in Gnostic terms, so construed, Paul's concern was not with YHWH's irrevocable promises to Israel as the people of his covenant and, in this way, for creation as a whole and in all of its particularities. Instead, his concern, the Gnostics contended, was over the election of the true, pneumatic Christians— that is, the Gnostics. They are the "new" Israel—the true church beyond Israel, the gathering of pneumatics who are an image of the nonmaterial "Ecclesia". ...
>
> (p.23)

Although Carter's account is worthy of sustained attention, unfortunately it is also too richly detailed to take up here. However, for him, supersessionism, in the end, is a Gnostic heresy. By mimetic appropriation in the theological curriculum, it has had a poisonous career in theological history in reproducing the supremacy of Jesus' divinity over his Jewish flesh, the replacement of the church over national Israel or Judea, universal election over the election of Israel, the supersession of the West over the East and the subaltern, and white over black.

Christian supersession being founded on a bad metaphor, Carter rejects it as a Gnostic heresy. For him, it is not so much that Christ's new covenant supersedes God's promises, covenants, and dealings with biblical Israel in a new creation and a new Israel. Rather, Christ is the "recapitulation" of all God's promises in his one body. As the recapitulation of salvation history (God's soteriological aim), the crucified, risen, and ascended Christ is savior of all and, simultaneously, is the fulfillment of God's promises and covenants to biblical Israel. However, one must wonder whether a change of verbs, from "supersede" to "recapitulate" does not, in Carter's case, reinscribe supersession by imitation. Consider his discussion:

> John Behr observes that "recapitulation" (anakephlaiôsis) describes for Irenaus the relationship between the Scriptures of the Old Testament and the Gospels of the New, as both are held together through the events of Christ's flesh as those events culminate with the cross: "Recapitulation *summarizes* the whole [of a case], presenting [a restatement of it] in *epitome*, bringing together the *whole* argument in one conspectus, so that, while the particular details made little

impact [alone], *the picture as a whole might be more forceful.* Recapitulation provides a *résumé* which, because shorter, is clear and therefore *more effective.*"

(Carter, 2008, p.26)

In terms (which I italicize for emphasis) such as *summarizes, epitome, the whole, résumé* and phrases such as *the picture as a whole might be more forceful* and *more effective,* one captures immediately the difficulty of escaping the mimetic history of supersessionism in Christology, even for a theologian such as Carter who is keenly aware of its poisonous effects in the mimesis of salvation and dissimilitude. For what is shown is that the whole is greater than its parts.

Although an inheritance of the Christological debates in early Christianity, the mimesis of Christian supersessionism traveled in theological history to become a historical scheme in Portuguese trafficking in sub-Saharan African slavery and the Spanish conquest of Peru. Willie J. Jennings (2010) describes this mimesis as a reconfiguration of the logic of supersessionism (p.32). He writes:

> Christian Spain and Portugal as well as in other parts of medieval Europe indicated a profound theological distortion. Here was a process of discerning Christian identity that, because it had jettisoned Israel from its calculus of the formation of Christian life, created a conceptual vacuum that was filled by the European. But not simply qua European; rather the very process of becoming Christian took on new ontic markers. Those markers of being were aesthetic and racial. This was not a straightforward matter of replacement (European for Jew) but, as I have suggested, of displacement and now theological reconfiguration. European Christians reconfigured the vision of God's attention and love for Israel, that is, they reconfigured a vision of Israel's election. If Israel had been the visibly elect of God, then that visibility in the European imagination migrated without return to a new home shaped now by new visible markers. If Israel's election had been the compass around which Christian identity gained its bearings and gained its trajectory, now with this reconfiguration the body of the European would be the compass marking divine election. More importantly, that new elected body, the white body, would be the discerning body, able to detect holy effects and saving grace.

(p.33)

For Jennings, the mimesis of supersessionism does not only reach its apex in a theological history of salvation and dissimilitude within Christian Europe and its alterns (Jews, Muslim, and savages), but within its own history of mimesis, the theological doctrine recoiled into a philosophy of history in which modern Europe supersedes all prior histories of peoples and races.

Supersessionism organizes the history of peoples by progressive ages and stages until arriving at civilization, which means Western European civilization and culture (whiteness). Hegel's philosophy of history stands as a monumental achievement of this mimesis of Christian supersessionism. Here, the motives of all particular societies lay not so much in their empirical life as in their psychological, mental contributions to the furtherance of civilization. This process signifies a *neognostism*, as Carter (2008) describes it (p.14). Social arrangements become politics, rituals become theological, artifacts become art, customs and habits become ethics, and ways of thinking become philosophy. And all are driven by and toward the supersession of absolute spirit.

Prior to Kant (1960), who ridiculed African religion as just so much a relic of superstition and "fetishism" (pp.110–11), David Hume (1985), in his infamous footnote 10, describes African peoples:

> I am apt to suspect the Negroes to be naturally inferior to the whites. There scarcely ever was a civilized nation of that complexion, nor even any individual eminent either in action or speculation. No ingenious manufactures among them, no arts, no science. On the other hand, the most rude and barbarous of the white, such as the ancient GERMANS, the present TARTARS, have still something eminent about them, in their valour, form of government, or some other particular.
>
> *(p.208)*

Given the cultural logic of supersessionism, for Hegel, Africa falls completely outside the progress of universal history. Consider his final judgment.

> The particularity of African character is difficult to comprehend, for the very reason that in reference to it, we must quite give up the principle which naturally accompanies all our ideas—the category of universality. ... The Negro, as already observed, exhibits the natural man in his completely wild and untamed state. We must lay aside all thought of reverence and morality—all that we call feeling—if we would rightly comprehend him; there is nothing harmonious with humanity to be found in this type of character ... At this point we leave Africa, not to mention it again. For it has no historical part of the World; it has no movement or development to exhibit.
>
> *(Outlaw, 1995, p.314)*

I am proposing that if we are to critically interpret the significance of Christology and whiteness, we will find ourselves observing by repetition the mimesis of Christian supersessionism. Moreover, notwithstanding Carter's and Jennings' contempt for this doctrine and its cultural, racial, and ethnic logics, the doctrine seems inescapable from the Christian imagination; for it appears as the mimetic effect of the Gospels them-selves and of the person and work of Jesus. Does renouncing the supersession of Christ over all and the election of all in Christ, as was preached by Paul, require the renunciation of all mimetic desire, if by such a renunciation the violence spawned by it, in the Christian imaginary of nations, peoples, and races, is to be negated? These are questions that I put to French phenomenologist René Girard in the following section. I regard supersessionism to be a theologically determinative orientation of the Christian imaginary. I argue that it operates mimetically as a history of salvation and dissimilitude and otherness. Albeit in a preliminary manner, I argue that the mimesis of supersessionism in Christology is the scandal of the gospel of Jesus, that it is rooted in mimetic desire, and that it continues in its own mimetic history the violence of the gospel. These claims are positioned relative to Girard's renunciation of mimetic desire and violence as characteristic of Christian faith.

Girard and the renunciation of mimetic desire

René Girard (2003) insists that mimetic desire lies at the root of all violence generated by mimetic rivalry. Although Girard's mimetic theory is quite detailed and complex, he provides a helpful summary that is critical for the purposes of this short chapter. Hence, I quote him at length.

> If you survey the literature in imitation, you will quickly discover that acquisition and appropriation are never included among the modes of behavior that are likely to be imitated. If acquisition and appropriation were included, imitation as a social phenomenon would turn out to be more problematic that it appears, and above all conflictual. If the appropriative gesture of an individual named A is rooted in the imitation of an individual named B, it means that A and B must reach together for one and the same object. They become rivals for that object. If the tendency to imitate appropriation is present on both sides, imitative rivalry must tend to be reciprocal; it must be subject to the back and forth reinforcement that communication theorists call a positive feedback loop. In other words, the individual who first acts as a model will experience an increase in his own appropriative urge when he finds himself thwarted by his imitator and reciprocally. Each becomes the imitator of his own imitator and the model of his own model. Each tries to push aside the obstacle that the other places in his path. Violence is generated by this process; or rather violence is the process itself when two or more partners try to prevent one another from appropriating the object they desire through physical or other means. Under the influence of the judicial viewpoint and of our own psychological impulses, we always look for some original violence or at least for well-defined acts of violence that would be separate from nonviolent behavior. We want to distinguish the culprit from the innocent and, as a result, we substitute discontinuities and difference from the continuities and reciprocities of the mimetic escalation.
>
> *(p. 9)*

In a 1992 interview, Girard responds to the question whether his theory of mimetic violence requires the renunciation of all mimetic desire. He contends that mimetic desire lies at the root of every mimetic rivalry where the consequence is violence and that the gospel of Jesus renounces this history of violence. For him, the non-sacrificial death of Jesus mediates and reconciles mimetic desire to the nonviolence of the gospel of Jesus. For Girard, Jesus' death could not rightly be regarded as sacrificial; for it is Jesus, who of his own freedom paves the path toward his crucifixion. Being the word made flesh, he embodies a nonviolent God in whose name his own life of nonviolence is an imitation of the Father. His death, therefore, is the mimetic display of Jesus' mimetic desire to imitate the Father and renounce all mimetic rivalry and violence. On the question of whether all mimetic desire must be renounced, Girard (2003) explains:

> As to whether I am advocating "renunciation" of mimetic desire, yes and no. Not the renunciation of mimetic desire itself, because what Jesus advocates is mimetic desire. Imitate me, and imitate the Father through me, he says, so it's twice mimetic. Jesus seems to say that the only way to avoid violence is to imitate me, and imitate the Father. So the idea that mimetic desire itself is bad makes no sense. It's true, however, that occasionally I say "mimetic desire" when I really mean only the type of mimetic desire that generates mimetic rivalry, and in turn, is generated by it.
>
> (p.63)

I want to propose that, in the mimetic history of the imitation of Christ, followers of Jesus are oriented toward a mimetic desire in which violence and rivalry are carried along into the scandalous gospel of Jesus and consequently into every future mimesis of salvation and dissimilitude. Responding to whether all mimetic desire produces violence, Girard (2003) says:

> No, that impression is not true. ... Jesus says that scandals must happen, and he tells his disciples that they will all be scandalized when he is arrested; but at the same time he says: happy are those to whom I will not be a scandal. So there are nevertheless a few who are not scandalized. That scandals must happen might sound like determinism, but it is not.
>
> (p.62)

In the above quote, scandal signifies, for Girard, "human failure to walk away from mimetic rivalry" and violence (Girard, 2003, p.215). He insists that: "mimetic rivalry is not sin but rather a permanent occasion of sin. The sin occurs when our relentlessness makes the rivalry obsessive. Its name is envy, jealousy, pride, anger, and despair. For this satanic exasperation of mimetic rivalry, the Gospels have a marvelous word, *skandalon*" (Girard, 2003, p.215). Scandals of mimetic desire may be personal and addictive as in "drugs, sex, power, and above all, morbid competiveness," but they may also be corporal as well, "professional, political, intellectual and spiritual," says Girard (p.215). "Being mimetic from the start, scandals become more so as they multiply and intensify. They become impersonal, anonymous, undifferentiated, and interchangeable," Girard insists (p.216). Moreover, "beyond a certain threshold they substitute for one another, with little or no awareness on our part. Scandals begin small, with two or three individuals, but as they turn gregarious, they can grow very large. People become so burdened with scandals that they desperately, if unconsciously, seek public substitutes, collective targets upon whom to unburden themselves" (p.216). Such are the effects of mimetic desire. And the consequent is mimetic violence in which, as Girard has argued, "we want to distinguish the culprit from the innocent " and "substitute discontinuities and differences for the continuities and reciprocities" (p.9).

For Girard, mimetic desire is dangerously oriented toward mimetic rivalry and violence (1972; 2003).[1] It is the rivalry of the copy toward the model, the type toward its antitype, or the truly real toward appearances. Girard proposes that the mimetic desire to imitate Jesus directs us away from such rivalry and violence generated by mimetic desire. However, I propose that Girard's identification of mimesis with the term "imitation" may be too constraining for all that mimesis allows. As Michael Potolsky (2005) argues, mimesis produces a surplus of effects. It "takes on different guises in different historical contexts, masquerading under a variety of related terms and translations: emulation, mimicry, dissimulation, doubling, theatricality, realism, identification, correspondence, depiction, verisimilitude, resemblance" (p.1). Potolsky (2005) argues: "no one translation and no one interpretation is sufficient to encompass its complexity and tradition of commentary it has inspired. Nor can any one translation account for the range of attitudes mimesis evokes" (p.1).

Although Girard insists that not every mimetic desire is dangerously oriented toward rivalry and violence, I suggest that even Christian mimetic desire, directed toward the renunciation of mimetic rivalry and violence, carries within itself its own history of rivalries, reversals, renunciations, repetitions, and dissimilitude. In his discussion of Nietzsche's revaluation of values, Walter Kaufmann (1968) well explains this historical effect in the mimesis of salvation and dissimilitude. He says that "the revaluation is the alleged discovery that our morality is but its own standard, poisonously immoral: that Christian love is the mimicry of impotent hatred; that most unselfishness is but the particularly vicious form of selfishness; and that resentment is at the core of our morals" (Kaufmann, 1968, p.113). Moreover, in his discussion of "Nietzsche's Repudiation of Christ," Kaufmann suggests that the mimesis of the gospel succeeds not only by a repetition of supersession but also by a *renunciation* of the "truth of the gospel." This renunciation is poignantly articulated in Nietzsche's critique of the *For's*. Consider Nietzsche:

> I give some examples of what the little people put into their heads, what they put into the mouth of their master: without exception, confessions of "beautiful souls":
>
> "And whosoever shall not receive you nor hear you, when ye depart thence, shake off the dust under your feet for a testimony against them. Verily I say unto you, It shall be more tolerable for Sodom and Gomorrah in the Day of Judgment, than for that city" (Mark 6:11)—*how evangelic!* ...
>
> "Whosoever will come after me let him deny himself, and take up his cross, and follow me, For –" (... Christian morality is refuted by it's *For's*: its "reason" refute. ...) (Mark 8:34).
>
> "*For* if ye love them which love you, what reward have ye? ... " (Matt. 5:46) – "Principle of Christian love": *it wants in the end to be paid well.*

> "But if ye forgive not men their trespasses, neither will your Father forgive your trespasses" (Matt. 6:15) – *Very compromising* for said "Father". ...
>
> *(Kaufmann, 1968, p. 347, citing Nietzsche's* Antichrist,
> *p. 45 (emphasis mine))*

On Kaufmann's reading of "Nietzsche vs. the Christ", the gospel of Jesus carries in its history the mimesis of rivalry, violence, retribution, and the renunciation of mimetic desire. According to him, "Nietzsche charges that the Christian 'faith' made it possible for men not only to persist in their unchristian behavior, but also to indulge their lust for revenge by hoping for the eventual torture and destruction of their persecutors" (Kaufmann, 1968, p.347). Kaufmann (1968) thinks that Nietzsche "may have had in mind Paul's admonition: 'Bless them which persecute you: bless, and curse not. ... Avenge not yourselves, but rather give place unto wrath: for it is written, Vengeance is mine: I will repay, saith the Lord. Therefore if thine enemy hunger, feed him; if he thirst, give him drink: *for* in so doing thou shalt heap coals of fire on his head'" (Rom. 12:14 and 19–20) (p.347, emphasis mine). For Nietzsche, such a sentiment betrays a "revaluation of the evangel by addition of a most unevangelistic promise" (Kaufmann, 1968, p.347–48). Mimetic rivalry, violence, retribution, and renunciation are internal to the mimesis of salvation and dissimilitude in the scandalous gospel of Jesus.

I propose that the scandal of the gospel of Jesus is this repetition of a mimetic history of rivalry and violence in salvation history, where the gospel that was preached by Jesus scandalizes the world, demanding its renunciation by repentance and turning. It requires an over-turning of the present order with the supersession of a new one. This mimetic desire carries within itself the history of its own mimesis, which produces a repetition of renunciations, reversals and alterity (dissimilitude). Imitating Jesus requires that believers put to death the flesh and deny themselves to be like Christ.

The scandalous gospel of Jesus

Peter J. Gomes (2007) begins his book *The Scandalous Gospel of Jesus* where most do, namely, with the Bible. Unlike so many, he holds no idolatrous orientation toward it. Although the Bible is iconic for many Christians, Gomes thinks that ordinary Christians have a misplaced attention toward it. They see the Bible itself as gospel rather than the gospel being what Jesus preached and taught. He says:

> We start with the Bible because, like Everest it is there, and it looms large. There is no point in pretending otherwise, but while we may begin there, are we meant to end up there as well? If it is a means, to what is it a means? I suggest that the Bible, in its entire complex splendor, is but a means to a greater end, which is good news, the glad tidings, the gospel. Jesus came preaching—we are told this in all the Gospels—but nowhere in the Gospels is there a claim that he came preaching the New Testament, or even Christianity. It still shocks some Christians to realize that Jesus was not a Christian, that he did not know

"our" Bible, and that what he preached was substantially at odds with his biblical culture and with ours as well.

(Gomes, 2007, p.11)

Girard has argued that every mimesis requires mediation or a mediator. Thus, for Gomes, the Bible is mediatory. It stands between two histories. In Augustine's *City of God*, scripture mediates the mimetic rivalry of the kingdoms of righteousness and the human city. The Gospels are also mediatory. They mediate the preaching and teaching of Jesus and God's soteriological aim. In the gospel, that is, the good news is revealed in mimetic acts, events, desires, and aims that constitute the repetition of reversals of times, powers, authorities, status, wealth, and, yes, the election of nations. The kingdom of righteousness supersedes the kingdoms of this world, putting Jesus in danger with "his biblical culture and with ours as well," say Gomes (2007, p.11).

What is already understood as the truth of gospel is gained through a multiplicity of mediations. Biblical texts do not only purport what interpreters claim are their meanings. More importantly, interpretations multiply as interpreters (mediators) adjust themselves to uncomfortable subject positions into which they are signified by the gospel. The many gospels understood and preached, consequently, carry within them a history of mimetic effects, acts, events, desires, and aims. Gomes (2007) describes it this way:

> Depending, then, upon how one reads and interprets, either the Bible is a textbook for the status quo, a book of quiescent pieties and promises, or it is a recipe for social change and transformation. There are churches dedicated to each point of view, each claiming its share of the good news; but what is good news for some is often bad news for somebody else. We will see how this double-edge sword of the gospel makes Jesus' own preaching and teaching so dangerous, not only way back then but right here and now, and we will see why it is a very dangerous thing to take seriously the question: "What would Jesus Do?"

(p.12)

A number of questions open up: dangerous in what way, for whom, against whom? However such questions are answered, no answer escapes the mimetic desires of interpreters of the good news. None escapes the history of mimetic rivalry or the rupturing violence that the gospel produces and carries along in the mimesis of salvation and dissimilitude.

Gomes is most concerned about contemporary Christians' forgetfulness of the dangerous orientation of the gospel. With the Constantinian change, "the church is made an agency of continuity rather than of change, conformity rather than transformation becomes the reigning ideology of the day, and the church that is comfortable with the powers-that-be is no threat to them" (Gomes, 2007, p.20). One notes here a repetition of power, of continuity to change, and conformity to transformation. The church is constituted a danger, a scandal in its being toward the world, the state, the empire, and the status quo. It carries within the history of one reversal after another, the reversals of power, authority, status, and election. By its conformity to the world, Gomes (2007) argues that "rarely has the Christian church risked its temporary position to proclaim the glad tidings of Jesus' preaching and teaching, the risk of the status quo is almost always too great. The danger of the gospel is that if we take it seriously, then like Jesus, we will risk all and might even lose all" (p.22).

Although imitation is too narrow a word for all that we want mimesis to do, still, the gospel can be said to *mirror* God's soteriological aims. That is, the ministry of Jesus represents these aims as mimetic displays in which the blind see, the sick are healed, the lame walk, demons are exorcised, the dead are raised, and the poor are preached the good news. Those enlightened enough to grasp this truth, says Gomes, "will take no offense with the one who proclaims these truths and performs these deeds." That is, they will not be scandalized by this truth, but will become a scandal to others, for the gospel of Jesus is an offending gospel. Mimetic reversals or doublings permeate the Gospels by repetition. Consider the "beatitudes," and what Gomes (2007) calls the "woebetudes:"

- (Happy) are you poor; the kingdom of God is yours, (Woe) How terrible for you who are rich; you have had your easy life.
- (Happy) are you who are hungry now; you will be filled, (Woe) How terrible for you who are full now, you will go hungry.
- (Happy) are you who weep now; you will laugh, (Woe) How terrible when all men speak well of you; because their ancestors said the same things to the false prophets.

(p.29)

These doublings do not only present a mimesis of desire and rivalry, but also dissimilitude. In them, the mimetic desire of the blessed produces its own alterity that distinguishes culprit from the innocent and substituting discontinuities and differences for continuities and reciprocities. Dissimilitude marks Pharisees and Sadducees, the rich and the synagogue, the empire and the Jews, the Jews and Gentiles, and the election of nations and peoples. What is reproduced in the mimesis of salvation and dissimilitude is a surplus of mimetic otherness, of dissimilitude, that results in perpetual supersessionisms.

Although, the message of the beatitudes was intended as good news for those on the losing end of life, it doubles. This is a mimetic effect, a reversing of the relation or standing of others within God's soteriological aims. Consider Gomes' interpretation of the Sermon on the Mount:

> The sermon was not hard to preach, in the sense that the meaning of the text is quite clear. Those who appear to win by worldly standards, who are now the haves and not the haves-not, have every reason to be anxious about tomorrow, for if the good news, the gospel, is that worldly victories are only temporary and subject to reversal, then those who win today will lose tomorrow. Those who have it made today will have it unmade tomorrow. If you are at this

moment at ease and satisfied, enjoy it, for it will not last; now is your reward, but now is not forever.

(Gomes, 2007, p.30)

This repetition of mimetic reversals or doublings structurally relates this scandalous gospel of Jesus and intra-human relations into every future mimesis in the history of salvation and dissimilitude. The result is mimetic rivalry and violence rupturing repetitively into one supersession after another, until finally the Kingdom of God supersedes the kingdoms of this world. The book of Revelation celebrates this ultimate supersession of all reversals:

Woe! Woe! O great city, dressed in fine linen, purple and scarlet, and glittering with gold, precious stones and pearls! In one hour such great wealth has been brought to ruin ... Woe! Woe! O great city where all who had ships on the sea became rich through her wealth! In one hour she has been brought to ruin! Rejoice over her, O heaven! Rejoice, saints and apostles and prophets! God has judged her for the way she treated you.

(Revelation 18:16–20)

The scandalous gospel of Jesus carries over into every future mimesis of salvation and dissimilitude a dangerous history of repetitions, reversals, renunciations, and racial supersessions that reproduced, as it were in my childhood recollections, an iconography of white Jesus. In the last section, I show how this mimesis of salvation and dissimilitude is satirically carried over into the scandalous gospel of Reverend Ruckus in Aaron McGruder's *Boondocks* episode, "The Passion of Reverend Ruckus."

The scandalous gospel of Reverend Ruckus

Originally airing on March 19, 2006, Uncle Ruckus (the aged, self-hating, black male character of McGruder's creation, known for his constant deriding of everything black and total disregard for "niggers") dreams that he has gone to heaven. He is met at the gates by his iconic and messianic hero, President Ronald Reagan. Reagan is the emissary of "White God" and his son, "White Jesus." Reagan tells Ruckus that he is in white heaven and that because there are many types of people, God has made separate but "relatively equal" heavens. He assures Ruckus that God doesn't have a problem with racism, but that he personally hates black people and worked behind the scene of social problems that plagued black communities from crack cocaine and AIDs to Reaganomics. Ruckus' admiration for Reagan increases with awe. Then Reagan proposes to Ruckus that he too can join him in white heaven if he spreads the message that "God loves white people" and renounces everything black. Ruckus is led to a clear pool. Looking in, he sees himself transformed into a white-skinned, blond-haired and blue-eyed (Ruckus only has one good eye) image.

Awakened from his dream, Ruckus appears with a Bible in hand at the door of Robert Freeman, the retired grandfather of his adopted nephews, Huey (the mimesis of Black Panther Party leader Huey Newton) and his little Hip Hop thug brother, Reilly. Ruckus tells Robert that he has just returned from the doctor and is dying from a cancer on his back, and that he is on a mission from white God. He urges Robert to follow him to the street, where, standing on the back of a pickup truck, he announces his call to preach the gospel of white God and his son, white Jesus. His message is simple: "God is white and loves the white man above all others"; God hates "darkies" and loves white people, which is why he made his son in the image of the white man; the good news is that "everyone with a skin black as coal can enter the gates of paradise if he hates his own blackness; hate the skin, not the sinner."

Reverend Ruckus' message strikes a chord with a handful of white listeners gathered on the street to hear his message. He absolves them of any guilt they may have for their race prejudice toward black people. The message spreads quickly and Reverend Ruckus gains a large following of both whites and blacks. With the aid of television news entrepreneur Armstrong Elder, Reverend Ruckus' ministry flourishes. He plans a great revival. The tent meeting is packed, and he preaches to the attentive throngs, while Armstrong Elder manages sales of Ruckus' book. Dressed in a white suit and preaching with ecstatic, ejaculatory moves, Ruckus admonishes the audience to renounce blackness and to think of at least five "niggers" whom they would personally like to smack the black off their faces. Tom (the light-skinned, middle-class attorney, married to a white wife and friend of Robert, whom he accompanies to the meeting in order to bring Ruckus to his senses) gets enthusiastically caught up in the reverend's message. Jumping from his seat, feeling the spirit, and naming several black people whom he personally would want to slap the black off, he shouts: "He's Right!" as Robert tries to gain control over him.

Ruckus then announces an altar call, inviting all who want to renounce their blackness to come to the front of the auditorium. All those "black of skin and full of sin" are invited so that Ruckus may lay hands on them. In violent sweeps, he begins slapping their faces in order to symbolically slap the black off, shouting "Black be gone! Black be gone!" He excites all at the revival meeting to follow him, to imitate him. The meeting erupts in an orgiastic display of violence as the audience gets caught up in a slapping frenzy. Simultaneously, Reverend Ruckus begins praying to white God. He utters that if his message is a lie, may God strike him with lightning. Suddenly, a bolt of lightning strikes him. Immediately, the frenzy stops, and gatherers leave disappointed. Only Tom and Robert remain behind, after coming back to their senses, to care for lightning-struck Reverend Ruckus. It appears that the lightning strike did not only put an end to Reverend Ruckus' scandalous gospel of white Jesus; it also cured his cancer.

McGruder's "The Passion of Ruckus" is satirical. Yet, it adequately displays a mimesis of salvation and dissimilitude that reproduces an ancient tale of Christological and soteriological significance. Salvation and dissimilitude connect simultaneously in repetitions of rivalry, renunciation, and violence. Within the theatre of salvation, God washes away every stain and makes all good people white as snow. Ruckus participates in an imitation of this scandal, for while the good news is good for some, it is bad news for others, in this case, black people. While a mimicry of both contemporary performances of mass televangelism and the commoditization of the gospel, Reverend Ruckus' message is a mimesis, a repetition of a history of supersession. It repeats a history of mimetic desire that positions white over black and calls for a renunciation, turning, and reversal of everything black for the blessedness of whiteness. McGruder's "Passion of Ruckus" may be satirical, but it shows well how the imitation of Christ carries within its own history of mimetic desire, the rivalry, violence, renunciation, and scandal of supersessionism that is the gospel of Jesus.

To conclude, Zora Neale Hurston (1996) once wrote that "the Negro's universal mimicry is not so much a thing itself as an evidence of something that permeates his entire self. And that thing is drama" (p.24). So it is with McGruder's "Reverend Ruckus" and his scandalous gospel of white Jesus. I have argued that Christology is Christian discourse framed by the person and work of Jesus. Moreover, Jesus is the embodiment of God's soteriological aim, which is the good news of the kingdom of God that is preached and where the aim is to reconcile all people to God. Christian theologians have interpreted this ministry and the exaltation of Christ in terms of Christian supersession. I have argued that supersessionism runs deep into the constructions and multiplicity of gospels. It is preached in the Gospels and by Paul and culminates in John's apocalyptic rupturing, reversals, and overcoming of this world by the kingdom of God. Jesus preached a scandalous, offending gospel in which the mimetic desire to follow Christ is good news for some, but for others, it reproduces a history of dissimilitude or otherness.

Theologians such as Carter and Jennings have shown how supersessionism eventually enters into the modern formations of race and racism. And Girard insists that the only way to overcome this poisonous doctrine is to imitate Christ's nonviolent gospel, which renounces mimetic rivalry and violence. However, I have argued that supersessionism may itself constitute the very scandal of the gospel, and that the history of this scandal carries within itself its own repetitions into every future mimesis of salvation and dissimilitude within new contexts, themes, plots, and staging each filled with a surplus of mimetic possibilities and makings. I then turned to the supersession of white over black in the scandalous gospel of Reverend Ruckus. It is a satirical representation of the mimesis of salvation and dissimilitude in the scandalous gospel of Jesus that positions Ruckus as yet another imitation of its dangers and scandal.

And now I look once more at the two icons of Jesus and the blessed Mother in my shed. I recall Jesus seated at the Last Supper, the soft, gentle Jesus holding a lamb in his arms, the Jesus around whom different races of children are gathered, and Jesus sitting in solitude on a hill looking over the plains of Galilee or toward Jerusalem. I am aware of his blond hair and European features. I am now all too conscious of Christ's iconic whiteness and the scandal it represents in these icons. Still, I smile with affection, musing: What would Jesus do? What would he have me to do? Must I renounce all mimetic desire, if by doing so I might escape the rivalry, violence, and scandal that the mimetic desire to follow Christ occasions? I think not. For such a renunciation would, indeed, be the most dangerous and scandalous mimetic effect of the offending gospel of Jesus for my Christian faith. Rather than renounce every mimetic desire in imitating Christ, it is perhaps enough that I am conscious of the mimesis of supersecession, its dangers and scandals, in the scandalous gospel of Jesus. And perhaps such awareness is enough to form a critical stereoscopic orientation toward Christology and the poisonous effects of supersessionism and the whiteness they created.

Note

1 See chapters 1, 3 and 6 in Girard (1972), and Parts I and II in Girard (2003).

References

Carter, J. Kameron (2008). *Race: A Theological Account*. New York, NY: Oxford University Press.

Girard, René. (2003). *The René Girard Reader*. James G. Williams, ed. New York, NY: The Crossroad Publishing Company.

——(1972). *Violence and the Sacred*. Baltimore, MD: Johns Hopkins University Press.

Gomes, Peter J. (2007). *The Scandalous Gospel of Jesus: What's so Good about the Good News?* New York, NY: HarperCollins Publishers.

Hume, David. (1985). "On National Character." In *Essays: Moral, Political, and Literary*, Eugene F. Miller, ed. Indianapolis, IN: Liberty Fund.

Hurston, Zora Neale. (1969). "Characteristics of Negro Expression." In Nancy Cunard, ed., *Negro: An Anthology*. New York, NY: Continuum.

Jennings, Willie James. (2010) *The Christian Imagination: Theology and the Origins of Race*. New Haven, CT: Yale University Press.

Kant, Immanuel. (1960). *Observations on the Felling of the Beautiful and Sublime*. John T. Goldthwait, trans. Berkeley, CA: University of California Press.

Kaufmann, Walter. (1968). *Nietzsche: Philosopher, Psychologist, Antichrist*. Princeton, NJ: Princeton University Press.

Outlaw, Lucius T. (1995). "Philosophy, Ethnicity, and Race." In *I Am Because We Are: Readings in Black Philosophy*, Fred Lee Hord and Jonathan Scott Lee, eds. Amherst, MA: University of Massachusetts Press.

Potolsky, Matthew. (2005). *Mimesis*. New York, NY: Routledge.

Vlach, Michael J. (2011). "Defining Supersessionism." *Theological Studies*. http://theological studies.org/resource-library/supersessionism/324-defining-supersessionism.

INDEX

by males in religion, 101; durable inequality of, 68; economic consequences of abandonment of polygamy on women, 120; exclusion, 102; hierarchies, 115; oppression, 27, 111; sexism, 150; shortcomings of women, 101; social roles of, 13; suffering and, 13; superiority, 162; surrogacy role of black women, 174; violence and, 15
Genocide, 43, 89, 139
Gentrification, 151, 152
Georgakas, Dan, 181
Gilkes, Cheryl Townsend, 13, 59–73
Girard, René, 174, 201, 202–5
Glaude, Eddie, Jr., 81n2
God: all being made in image of, 11; covenants of, 198; intentions regarding freedom, 134; love for underclass, 78; openness to, 3; opposition to whiteness, 27, 28; partiality toward victims of oppressive human structures, 27; prophetic dealings with lepers, 61; sovereignty of, 68; as Truth, 110
Goffman, Erving, 174, 175
Goldberg, David Theo, 44, 50, 55n24
Gomes, Peter, 205, 206, 207, 208
Gorsline, Robin Hawley, 22
Gossett, Thomas, 69
Grace, Wendy, 176
Graham, Lawrence Otis, 79
Grant, Jacquelyn, 27, 173
Great Sermon, 145
Green, Garrett, 11
Greenlee, Sam, 59
Guider, Meg, 50

Haley, Leon, 80
Hamilton, Charles, 67, 181, 186, 190
Harding, Vincent, 16, 160, 181, 187, 188, 189, 191
Harris, Cheryl, 54n1, 140
Harrison, Beverly, 52
Harrison, Renee, 121
Harrison, W.P., 119
Hart, William David, 15, 156–67
Harvey, Jennifer, 14, 28, 84–99
Harvey, Paul, 86
Harwood, Richard, 41, 55n17
Headley, Clevis, 6
Hegel, G.W.F., 200, 201
Hegemony: dismantling, 16; in governance, 11; of light/dark binary of meaning and, 153; of whiteness, 5, 13, 21, 59–73, 64

Helms, Janet, 93, 97
Hendricks, Obery, 61, 65, 72
Herzog, William, 88, 89
Heschel, Abraham Joshua, 71
Heshel, Susannah, 160, 161
Hinga, Teresa, 120, 122
Hobgood, Mary Elizabeth, 4, 6, 36, 52
Holly, James Theodore, 171
Holocaust, 15
Homophobia, 33n22, 111, 123, 150
Horsley, Richard, 144, 146, 154n7
Hughes, Langston, 65
Hume, David, 201
Humility, 8, 51, 71
Hurston, Zora Neale, 28, 210

"Icon of Starvation," 38, 40–46
Icons: defining, 40; as windows on the Divine, 40
Identity: affirmation of, 90; cultural, 104, 108, 124; development, 85; group, 121; markers, 104; national, 89; normative, 139; political meaning of, 85; positive/negative white, 93, 97; racial, 84, 85, 86, 91, 92, 95, 96; social, 117; white, 4, 9, 48; white Christian, 11
Idolatry: white racism as, 3, 4
Idowu, E. Bojaji, 108
Ignatiev, Noel, 69, 85, 97, 99n1, 104
Image(s): of black children as primitive, 45; connections to history through, 49; in contradiction of text, 38, 42, 43, 44; controversies over, 41, 42; as cultural representations, 40; destabilization of privilege and, 37; as interpretations of reality, 41; Jesus, 169–77; normalization of others' anguish, 37; overwhelming experience of viewing, 52; questioning intent of, 46; racial knowledge of, 44; reinscription of systems of oppression in, 39, 40; representational practices in, 38, 42; responses to, 36–53; responsibility and, 36; of suffering, 36–53, 54n3; understanding function of, 49; understanding privilege and, 40; used to shift to position of shared vulnerability with subjects, 45, 46–53; of what one wishes to see, 170
Imaginary: white, 5
Imagination: Biblical, 70; Jesus Christ in, 170; sacramental, 16
Imago Dei, 4, 10, 171; Christological repositioning of, 176